Rapture, Revelation, and the End Times

Exploring the Left Behind Series

Edited by
Bruce David Forbes
and
Jeanne Halgren Kilde

First published 2004 by
PALGRAVE MACMILLAN™
175 Fifth Avenue, New York, N.Y. 10010 and
Houndmills, Basingstoke, Hampshire, England RG21 6XS
Companies and representatives throughout the world

PALGRAVE MACMILLAN is the global academic imprint of the Palgrave Macmillan division of St. Martin's Press, LLC and of Palgrave Macmillan Ltd. Macmillan® is a registered trademark in the United States, United Kingdom and other countries. Palgrave is a registered trademark in the European Union and other countries.

ISBN 1–4039–6525–0 hardback

Library of Congress Cataloging-in-Publication Data
    Rapture, Revelation, and the end times : exploring the Left behind series / edited by Bruce David Forbes and Jeanne Halgren Kilde.
        p.cm
    Includes bibliographical references and index.
    ISBN 1–4039–6525–0
        1. End of the world. I. Forbes, Bruce David. II. Kilde, Jeanne Halgren, 1957

BT877.R37 2004
236'.9—dc22   2003064798

A catalogue record for this book is available from the British Library.

Design by Newgen Imaging Systems (P) Ltd., Chennai, India.

First edition: June 2004
10 9 8 7 6 5 4 3 2 1

Printed in the United States of America.

all the novels, including a separate series for younger readers, are more than 60 million at this writing, and continuing.

The Indwelling, the seventh book, reached the number one position on four major best-seller lists in fiction: the *New York Times, Publishers Weekly*, the *Wall Street Journal*, and *USA Today*'s Top 150 list. The volumes that followed have each repeated the feat. *Desecration*, the tenth novel, was the best-selling fiction title in the United States in 2001, the first year since 1995 that John Grisham has not held that distinction. The Left Behind books are the first Christian novels, narrowly defined, to reach the top position on such best-seller lists. What is remarkable is that Christian bookstores are not included in the tracking for these major lists, but Tyndale House, the publisher of the Left Behind books, claims that a third of its sales are made through Christian booksellers. Thus, the Left Behind volumes moved to the top of these lists through sales at stores such as Barnes & Noble, Wal-Mart, and Target, an indication of a crossover audience beyond predictable conservative Christian readers.

Tyndale has been aggressive in producing a number of related products, including audiotapes of the books and separate dramatized versions, an entire series of Left Behind novels written especially for youth, plus graphic novels (which are essentially thick comic books) and daily calendars with Left Behind quotations. Two Left Behind movies have been produced, mostly for video and DVD sales, with only the first movie reaching limited showings in commercial theaters through sponsorships by interested churches.

Beyond sales statistics, do we know what portion of the American population has been exposed to the books? According to a survey conducted by the Barna Research Group in May 2001, 24 percent of American adults were aware of the Left Behind books. For comparison, 69 percent of American adults were aware of the Harry Potter books by J. K. Rowling, but only 13 percent were aware of Bruce Wilkinson's *The Prayer of Jabez*, another recent sales phenomenon. (Barna Research Group is a marketing research company known for its work in conservative

Jenkins and LaHaye and their publisher, Tyndale House, are considering two more volumes, *Left Behind: The Prequel* and a concluding volume, *Final Judgment*. Whether they appear or not, at least four additional fiction series already have been launched because of the success of the Left Behind books. Two series are direct spin-offs from the Left Behind storyline, one with a military focus and one political, written by newly recruited authors. In addition, Jenkins and LaHaye each have begun separate series of novels, with new stories and characters unrelated to the Left Behind narrative but still about climactic events in the future.[2]

Christians express a variety of viewpoints about the future, about an end to human history. One perspective expects a "rapture," when true Christians are lifted from the earth in an instant. In one version of this view, all other people who remain on the earth then would experience a seven-year period of great difficulties (tribulation) before Jesus returns to defeat Satan and begin a glorious thousand-year reign. The Left Behind novels provide a fictionalized account of what might happen during and after such a rapture. At the very beginning of the first book, people all over the world mysteriously disappear, leaving behind clothing, eyeglasses, and hearing aids wherever they were seated or standing at the moment of disappearance. Two major protagonists in the books are Rayford Steele, an airline pilot, and "Buck" Williams, a journalist, and they eventually discern the reason for these mysterious happenings: the rapture. Some of those left behind receive the event as a wake-up call and turn to God, but the world in which they live is thrown into turmoil as the antichrist arises to control the earth, with much deception, oppression, violence, and death. The books describe the seven years of tribulation; it is the story of those who are "left behind."

The sales success of the Left Behind series has been phenomenal. First print runs of the early books were 150,000 to 200,000 each. In contrast, the eighth book in the series, *The Mark*, had an initial print run of 2.5 million copies, and 2.4 million were pre-sold eight weeks before the volume's release. Total sales of looked at the book of Revelation before. I became very curious about the popularity of these books. Who is reading them, and what is the appeal? What impact do they have on the individuals who read them, and on American society in general?

The Books and Their Popularity

For those who might be unfamiliar with the Left Behind books, the basic story of their appearance is this: Tim LaHaye, whose name is widely recognized in conservative Christian circles because of a long career as an author and speaker, wanted to produce a fictionalized account of the end times. "Sitting on airplanes and watching the pilots, I'd think to myself, 'What if the Rapture occurred on an airplane?' " After several years seeking a co-author, LaHaye was introduced to writer Jerry Jenkins, who accepted the task but initially was delayed because he was in the midst of completing work with Billy Graham on Graham's autobiography, *Just As I Am.*[1] The first of a projected short series of novels, *Left Behind* appeared in 1995. Both LaHaye and Jenkins were listed as co-authors, but the book jackets identify LaHaye as the person "who conceived the Left Behind series" and Jenkins as the "writer of the series." Sales were so strong that the co-creators eventually extended the plan for the series to twelve volumes:

Left Behind: A Novel of the Earth's Last Days (1995)
Tribulation Force: The Continuing Drama of Those Left Behind (1996)
Nicolae: The Rise of Antichrist (1997)
Soul Harvest: The World Takes Sides (1998)
Apollyon: The Destroyer Is Unleashed (1999)
Assassins: Assignment: Jerusalem, Target: Antichrist (1999)
The Indwelling: The Beast Takes Possession (2000)
The Mark: The Beast Rules the World (2000)
Desecration: Antichrist Takes the Throne (2001)
The Remnant: On the Brink of Armageddon (2002)
Armageddon: The Cosmic Battle of the Ages (2003)
Glorious Appearing: The End of Days (2004)

1

How Popular Are the Left Behind Books . . . and Why?

A Discussion of Popular Culture

Bruce David Forbes

A few years ago, a stranger seated next to me on an airplane looked up from the novel he was reading and asked, "Have you read any of the Left Behind books?" I replied that I had heard of them but had never read one. He held up the latest installment, told me that he was hooked, and said that he had recommended the novels to several family members and friends who now were reading the entire series as well. When I asked about his personal religious background, he said that he was not much of a church-going person, but the books fascinated him.

As that kind of encounter occurred again and again, my curiosity was piqued by the number of unexpected persons who were enthusiastic about the Left Behind books. I am aware that many conservative Christians believe in dramatic events at the end of history and a literal return of Christ, but so many comments came from people who did not fit in that category: an inactive Catholic, a friend who was skeptical about all institutional religion, a mainline Protestant who had never really to provide background, answer questions, and raise new areas of inquiry for readers' further investigation.

Bringing together these disciplines highlights some interesting differences among them regarding language use. For instance, readers will notice that while historian Kilde uses the term "premillennial dispensationalism," evangelical theologian Grenz prefers "dispensationalist premillennialism." This difference highlights the contrasting backgrounds of the authors, because different academic fields and different theological perspectives vary in their preferences in terminology. In another example, the term "proof text" is seen by some theologians as a pejorative label, while many historians and literary scholars use it as a neutral, descriptive phrase to denote one approach to biblical interpretation. In this collection, the editors have elected to allow each author to use the language with which he or she is most comfortable, in spite of the fact that this results in some inconsistencies. Readers should keep in mind these disciplinary differences.

Readers' questions form the foundation of this collection's exploration of the series. In addition to questions that are addressed in the chapters themselves, a list of discussion questions is provided at the end of the book, to encourage personal reflection or to provide a guide for small-group discussion. But these are only a starting point. The authors of this book encourage readers to go beyond the basic issues presented here to think about how the religious, social, and political positions presented in the Left Behind series relate to their own values and views regarding religion and society. To aid in further inquiries, a book list appears at the end of this volume, offering suggestions for additional sources written from a variety of viewpoints.

This book, then, is intended as a kind of "first stop" for readers attempting to fully understand the series in all its religious, social, and political implications. Answering some of the basic questions about Left Behind's religious perspective, it provides tools readers require to make their own judgments about the religious messages embedded in the books and at the same time launches readers into several new and unexpected areas of inquiry.

eternal damnation? Do all Christians believe that the Bible predicts that true Christians will be swept up to heaven prior to a period of unparalleled horror and tribulation on earth? How did the Left Behind perspective on these end times events develop? Why are other groups, particularly the Jewish people, included in the apocalyptic events? Why are so many social and political issues woven into these books? And, perhaps most interesting, just why have these novels gotten so popular? On what levels does it appeal to contemporary society?

The goal of this "guide" is to answer these questions, providing the background and contextual information readers need to make their own critical assessments of the Left Behind series in particular and of end-times fiction and premillennial dispensationalism in general. By offering this material, the contributors to this volume hope to deepen readers' understanding of the Left Behind series as both a religious and a cultural phenomenon. The essays are intended neither to advance nor to dispute the views of the end times presented in the series. Rather, the authors in this volume strive to provide readers with a balanced survey of the diversity of perspectives available on this subject. Several of the contributors summarize their own viewpoints, but they also try to be fair in discussing alternatives.

Because religious beliefs intersect with many aspects of life, the chapters in this volume are written from several disciplinary perspectives. The study of popular culture and of literary genres is represented in chapters by Bruce David Forbes and Amy Johnson Frykholm, which focus on Left Behind's popularity and its debt to the social and political themes common within religious fiction. The history of Left Behind's perspective is examined by Jeanne Halgren Kilde, who traces the development of premillennial dispensationalism and millenarian thought through Christian history, and by Yaakov Ariel, who investigates the specific role assigned to the Jewish people within millenarian thought. New Testament scholar Mark Reasoner examines the interpretive position of the Left Behind authors, and theologian Stanley Grenz compares this interpretive position to other evangelical Christian perspectives. This multidisciplinary approach is meant will be called to heaven in an event referred to as "the rapture" and thus spared the pain and horror of this apocalyptic period. This religious perspective, called "premillennial dispensational-ism," motivates all of the action, events, and relationships depicted in the series.

On one level, the novels are intended as entertainment. They tell an exciting adventure story about people who convert to Christianity after the rapture and remain on earth to fight the antichrist. On another level, their religious message is central. For those who believe in the authors' perspective, the novels demonstrate the high stakes at play in the process of religious conversion, affirming the crucial importance of devotion to Christ. Perhaps even more important, the books are intended to convince readers that in real life, Jesus' return and the commence-ment of the end times may happen at any minute, so it is neces-sary to embrace immediately the particular style of Christianity represented in the books. In this vein, the novels are intended as a wake-up call for nonbelieving readers, a warning that time is short and that the consequences of putting off consideration of one's salvation are eternal.

Given the enthusiastic expressions of appreciation of these books on the Left Behind website and in conservative Christian circles throughout the world, it appears that many of the millions of readers of this series have embraced this particular message of conversion and salvation. These readers fully expect the rapture to happen in the near future and the apocalyptic events of Revelation to proceed.

Many other readers, however, enjoy the adventure story but find the religious content curious or confusing. These readers understand that the series advocates a specific perspective on Christianity and society but feel ill-equipped to evaluate it. Many are frustrated that they do not have the knowledge of the-ology, biblical interpretation, or the history of Christian thought to fully appraise the religious perspective conveyed through the series.

Numerous questions arise: Do all Christian groups share the theology that requires Christian conversion in order to avoid

Introduction

Rapture, Revelation, and the End Times: Exploring the Left Behind Series

Jeanne Halgren Kilde and
Bruce David Forbes

The Left Behind books by Tim LaHaye and Jerry B. Jenkins have now sold more than 60 million copies in their various forms. Based on one particular view of biblical prophecy, these books provide a fictional narrative of the end times: God has raptured his faithful church to heaven, and readers follow the struggles of a small group of belated converts as they battle the antichrist during the seven years of tribulation that precede Christ's return in glory. Sold at Target, Wal-Mart, and Barnes & Noble, the series has reached well beyond conservative Christian audiences to the general public. In fact, the most recent volumes all have attained the number-one position in major rankings of best-selling fiction in the United States, even though those rankings do not include sales in Christian bookstores.

Although these novels are fiction, they present a scheme of future events that the Left Behind authors believe to be biblically based. These writers believe that God will send his son, Jesus Christ, back to earth to finally conquer all sin and evil in a series of apocalyptic events that will shatter human society. Those who have previously become truly confessing Christians

Acknowledgments

In putting together this collection, we have received generous assistance from many individuals. We would like to thank the contributors for their chapters as well as for their conversations throughout the development of this book. In particular, we appreciate Mark Reasoner's engagement since the beginning of the project and Amy Johnson Frykholm's substantial participation in reviewing many portions of the book. We also want to thank Reinder VanTil and Jeanne Barker Nunn for their suggestions regarding early drafts. Finally, we want to express our deep appreciation to the following individuals for their interest in and support for the project in numerous ways: Calvin Roetzel, Paul Kilde, Jan Carrier, Heather Reid, John Lawrence, Jim Fisk, Brooke Golliher Williams, and Lynn Kogelmann.

Bruce David Forbes
Jeanne Halgren Kilde

Contents

Christian circles. Tyndale House commissioned the study cited here, but Barna generally is regarded as an independent company with reliable methodologies, although some of its categories and interpretations clearly reveal evangelical Christian perspectives.)

In addition to indications that approximately one quarter of the American adult population is aware of the Left Behind books, Barna's research found that 9 percent of the general public had *read* at least one of the books. Yes, that is almost one out of every ten American adults. Not surprisingly, most readers were "born-again Christians," persons who attend non–mainstream Protestant churches, and residents of the South and the West. Those least likely to have read the books were non-born-again Christians, Catholics, and residents of the Northeast.

Yet, although Left Behind readers were drawn mostly from the ranks of conservative Christians, Barna's research estimated that 3 million "non-born-again adults" had read one or more of the books. George Barna, the director of the survey, noted that "the series represents one of the most widely experienced religious teaching or evangelistic tools among adults who are not born again Christians." He said that the series "has reached a larger unduplicated audience of non-believers than most religious television or radio ministries draw through their programs." Barna added, "The survey suggests that nearly one-tenth of the audience for the series are atheists and people associated with non-Christian faiths, while more than two million of the readers are individuals who consider themselves to be Christian but have never accepted Jesus Christ as their savior. Although three-quarters of the *Left Behind* audience attends Protestant churches, these books have also piqued the interest of hundreds of thousands of people who do not normally read books with religious themes that reflect one stream of Protestant theology."[3]

The Left Behind series had a number of predecessors expressing and promoting beliefs in a pretribulation rapture through books, music, and film. The two most notable popular culture examples were a book and a film that appeared in the 1970s.

Yet as important as both of them were, neither broke through into the general popular culture as much as the novels by LaHaye and Jenkins have.

In 1970 Hal Lindsey (with Carole C. Carlson) published *The Late Great Planet Earth*, a runaway best-seller that sold more than 20 million copies and was named by the *New York Times* as the best-selling nonfiction book of the 1970s.[4] Lindsey believed that a key to predicting the end times was the re-establishment of Israel in 1948, and from that basis he related numerous biblical references to specific current events. While he did not explicitly name the dates, he strongly implied that both a rapture and a period of tribulation would take place in the 1980s, and his book provided a persuasive scenario that led to many water-cooler conversations about whether the end times were near. Even though Lindsay's seemingly failed prediction thereafter made many Christians wary of being too specific in their expectations, the book still was effective in promoting the particular view of the end times that included a rapture and a tribulation. Many readers were left with the impression that this general outline of events was the only biblical view, even if Lindsey's specific dates had turned out to be mistaken.

The second notable predecessor is the film *A Thief in the Night*, produced in 1972 and distributed in 1973. This low-budget movie was not released in theaters; it was shown to local church youth groups, at Sunday evening services, and at Bible camps and rallies throughout the 1970s and 1980s. The film begins with a close-up of a clock ticking. A woman awakes and, searching for her husband, finds only his razor buzzing in the bathroom sink. The rapture has occurred. The plot then steps back to tell the story of several persons' lives prior to the rapture and, after the event, the frightening experiences of those who are left behind. Near the end of the film the woman awakes to learn that it has all been a dream. However, in trying to locate her husband, she finds only his razor, buzzing, and she screams, knowing that the dream has turned into reality.

Many mainline Protestant and Catholic youth who were raised in that era never heard of the movie, but among the evangelical subculture in the United States almost *everyone* remembers it vividly. Because of the manner of the film's distribution, it is impossible to ascertain how many people saw *A Thief in the Night*. When pressed, one of the partners who produced the film estimated 100 million viewers, including duplications by persons who saw it more than once. Randall Balmer, a historian of American evangelicalism, suggests that "even if you slash that number in half to account for hyperbole, fifty million is still a staggering figure, a viewership that would be the envy of many Hollywood producers."[5] The movie's creators, Donald Thompson and Russell Doughten, were more interested in the number of conversions prompted by the film, and they claim over 4 million. Again, there is no way to verify such a number, but the film was frightening, and it was particularly effective when followed by an altar call encouraging people to make a decision for Christ.

Both of these cultural phenomena, the film and the book, helped confirm beliefs about a pretribulation rapture as the dominant view of the end times held by American evangelicals. Yet *A Thief in the Night*, although enormously influential in the evangelical subculture, never reached far beyond it. Sales success of *The Late Great Planet Earth* showed some signs of reaching further into the general culture, but the impact was limited, especially after Lindsey's specific predictions failed to materialize. Both helped pave the way for the Left Behind books, but LaHaye and Jenkins's novels have now gone further than their predecessors, receiving a devoted following among conservative Christians but also drawing the interest of great numbers of curious readers in the general population.

Backgrounds of the Authors

Although the readers of the Left Behind novels are diverse, the two authors of the books represent a very specific segment of Christianity, with a particular theology and particular social and political viewpoints. The perspectives of LaHaye and Jenkins are not identical, and some commentators have speculated about the relative influence of each man in the inclusion of various themes and story lines. Yet both creators have deep roots in conservative Christianity, and their backgrounds help us understand their theological and cultural intentions in writing the series.

The best known of the two authors is Tim LaHaye, now in his seventies, whose long career has influenced a wide range of Christian evangelical causes. A graduate of Bob Jones University, LaHaye served as a minister in Minnesota and then as pastor at Scott Memorial Baptist Church in San Diego, California, for about twenty-five years. He founded several private Christian schools and Christian Heritage College of El Cajon, California. He holds a Doctor of Ministry degree from Western Theological Seminary and an honorary doctorate from Jerry Falwell's Liberty University. Through speaking tours, organizational efforts, and the publication of more than forty books, LaHaye has been involved in most of conservative Christianity's major issues and causes in recent decades:

- *Family Life*. In 1966 LaHaye published a book titled *Spirit-Controlled Temperament*, which fused psychological approaches with biblical themes and became instrumental in making a "therapeutic mindset" acceptable among Christian evangelicals.[6] He followed with other volumes on similar themes, such as *Understanding the Male Temperament* and *Spirit-Controlled Family Living*.[7] In 1976 he and his wife, Beverly, co-authored *The Act of Marriage: The Beauty of Sexual Love*, called "the first best-selling evangelical sex manual," and they gained national prominence by leading Family Life Seminars and workshops on Christian marriage throughout the nation.[8] Tim and Beverly LaHaye opposed the Equal Rights Amendment to the U.S. Constitution, and although they support women's engagement in conservative Christian political activism, they also advocate traditional gender roles within marriage.[9]
- *Creationism*. LaHaye was involved, along with Henry Morris, in the establishment of the Institute for Creation Research, an

influential source of materials for those conservative Christians who reject evolution and who seek support for a literal reading of the creation account in Genesis. LaHaye was featured significantly in a widely distributed film of the 1970s, *The Search for Noah's Ark*, and he co-wrote a book with Henry Morris's son on the same subject, *The Ark on Ararat*, also seeking to prove the literal truth of Genesis.[10]

- *Battles.* In the late 1970s and early 1980s he wrote a series of books positioning conservative Christians in a combative struggle with cultural forces: *The Battle for the Mind, The Battle for the Family,* and *The Battle for the Public Schools.*[11] He also was an early voice raising an alarm about homosexuality, publishing *The Unhappy Gays: What Everyone Should Know about Homosexuality.*[12] His most recent book in this combative genre is *Mind Seige*, co-authored with David Noebel, which argues that secular humanism thoroughly pervades American society and should be opposed by Christians. The book claims that the "five basic tenets" of secular humanism are atheism, evolution, amorality, human autonomy, and globalism.[13]

- *Politics.* Holding the views cited above, LaHaye shared the concerns of many politically conservative Christians who became increasingly active in the movement often labeled the Religious Right or the New Christian Right. He was a board member of Jerry Falwell's Moral Majority, created the Council for National Policy (a coalition of leaders of the religious right), and became head of the American Coalition for Traditional Values. His wife, Beverly LaHaye, is the founder and "chairman of the board" of Concerned Women for America, which calls itself "the U.S.A.'s largest politically active women's organization" and shares the perspectives of the Religious Right. In 2001 the LaHayes further demonstrated their close relationship with Jerry Falwell with a $4.5 million gift to Falwell's Liberty University for the construction of a student center. Mark Noll, a noted historian of American evangelicalism, lists LaHaye along with Jerry Falwell and James Dobson as examples of conservative religious leaders who "entered politics with a vengeance during the 1970s and 1980s." They "created the New Religious Right and have made conservative evangelical support so important for the Republican Party since the campaigns of Ronald Reagan."[14] Some of LaHaye's forays into politics, however, have not gone well. Controversy arose when it was revealed that LaHaye had accepted funds from the Reverend Sun Myung Moon and served on the boards of two of his organizations. He also resigned as co-chairman of Jack Kemp's 1988 presidential campaign after press accounts reported that LaHaye had called Roman Catholicism a "false religion" and had, on one occasion, asserted that Jews were responsible for the death of Jesus.[15]

In addition to these causes, LaHaye is a passionate advocate of "dispensational premillennialism," also called "premillennial dispensationalism" or simply "dispensationalism," a specific end times viewpoint that arose in the 1830s. (See chapter 2 for a fuller description of the belief system and its history.) Dispensational premillennialism is the interpretation that underlies the Left Behind books, expecting a rapture, followed by a seven-year period of tribulation, concluding with a "glorious appearing" by Christ who will defeat Satan and inaugurate a thousand-year reign on the earth. In 1973 LaHaye argued for such views in a commentary on the biblical book of Revelation, and in the 1990s he published at least three more books about prophecy and the end times, including a volume entitled *Rapture under Attack*.[16] He is a co-founder of the Pre-Trib Research Center, "established for the express purpose of exposing ministers to teachings of good Bible prophecy" and to keep people from "being deceived as we approach the end of the age," exposing "false prophets and their harmful teaching."

Because of LaHaye's wide-ranging career, Larry Eskridge of the *Evangelical Studies Bulletin* wrote an essay in 2001 claiming that Tim LaHaye has been the most influential American evangelical of the last twenty-five years. Eskridge would name Billy Graham the most influential American evangelical of the twentieth century, but much of Graham's prominence came earlier. Focusing on the last twenty-five years, Eskridge argued that LaHaye has been more influential than better-known names like Jerry Falwell, Pat Robertson, James Dobson, and Bill Bright, because of his involvement in so many evangelical causes. LaHaye is someone "who was influenced by all the changes swirling around evangelicalism, rose out of the ranks of the movement, and then in turn played a strategic role at key points that have cemented—for good or ill—the direction [evangelicals] will be taking in the next few decades."[17]

LaHaye's co-creator, Jerry Jenkins, is the actual writer of the series. Although Jenkins's name was not as widely recognized as LaHaye's prior to the success of the Left Behind books, he also had an established career as a prolific author. Before his involvement with the Left Behind series, Jenkins's conservative Christian credentials came especially through his involvement with the Moody Bible Institute in Chicago. Founded by the prominent nineteenth-century evangelist Dwight L. Moody, the institute offers a curriculum and publications focused on missions, evangelism, and Bible prophecy. Formerly the vice president for publishing and now a "writer-at-large" for Moody, Jenkins is the author of more than a hundred books in four genres: biographies, marriage and family titles, fiction for children, and fiction for adults. These include series of "Christian mysteries" for adults and for children, published by Moody, as well as devotional books and other Christian literature. Yet his freelance writing efforts have ranged even more widely, including articles in *Reader's Digest, Parade*, and American and United in-flight magazines. Jenkins has written numerous sports biographies, with stars such as Hank Aaron, Walter Payton, Meadowlark Lemon, Orel Hershiser, and Nolan Ryan, and he is the writer of the nationally syndicated sport story comic strip *Gil Thorp*. As mentioned previously, he also assisted Billy Graham with his autobiography. With the success of the Left Behind volumes, Jenkins and his family have relocated from the Chicago area to Colorado, where Jenkins has been a frequent guest on James Dobson's *Focus on the Family* radio program.[18]

Response from Fans and Critics

It is a generalization, but within Christian circles one might discuss three different responses to the Left Behind books: (1) devoted appreciation from fans, (2) disagreement about apocalyptic details from some conservative Christians who otherwise affirm a literal final judgment and second coming of Christ, and (3) striking silence from mainline or liberal Christians.

The response of fans, by definition, is enthusiastic. They constitute the core audience that continues to buy the books, even as the series seemed to get longer and longer. Tyndale House maintains a website with message boards for discussion, filled with comments about "awesome books" and appreciation "for changing my life." Readers also identify with characters in the books. One person commented to Jerry Jenkins that "I've been known to instantly begin praying for a character when they disappeared or became injured. . . . Do you ever forget that your characters are not real and find yourself thinking of them as people you really know?" Jenkins replied that "we have heard from people who found themselves praying for characters or even watching the news to see what Carpathia [the antichrist in the novels] is up to."[19]

Some testify that they were converted by the books. Ida Bailey, in an opinion piece written for Beliefnet.com, indicated that she identified with Pastor Barnes, a minister in the series who found himself left behind after the rapture. Bailey wrote: "I had grown up in a Christian family. Had a pollster asked me my religious identity, I would have said 'Protestant.' But I was not a real Christian. I would have been left behind, just like Pastor Barnes, having claimed to be a Christian but having failed to live a life in personal communion with the Lord. On October 1, 1996, I put down my copy of *Left Behind*, picked up a copy of the Bible, and dedicated my life to following Jesus. I began going to church, praying every morning, and reading whatever Christian books I could get my hands on." She disagreed that such a conversion was based on scare tactics. "I was not brought to Christ through fear, exactly, but through sorrow. . . .

I was moved to rededicate my life to Christ not because I feared getting left behind after the Rapture but because I wanted my pre-Rapture life to be meaningful."[20]

Many readers also apparently accept the claim that, although the books are fiction, the underlying outline of end time events is the only self-evident biblical view. Crossings, a Christian book club, made the following claim in a recent book advertisement (the first sentence was printed in bold in the advertisement): "The series is guaranteed to be theologically sound. Dr. LaHaye is a minister and noted authority on Bible prophecy."[21] The importance of the LaHaye name in association with the Left Behind books is the reliance his admirers give to his authority as an expert on biblical prophecy. LaHaye encourages it, indicating that his investigation of Bible prophecy is "the greatest research project of my life." "Now, after ten thousand pages of reading, visits to both congressional and Christian college and university libraries, computer book researches, a canvas of used bookstores, reading hundreds of letters, and through many conversations both in this country and the British Isles, and after a careful examination of every Bible verse related to the subject, I can honestly say I am more convinced than ever of the pre-Tribulation rapture position."[22] Jenkins defers to LaHaye as a consultant and guide on such matters.

Yet the theology of the books is not endorsed by all, even among conservative Christians who, on many other significant issues, share the general perspectives of LaHaye and Jenkins. Some accept almost all of the Left Behind viewpoint but debate the timing of a rapture in relationship to other events at the end of history. Will the rapture occur first, followed by a seven-year tribulation (a *pretribulation rapture*, the assumption behind the Left Behind books)? Or will the rapture occur in the middle of the tribulation (*midtribulation*) or at the end of the tribulation period (*posttribulation*)? Disagreements among "pre-trib," "mid-trib," and "post-trib" views matter a great deal to some people, including LaHaye, who devotes the last portion of his book *Rapture under Attack* to a refutation of the rival perspectives.

An example of a fuller conservative Christian rejection of Left Behind theology is provided by A. L. Barry, now deceased, who was president of the Lutheran Church—Missouri Synod in 2000, the year of publication for *The Mark*, the eighth volume in the series. Barry released a statement saying that "the entire *Left Behind* series . . . is an unbiblical flight of fancy (known by the term 'dispensational premillennialism') receiving far more press than it deserves." Disagreeing with the claim of the authors that the books are "true to prophecy," Barry offered three objections. First, he said, "the fascinating book of Revelation is not meant to be read as a literal account. Instead, it is written in highly symbolic language and, through grand visions and pictures, presents important truths about the power of God and of His Son, Jesus Christ." This is a significant statement, because the Lutheran Church—Missouri Synod generally supports a literal reading of the Bible except in cases where the Bible itself clearly indicates that it should be read in another way. Here Barry indicates that the book of Revelation is one of those exceptions.

Second, he objected that the authors of the Left Behind novels, with their emphasis on the frightening aspects of Revelation's imagery, "sidetrack their readers from the positive Gospel encouragement of the Apocalypse: the joy of the Lord's return." Because the length of the series dwells on traumatic happenings, it de-emphasizes "eternally joyful events."

Third, Barry pointed to "an even greater error and danger": "the idea that there will be a 'second chance' for people who do not have trusting faith in Jesus Christ." He found this notion to be "completely contrary to the Bible. . . . there is just one occurrence at the end of history: Judgment Day. That day, for all its power and majesty, will be far simpler and more conclusive than the complex, ongoing chain of events envisioned in the *Left Behind* books." Barry found no biblical support for the complicated scenario of people vanishing into thin air in a rapture, followed by chaos and hysteria. "This sort of haunting imagery may sell books, but it is not what the Bible says." Barry affirmed a single Judgment Day, and on that day "all things will come to an end, with no second chances."[23]

The most thorough recent attempt by a conservative Christian to offer a specific biblical critique of the Left Behind books is *End Times Fiction: A Biblical Consideration of the Left Behind Theology*, written by Gary DeMar. Like many other critics, DeMar shares many assumptions with LaHaye and Jenkins. "Even though Tim LaHaye and I disagree on prophecy issues, we agree on the basics of the Christian faith that put both of us in the Evangelical camp. . . . To demonstrate that we do not disagree on everything, he quotes me favorably in his newest nonfiction book, *Mind Siege*. . . ."[24] Because of the shared assumptions, DeMar finds it important to respond with detailed biblical arguments to LaHaye's views of Bible prophecy. DeMar offers alternative perspectives on "ten major components of the pre-tribulation rapture theology," arguing that most of the biblical prophecies emphasized by LaHaye already have been fulfilled and do not point to further events in the future. DeMar's conclusion is that "*Left Behind* is a work of fiction. As long as it's read with this point in mind, there is no harm. But if the interpretive methodology set forth in the series is embraced as the Bible's method, then I believe many people will be disappointed and disillusioned when the scenario out-lined by LaHaye does not come to pass."[25]

Although some conservative Christians have been critical of the details about the end-times expectation undergirding the Left Behind books, mainline Christians and their denomina-tional leaders have tended to ignore them. Ask the average member of a mainline congregation when they last heard a ser-mon about the book of Revelation or the end times, and most will have difficulty remembering a single example. When asked what they believe about the possibility of end-times events, many will say that they have not done much thinking about it.

The category of "mainline Christians" is a bit confusing. First of all, because membership in many of these groups has slipped in recent years, some of their rivals have begun calling them "oldline" or "sideline." Denominations that often are labeled mainline include Catholics, United Methodists, ELCA Lutherans, Episcopalians, Presbyterians, the United Church of Christ, and others. Yet denominations of that size have great diversity of perspectives within them, and their leadership often represents views quite different from significant portions of their membership. Even with its diversity of views, the mainline represents a tendency to read more portions of the Bible symbolically and to concentrate less on questions about an afterlife, giving more attention to finding meaning in this life now and expressing their faith through social involvements. These very tendencies help explain why mainline Christians have given less attention to end-times speculation.

However, one might expect some mainline responses to the Left Behind books for two reasons. First, whatever the inclinations of the leadership, many members of mainline congregations have read the books and are asking questions. Jay Phelan Jr., president of North Park Theological Seminary (a seminary of the Covenant denomination, an offshoot of Swedish Lutheranism), has led a number of seminars in local churches about eschatology, beliefs about the future, but he recognizes that such sessions are unusual in mainline settings. He says: "I think that the neglect of the study of eschatology in the church is a serious mistake, and it's one of the reasons that stuff like *Left Behind* becomes so popular. People are hungry to have some information about what the Bible says about the future. And if you don't give them something good to eat, they'll eat junk food. And the *Left Behind* series are kind of the Twinkies and the Hostess Cupcakes of the theological world."[26]

Second, mainline or liberal Christian views are directly criticized in the books. For example, in *Nicolae*, the third volume in the series, journalist Buck Williams has an extended conversation with a religious leader named Peter Mathews. Mathews criticizes "your right-wing, fanatical, fundamentalist factions who have always taken the Bible literally. These same preachers, and I daresay many of their parishioners, are the ones who take the creation account—the Adam and Eve myth, if you will—literally." Mathews said that the book of Revelation is "wonderful, archaic, beautiful literature, to be taken symbolically, figuratively, metaphorically." In discussing an earthquake that had just occurred, Mathews commented, "Regardless of your view on the person or concept of God, or *a* god, hardly anyone today would imagine a supreme spirit-being full of goodness and light subjecting the entire earth—already suffering from so recent a devastating war—to a calamity like an earthquake."[27] These are views frequently associated with mainline Christianity. And, in this novel, just who is Peter Mathews, the person who holds these views? He is a former pope who has become the Pontifex Maximus, the leader of the new One World Faith centered on the antichrist.

One exception to the general silence of mainline Christians came at the June 2001 national meeting of the Presbyterian Church (USA). Representatives at their General Assembly voted to communicate to Presbyterian pastors and local churches that books in the Left Behind series are based on an interpretation of the Bible that "is not in accord with our Reformed understanding of Covenant theology." They encouraged congregations to sponsor Bible studies "that give a Reformed understanding of the book of Revelation and show how this is different from that of the dispensationalist view."

In comments preceding the Presbyterian vote, an employee of Barnes & Noble in Grapevine, Texas, indicated that his "little store sells more copies of the *Left Behind* series than any other store" in the United States. He stated that he was expected to maintain at least 85 copies of each book on the bookstore's shelves; with eight books available in the summer of 2001, that amounted to approximately 680 copies of the Left Behind books in stock, compared to about 150 copies of the Bible. The employee said he was concerned that people would be confused by the books' "misguided understanding."[28]

Some Catholic responses have appeared as well. Tyndale House reports that 11 percent of Left Behind readers are Catholic, but there have been few official Catholic pronouncements on the series. Two independent Catholic authors, Carl Olson and Paul Thigpen, have written books to refute the Left Behind views, but not until June 2003 did a group of Catholic bishops in Illinois issue a statement critical of the LaHaye-Jenkins novels. "Finally!" was Olson's response. The bishops, along with Olson and Thigpen, are concerned to inform Catholics that the novels' theology is inconsistent with Catholic teaching. In addition, they see the Left Behind books as anti-Catholic. They argue that, although the pope was among the persons raptured in the first novel, he was only recently installed and had become a born-again Christian who seemed to advocate Protestant doctrines. The Catholic leader who replaced the raptured pope was a morally flawed person who eventually became an assistant to the antichrist. This portrayal of Catholicism, together with statements made by LaHaye in his nonfiction writings, convinced the Illinois bishops that the novels are anti-Catholic. LaHaye believes he has been misunderstood, saying that "every church has some renegade people in it, and we just picked one of theirs."[29]

Analyzing the Popularity

The Left Behind books have achieved remarkable sales and influence, which has also prompted its share of critiques. But what does all of this mean? Why has the Left Behind series become so popular? What does it say about the persons who have been drawn to the books, or about American society in general? What needs do the Left Behind books fill? Have the novels influenced individuals and society? Should we be inspired by or wary of their influence?

First of all, let us pause for a moment to consider how popular culture works, in general, and then we can apply these understandings to the Left Behind phenomenon. One of the most basic principles in analyzing popular culture is that *popular culture both reflects us and shapes us*. We usually think first about the latter part of that statement, about how popular culture might influence us, for good or for ill. For instance, many persons are concerned that violent content in movies and television programs helps create a more violent society. Others complain when popular culture regularly portrays women as victims rather than as heroes, because such portrayals limit the imagination of young girls when they dream about their futures.

More positively, sympathetic movie portrayals of cultures different from our own may help us understand the experiences of others. All of these are examples of how popular culture may shape or influence us, negatively or positively.

Yet popular culture also reflects us. In essence, "we" choose what becomes popular. Television networks announce new TV series at the beginning of a season, with extensive publicity and manipulation of time slots, but few of the shows actually succeed. The public makes choices and determines whether something becomes popular, and the viewers are not mere pawns under the network executives' control. The question then arises: *Why* did one series succeed when another did not? How did it resonate with the values of the public, or what needs did it fill? In a sense, looking at popular culture is like holding up a mirror, in which the general public sees itself: its needs, its desires, its beliefs, its yearnings. What does popular culture tell us about ourselves?

These are good questions to ask about the Left Behind books. Because the novels are so popular, with so many people reading and talking about them, do they influence the readers and society as a whole? And what does the fact that we have made them so popular tell us about ourselves and our society? Other chapters in this book will have some suggestions along the way, and I would like to offer a few comments as well.

Let us start with the question about why the Left Behind books are so popular and what their popularity says about us. One could make several suggestions, but I would argue that it is important to see these novels in the larger context of apocalyptic themes in popular culture. This is not just about conservative Christians, or Christianity in general, but also about broad themes in American culture. Struggles between good and evil are not limited to explicitly Christian books or films; they pervade American popular culture in its many forms. For example, consider westerns, Disney animated movies, comic books, science fiction serials, and action–adventure novels. Whether they portray cosmic battles between good and evil or conflicts on a more human plane, certain themes seem to arise repeatedly in American popular culture's portrayals of these struggles:

- *Evil comes from the outside.* In a western, an outlaw gang terrorizes the town, but there is nothing basically wrong with the innocent townspeople except perhaps for their weakness. In Disney's animated movie *Aladdin*, the villain Jafar may have manipulated his way into the Sultan's court, but he is clearly an outsider in both character and appearance. This repeated theme of the external source of evil is psychologically comforting, because "we" are not the problem.

- *People are either good or evil, not both.* Think of the villains in James Bond or Indiana Jones movies, or Lex Luthor battling Superman in comic books, or people wearing black hats and white hats in old-time westerns. More recently, think of the terrorist villains in any number of movies and television programs. The "evil" characters are not people one would expect to have heart-to-heart conversations with, to change their ways. Decisions are much easier when there is a clear-cut distinction between our enemies and our friends.

- *The solution is the destruction of the evil-doers.* When the distinction between good and bad people is clear-cut, it usually means that the bad people are beyond redemption. Thus, there is only one solution to eliminate evil-doers: kill them. In how many action-adventure movies are the villains transformed to a new way of living? (Very few.) How often do they die? (Most of the time.) Situations are resolved through "redemptive violence."

- *Good wins.* Movie audiences cheer when the evil space station blows up, or when the villain falls from a skyscraper to his death, and the heroes gather to congratulate one another. A clear victory is more emotionally satisfying than ambiguous endings, unless a sequel is planned.

Of course we can think of exceptions to each of these themes, but are they not the exceptions rather than the rule? I would contend that the themes listed above are dominant in American popular culture, although they are challenged regularly by dissenting examples.

The point here is that the Left Behind books did not introduce these themes; the books participate in well-established themes already pervasive in American popular culture. The Left Behind series is not unique in offering the story of a climactic battle between good and evil, with the four common features just described. Rather, the books reflect broader patterns in American culture. In a sense, the Left Behind books are just another Arnold Schwarzenegger movie in written form, with explicit religious imagery added.

Thus, much of the general public responds to the Left Behind books because they are familiar and comfortable, fitting with cultural patterns and themes we have heard from many sources. We embrace this kind of story line because it is emotionally satisfying to hear that others are the source of evil, not us, and that the difference between good and evil is easy to discern. And we are attracted by happy endings, the assurance that good will triumph and evil will be vanquished, even if violence is necessary to accomplish it.

The complicated question is whether these dominant cultural themes are true to reality and, for Christians, whether they really fit with basic proclamations of Christian theology. Does the source of evil always come from outside, or is it within us? Are human beings either good or evil, clearly one or the other? Or do individuals represent a mixture of strengths and good intentions along with weaknesses and tragic failings? Should we hope for the destruction of enemies or for their transformation? In the end, are we sure that the good will win?

These value-laden questions lead us to the issue of the impact of the Left Behind books on their readers and on American society in general. In published reviews and commentaries, and in informal conversations, three claims of impact seem to arise again and again: conversions, polarization, and political and social concerns.

Conversions

For Tim LaHaye and Jerry Jenkins and their supporters, the most important impact of the books is their evangelistic opportunity, their success in converting persons to Christ. In one online discussion, a reader asked Jerry Jenkins what had given him the most satisfaction in writing the books. Jenkins replied, "Between Dr. LaHaye and me we have personally heard from more than 2,500 people who tell us they have become believers through reading the series. That beats any royalty or bestseller."[30] Tim LaHaye has written that belief in the "any-moment-coming of Christ" is important because it "produces holy living in an unholy society like ours" and "produces an evangelistic church of soul-winning Christians."[31]

Tyndale has published a book titled *These Will Not Be Left Behind: True Stories of Changed Lives* to provide testimonies of conversions and transformations as a result of reading the Left Behind books. The volume's introduction states that the message of these books is: "Don't be left behind after the Rapture!" The introduction continues: "Is there someone you know who should read these stories so they won't be left behind? Could it be you? . . . As you read, pray for yourself, for your family, and for every person you meet, that all will surrender to Jesus Christ, our Savior and Lord."[32] Even though some persons read the series simply as an adventure story, the authors and publisher are explicit in stating their evangelical intention. And clearly, some readers have responded.

Other persons do not share a theology that hopes for the conversion of everyone to evangelical Christianity, but they still appreciate that the books may prompt readers to reflect on their priorities and ask questions about the meaning and purpose of life. After September 11, many Americans indicated that they re-evaluated whether they were spending enough time with their families, or how much they took life for granted. In a similar way, the books apparently have prompted life reassessments among some readers, even if they do not reach the same conclusions intended by LaHaye and Jenkins.

Polarization

Yet critics worry about negative impact on individuals and society, and a major concern is the encouragement of an us-versus-them mentality. An apocalyptic story that sorts the sheep from the goats encourages its readers to look at the whole world that way. One Catholic reviewer complained of the series' "mean-spirited vision of faith" and a "certain clubbiness with other believers." She said she found herself "slipping into the books' mindset and making a mental 'heaven or hell' note any time a character dies. When the story introduces a supernatural mark on the foreheads of all Christians, speculation ends: Now I can know for sure where everyone's going."[33]

Besides the general mentality, the books place in stark relief a basic theological issue that is debated within Christianity. Is Christianity the only valid religion, and do all others face eternal damnation? This is called an "exclusive" view, and it has been widely accepted in Christian history. However, other Christians advocate two alternatives: an "inclusive" view that sees Christ working in hidden ways in other religions, thus making them acceptable, and a "pluralist" view that sees Christianity as one among many valid religions. Of course, while the debate rages among Christians, adherents of other religions have their own views on this exclusive claim underlying the Left Behind books.

Gershom Gorenberg, a journalist based in Israel, provides an example of strong criticism of exclusive attitudes in an article about the Left Behind books titled "Intolerance: The Bestseller." He notes that in the books' storyline Jews must convert or die, to make up for the "national sin" of rejecting Jesus. Gorenberg adds that the books' "anti-Jewishness is exceeded by their anti-Catholicism. . . . In the world of *Left Behind*, there exists a single truth, based on a purportedly literal reading of Scripture; anyone who disagrees with that truth is deceived or evil."[34]

Political and Social Concerns

Critics also worry about seeing world events through an apocalyptic lens, and how American responses may be influenced by such an approach. Several chapters in this volume, especially the ones by Jeanne Kilde and Amy Frykholm, return to this theme.

Application to world events is encouraged by the Left Behind publishers. One paragraph on the Left Behind website states, "Reading the *Left Behind* series has been a haunting experience, especially since September 11, with the war on terror, the struggles between the U.S. and the United Nations, and the war in Iraq and its aftermath. Add to that the violence in Israel over the past two years with the current tensions over the 'roadmap to peace' and you get a sense that events described in the *Left Behind* series seem quite plausible."[35] For some, the end-times scenario helps one properly interpret current events. For others, the inclination to identify our human conflicts with a cosmic battle between good and evil is a dangerous escalation of our problems, making them worse. Is it helpful or not to see today's wars and struggles as part of God's intention, God's plan?

Evangelical Christians constitute a major portion of the readership of the Left Behind series, and they also constitute a significant political base for President George W. Bush, who numbers himself among them. Thus it should not be a surprise if, in the words of historian Paul Boyer, "belief in biblical prophecy is helping mold grass-roots attitudes toward current U.S. foreign policy. . . . all of us would do well to pay attention to the beliefs of the vast company of Americans who read the headlines and watch the news through a filter of prophetic belief."[36]

However, another critique about social and political impact moves in the opposite direction, asking if the theology of the books undercuts efforts to improve the earthly realm. If I believe that the rapture will come soon, leading to an unavoidable seven-year period of tribulation, resolved only by Christ at the end of the period of chaos and destruction, why would I be concerned about protecting the environment, or combating poverty, or working for world peace? All persons may not draw this conclusion, but some have. One television evangelist is reported to have said, "There'll be no peace until Jesus comes. Any preaching of peace prior to this return is heresy; it's against the word of God; it's Antichrist."[37]

The Left Behind series has become exceptionally popular in the United States, but it is unclear how many persons simply read the books as adventure stories and how many receive religious or social guidance from them, consciously or unconsciously. If the novels are to be taken seriously, whatever one's perspective, it would be helpful to learn about the background and intentions of the authors, to become informed about the theological position of the books in light of other alternatives, and to reflect on the social and cultural messages that accompany the story. Popular culture is seldom "just entertainment." If it has the possibility of reflecting tendencies of our society, and of influencing us, it certainly is worthy of discussion and debate.

Notes

1. The airplane quotation in this paragraph is from the Tim LaHaye Ministries website: www.timlahaye.com. Billy Graham, with Jerry Jenkins, *Just as I Am: The Autobiography of Billy Graham* (London: HarperCollins, 1997, 2002).
2. The first volume of the military-focused Left Behind series is Mel Odom, *Apocalypse Dawn* (Wheaton, Ill.: Tyndale House, 2003). The politically focused series begins with Neesa Hart, *End of State* (Wheaton, Ill.: Tyndale House, 2004). The first volume of Jerry Jenkins's new trilogy is *Soon: The Beginning of the End* (Wheaton, Ill.: Tyndale House, 2003). The first volume of Tim LaHaye's new series, actually written by co-author Greg Dinallo, is *Babylon Rising* (New York: Bantam, 2003).
3. "Different Groups Follow Harry Potter, Left Behind, and Jabez," (October 22, 2001), Barna Research Online, www.barna.org.
4. Hal Lindsey with Carole C. Carlson, *The Late Great Planet Earth* (Grand Rapids, Mich.: Zondervan, 1970). The sales statistics and *New York Times* assessment are repeated in many places, including William J. Petersen and Randy Petersen, *100 Christian Books That Changed the Century* (Grand Rapids, Mich.: Fleming H. Revell, 2000), 165–166.
5. Randall Balmer, *Mine Eyes Have Seen the Glory: A Journey into the Evangelical Subculture in America* (New York: Oxford University Press, 1993), 62. See chapter 3 for a discussion of the film and its director.
6. Tim LaHaye, *Spirit-controlled Temperament* (Wheaton, Ill.: Tyndale House, 1966).

7. Tim LaHaye, *Understanding the Male Temperament: What Every Man Would Like to Tell His Wife About Himself . . . But Won't* (Old Tappan, N.J.: Revell, 1977); Tim LaHaye and Beverly LaHaye, *Spirit-controlled Family Living* (Old Tappan, N.J.: Revell, 1978).

8. Tim LaHaye and Beverly LaHaye, *The Act of Marriage: The Beauty of Sexual Love* (Grand Rapids, Mich.: Zondervan, 1976). The quoted phrase is from Larry Eskridge, "And, the Most Influential American Evangelical of the Last 25 Years Is . . ." *Evangelical Studies Bulletin* (Winter 2001), 3. This article, plus Tim LaHaye's own website (www.timlahaye.com), provides much of the basic biographical information about LaHaye summarized here.

9. Glenn H. Utter and John W. Storey, *The Religious Right: A Reference Handbook* (Santa Barbara, Calif.: ABC-CLIO, 1995), 59.

10. Tim LaHaye and John David Morris, *The Ark on Ararat* (Nashville, Tenn.: Thomas Nelson, 1976).

11. Tim LaHaye, *The Battle for the Mind* (Old Tappan, N.J.: Revell, 1980); Tim LaHaye, *The Battle for the Family* (Old Tappan, N.J.: Revell, 1982); Tim LaHaye, *The Battle for the Public Schools* (Old Tappan, N.J.: Revell, 1983).

12. Tim LaHaye, *The Unhappy Gays: What Everyone Should Know about Homosexuality* (Wheaton, Ill.: Tyndale House, 1978).

13. Tim LaHaye and David Noebel, *Mind Seige: The Battle for Truth in the New Millennium* (Nashville, Tenn.: Word Publishing, 2000).

14. Mark A. Noll, *American Evangelical Christianity: An Introduction* (Malden, Mass.: Blackwell Publishers, 2001), 23.

15. Rob Boston, "If Best-Selling End-Times Author Tim LaHaye Has His Way, Church-State Separation Will Be Left Behind," *Church & State* 9 (February 2002), 33; Gerald M. Boyd, "Official in Kemp's Campaign Quits After Reports on Books," *New York Times* (8 December 1987), B13; Marjorie Hyer, "Unlikely Coalition Gathers for Protest of Moon Jailing," *Washington Post* (July 28, 1984), B6; Carolyn Weaver, "Unholy Alliance," *Mother Jones* 11 (January 1986), 14–17, 44, 46.

16. Tim LaHaye, *Rapture under Attack* (Sisters, Ore.: Multnomah Publishers, 1998). Previously published under the title *No Fear of the Storm*.

17. Eskridge, "And the Most Influential American Evangelical," 4.

18. See Jerry Jenkins's website: www.jerryjenkins.com.

19. "Desecration Live Global Chat—Transcript, November 1, 2001," Leftbehind.com.

20. Ida Bailey, "Rapturous Realizations: Don't Dismiss *Left Behind* as Ineffective Scare Tactics," www.Beliefnet.com.

21. Advertisement mailing from "Crossings: The Book Club for Today's Christian Family," Indianapolis, Ind.: December 2001.

22. LaHaye, *Rapture Under Attack*, 13.

23. "The 'Left Behind' View is Out of Left Field," The Lutheran Church—Missouri Synod, Office of the President, Statements, www.lcms.org/president/statements/leftbehind.asp; G. Brent McGuire, "Will You Be 'Left Behind'?" *The Lutheran Witness* (March 2001), 6–8, provides another Missouri Synod critique of the Left Behind books.

24. Gary DeMar, *End Times Fiction: A Biblical Consideration of the Left Behind Theology* (Nashville, Tenn.: Thomas Nelson Publishers, 2001), xviii.

25. Ibid., 207.

26. The Online Covenant Companion: Interview with Phalen about Left Behind, www.covchurch.org/cov/companion/article/0009phelanlb.html.

27. Tim LaHaye and Jerry Jenkins, *Nicolae: The Rise of Antichrist* (Wheaton, Ill.: Tyndale House, 1997), 359.

28. These comments by Chris Shelton can be found on the Presbyterian Church (USA) website: www.pcusa.org/ga213/audio/hearings/tiei01.htm.

29. Cathleen Falsani, "Bishops Warn Catholics about 'Left Behind' Books," *Chicago Sun-Times*, June 6, 2003; Carl E. Olson, *Will Catholics Be Left Behind?: A Critique of the Rapture and Today's Prophecy Preachers* (Ft. Collins, Colo.: Ignatius Press, 2003); Paul Thigpen, *The Rapture Trap: A Catholic Response to "End Times" Fever* (West Chester, Penn.: Ascension Press, 2001). It is interesting that both Olson and Thigpen are former evangelical or fundamentalist Protestants who converted to Catholicism.

30. "Desecration Live Global Chat—Transcript, November 1, 2001," Leftbehind.com.

31. LaHaye, *Rapture under Attack*, 23.

32. Tim LaHaye and Jerry B. Jenkins, with Norman B. Rohrer, *These Will Not Be Left Behind: True Stories of Changed Lives* (Wheaton, Ill.: Tyndale House, 2003), xii–xiii.

33. Teresa Malcolm, "Fearful Faith in End Times Novels," *National Catholic Reporter* (June 15, 2001), 13.

34. Gershom Gorenberg, "Intolerance: The Bestseller," *The American Prospect* (September 23, 2002), 44.

35. www.leftbehind.com/channelbooks.asp?channelID = 186.

36. Paul S. Boyer, "John Darby Meets Saddam Hussein: Foreign Policy and Bible Prophecy," *Chronicle of Higher Education* (14 February 2003).

37. This statement has been quoted repeatedly, for instance in Malcolm, "Fearful Faith in End Times Novels," 13. The common source seems to be Grace Halsell, *Prophecy and Politics: Militant Evangelists on the Road to Nuclear War* (Westport, Conn.: Lawrence Hill & Company, 1986), 16, who attributes the statement to James Robison. Unfortunately, Halsell's entire book contains no citations, so we are unaware of her exact source.

2

How Did Left Behind's Particular Vision of the End Times Develop?

A Historical Look at Millenarian Thought

JEANNE HALGREN KILDE

How will the world end? With a bang? With a whimper? Will God come out of the sky in a cloud? Will vast armies destroy all humanity? Will the sun's fire engulf the planet? Such questions have fascinated humankind for millennia. The Left Behind series presents in fictional form authors Tim LaHaye and Jerry B. Jenkins's heartfelt beliefs about what will happen at the end of time.

Like many Christian thinkers before them, LaHaye and Jenkins view the end of time as the termination of historical processes put into play by God himself. The promised return of the resurrected Jesus Christ is the essential culminating event of this history. As we shall see in this chapter, LaHaye and Jenkins's view is a distinctive understanding of Christ's return, which, although it is steeped in centuries of Christian thought, is very much a product of the nineteenth and twentieth centuries in which it developed.

The view is called "premillennial dispensationalism," and it is based on a process of biblical exegesis or interpretation that links together scriptural passages from a variety of New and Old Testament books to conclude that a specific series of events will take place in conjunction with Christ's return. These events constitute a period that has come to be known as the "end times."

We can trace several of these events through the Left Behind novels. The first is the rapture, in which all true Christian believers are called to heaven. This is immediately followed by a series of violent occurrences that take place during a seven-year period called the tribulation. During this period, an evil antichrist achieves world domination by perverting governments and global organizations for his own ends and ultimately brings destruction down on all humanity. At the end of seven horrific years, Jesus Christ returns in the second coming or Glorious Revelation to vanquish the antichrist in the battle of Armageddon and to judge the nations. Next follows the millennium, a thousand-year period of peace, during which Christ reigns on earth. At the close of the millennium, a final uprising of Satan occurs, but with his defeat by Christ, eternity is established.

Although Left Behind is an imaginative, fictional musing on the details of the end times, LaHaye and Jenkins believe the general outline of events themselves is divinely ordained and will necessarily come to pass. Theirs is certainly not the only Christian view of what will happen when Jesus makes his promised return. In fact, over the course of the last two thousand years, Christians frequently have been preoccupied, and at times obsessed, with ideas about the end of time, a category of theology called "eschatology." As a result, they have postulated a rich variety of ideas about God's culmination of human history. This chapter traces changing notions of Christian eschatology over the two thousand years of Christian history. As we will see, each of the interpretations examined has unique connections to the cultural context in which it developed, whether that be the first century or the twentieth. The view developed in the Left Behind series is no different; it is intimately linked to the political and social events of the late twentieth and early twenty-first centuries.

Several related conclusions also will arise from this historical examination:

- Although some Christians have viewed scriptural references to Christ's return as metaphorical, others have taken them as literal predictions of events.
- Whether living in the first century or the twenty-first, those who have seen scripture as predicting events usually have related those predictions to events occurring within their own times.
- Premillennial dispensationalism and its idea of a rapture as the watershed event in the return of Jesus Christ are relative newcomers in the 2,000-year history of Christian thought, developed only a century and a half ago.
- Premillennial dispensationalism is a powerful tool for evangelizing, but it is based on an understanding of history that, critics charge, relieves human society of responsibility for public life and can have serious social ramifications.

Most important, the historical perspective developed here demonstrates that theology and religious ideas are never monolithic. Understandings of God, Jesus, and the Bible develop out of social, cultural, and political debates prevalent at any given time. Linked as they are to historical contexts, they often come into conflict with one another. Even when believers share many views, they can disagree on crucial points. As readers contemplate the perspective presented in the Left Behind series, they should view it as one of many Christian perspectives, created by individuals strongly influenced by the worlds and times within which they live. By tracing the development of the end-times ideas that inform the series, this chapter will aid readers in better understanding LaHaye and Jenkins's imaginative treatment of the events they believe will come to pass.

Apocalypse and the Early Christians

The roots of Christian ideas about the end times are deep, going back to ancient Judaism and its stories about the divine punishment of enemies and the end of the world. These stories were called "apocalyptic," which meant "revelatory" or "revelation" in Greek, for they were thought to reveal God's ultimate intentions for humanity. Jewish apocalyptic writing flowered from about 250 B.C.E., or the time of Daniel, to around 100 C.E., in response to threats made on traditional Jewish culture. Thus, right from its earliest development, apocalyptic literature was closely linked to ongoing current events.

Early Jewish apocalyptic literature opposed Roman efforts to Hellenize, or impose Greek culture on, the ancient world. The book of Daniel condemned Hellenistic values and showed that God would reward and preserve Jewish culture and punish those who assimilated into Greek culture. In a vision, Daniel is assured that the beleaguered Jews, living under the rule of Greek emperor Antiochus IV, will be saved and rewarded after a period of tribulation: "At that time Michael, the great prince, the protector of your people, shall arise. There shall be a time of anguish such as has never occurred since nations first came into existence. But at that time your people shall be delivered, everyone who is found written in the book" (Dan. 12:1). The timing of these events is stressed: "From the time that the regular burnt offering is taken away and the abomination that desolates is set up, there shall be one thousand two hundred ninety days. Happy are those who persevere and attain the thousand three hundred thirty-five days. But you, go your way, and rest; you shall rise for your reward at the end of the days" (Dan. 12:11–13). Having persevered through suffering, the Jews would fulfill their role as God's chosen people.[1]

Apocalyptic texts like these helped the Jewish people make sense of their lives within the framework of God's purpose for the world. Early Christianity, which arose some generations later, owed much to those earlier writings. In particular, early Christians echoed ancient Jewish themes of a rescuing messiah who would save humankind. Jesus himself is described in Matthew 24 as having made a series of prophetic statements similar to the earlier ones in Daniel. These statements predict suffering, retribution, and reward for those who remain faithful to Jesus and his heavenly Father. After Jesus' death, those who believed he was this messiah eagerly awaited his imminent return, for Jesus said it would happen in their lifetime. Like others before them, they felt that God justified and legitimated their beliefs and would quickly return his son to punish those who sinned and to bestow his favor and reward on the faithful.

After the execution of Jesus, some of his followers—including Paul and the authors of the book of Matthew—continued writing in this apocalyptic tradition, describing his return, or the parousia, in an inspiring way that assured the early Christians that it would occur during their lifetimes and helped them maintain their faith through terrible persecutions. The imminence of Christ's return became an important theme. So when advancing time brought the deaths of some of the Christians at Thessalonica and there was concern for the salvation of the dead, Paul reassured the survivors that those who had died would be resurrected just as Christ had been resurrected and would enjoy God's vindication as well. He urged them to "encourage one another" with images borrowed from earlier Jewish apocalyptic writing: the trumpet calls of the archangel at God's descent from heaven to vindicate just believers. Similar descriptions of Christ's return appear in Matthew and later in Mark and Luke and also were intended to bolster the faith of early Christians.[2]

The best-known apocalyptic Christian text is the book of Revelation, which describes a series of fantastic and frightening visions experienced by a man named John of Patmos. Drawing, as did Paul, on earlier prophetic texts (particularly Matthew), this book describes many of the events that later interpreters, including Left Behind authors LaHaye and Jenkins, have pieced together in a time line of end-times occurrences—from the opening of the seven seals of the great scroll of divine wisdom to the coming of the four horsemen of the apocalypse. Most important, it predicts the millennium, a period of a thousand years during which Christ will reign on earth, bringing peace to all.

To be sure, then, Christians have viewed their God and messiah through what might be called a "prophetic lens" from the very earliest years. Jesus' promised return was understood in the context of ancient Jewish prophecies of the messiah who would save the nation of Israel. Recognizing and believing in Jesus' role in this divine plan, Christians would be saved, assured eternal life in paradise. Convinced it would happen during their lifetimes, Christians in the first and second centuries eagerly awaited Christ's return, for it would bring his judgment down on their enemies and their own eternal salvation.

The End Times and the Growth of Christian Orthodoxy

This view that Christ would come and the history of the world would soon end gained momentum from early Christians' struggle to disperse their message in a Roman world that was at best tolerant of the upstart religion and at worst persecutory. In this context, divine judgment and punishment of one's enemies, along with eternal reward for the faithful, were powerful motivators for early believers.

Yet as time passed, circumstances changed. In the fourth century, as Christianity became institutionalized throughout the Roman world under the Christian emperor Constantine, interest in the end times waned. It diminished in part because the position of Christianity in society had changed radically. No longer just another unofficial religion in the Roman empire, sometimes tolerated, sometimes not, the Christian church that Constantine established was increasingly wealthy, powerful, and cohesive across the Roman world. Christians, now enjoying high status, were little interested in contemplating the end times. Stories of divine punishment of enemies held little meaning as Christianity seemed to triumph over all other religions.

During this period, what little apocalyptic writing that appeared was frequently suppressed. Existing apocalyptic texts, like the book of Revelation, were widely interpreted not as literal indications of forthcoming events but as allegorical descriptions of spiritual development. The third-century Roman theologian Origen, for instance, argued that the establishment of the kingdom of God would be a spiritual event that would take place in the hearts and souls of believers, not in the real world at any real time. Later, in the early fifth century, Augustine, whose work would become an important foundation of orthodox Christian thought, argued that Revelation was an allegory and that the establishment of the Christian church itself constituted the advent of the millennium.[3] Its continued expansion and hegemony was the culmination of God's plan. As Mark Reasoner and Stanley Grenz explain in other chapters in this volume, interpretations like these, asserting that these texts offered metaphors for spiritual ideas, have remained popular and widespread throughout Christianity ever since and remain widely accepted today.

Despite opposition from the majority in the late Roman period, pockets of messianic or apocalyptic thought persisted. For instance, two important collections of prophetic writings dating from 350 to 340 C.E.—the Sibylline texts (a collection of Jewish, Christian, and pagan works) and the First Letter of John in the New Testament—developed several apocalyptic themes, including the messianic role of Constantine as a warrior god, the Golden Age of the Roman empire, the conversion of Jews to Christianity, the notion of the antichrist, a great end-times battle, and the second coming of Christ.

Such texts, however, represented only pockets on the fringes of Christian thought, for the orthodox church, growing powerful with the blessings of the empire, had little need for stories of retribution. Focusing on the spiritual character of salvation, orthodoxy viewed the church as, if not the culmination of a divine historical process, certainly a significant event in the divine plan— an event that mitigated the immediacy of the second coming. Indeed, the establishment of the church rendered previous ideas of the end times obsolete, for with the church in place, Christ's salvation could focus exclusively on the spiritual condition of human souls.

End Times Ideas in the Medieval Period

With the collapse of the Roman empire in the fifth century, Christianized portions of Europe were plunged into social and political chaos. Wave upon wave of marauding invaders assaulted towns, cities, and the isolated monasteries that had been established by Christians. Given the climate of violence, hunger, and despair, the thoughts of many Christians likely did turn again to the end times. But few expressions of these concern survived the turmoil of the period. We do know, however, that as social stability returned in the eleventh century, eschatological ideas had shifted considerably from those of the triumphant Roman times, taking on a new and distinctive character. End-times thinkers now were convinced that God had ordered history in a pattern of distinct periods (later called "dispensations") in which God dealt with humanity in specific ways. Schemes describing these eras were posed, indicating that Christians' understanding of end times and human history itself was changing.

In the 1100s a Cistercian abbot and mystic named Joachim of Fiore claimed that the Bible revealed a succession of three periods in history: the period of the Old Testament, which was ruled by God the Father; the period of the Church, which was revealed in the New Testament and ruled by Christ, the Son; and last, the coming kingdom of love or the millennium, to be ruled by the Holy Spirit. Joachim predicted that the beginning of this last era would be marked by a significant cataclysm, an event that would occur, he warned, around the year 1260. During this final period, he asserted, the Latin and Greek portions of the Christian church would be reunited, the Jews would be converted to Christianity, and Christ would bring a peaceful reign.

Joachim's ideas, although unorthodox, deeply connected to the growing interest in Trinitarian theology and briefly enjoyed some influence. In 1256, however, the Roman Catholic Church condemned the idea that the Bible predicted history. Chiliasm, or belief in a coming millennium, was pronounced a heresy. Orthodox Christianity, the church claimed, was a matter of here and now. One's personal, ongoing relationship with God through prayer and the sacraments was of utmost importance, not some future utopia. Later, Thomas Aquinas also refuted millenarian ideas, arguing that the Bible's messages were metaphorical and spiritual, not historical.[4]

Although our survey here is brief, we can see that Christian interest in apocalyptic understandings of biblical texts has waxed and waned since the earliest days of the church. Periods of strife often have seen an accompanying rise in such interest, while periods of Christian dominance have seen a decline in those views. In addition, a tension between literal and metaphorical understandings of scripture has characterized these pendulum swings in Christian thought.

The Protestant Reformation

Interest in apocalyptic thought and millenarianism arose anew with the social, political, and religious changes that swept over Europe in the fifteenth and sixteenth centuries—the period known as the Reformation. As population growth, civil dislocation, mass emigration, war, and religious reform changed the face of Europe in the late 1400s and early 1500s, biblical passages pertaining to the end times were cast into a new and prominent role. As in earlier times, civil and religious crises were viewed within the context of biblical interpretation, but now advancements in printing and increased literacy helped to spread those interpretations widely. With the growing criticism of the Roman Catholic Church and the political turmoil that followed, many Protestants developed a singularly apocalyptic state of mind, putting themselves "on the lookout," so to speak, for prophetic signs of the end times.[5]

Renaissance Europeans had new means at their disposal to spread their ideas. The printing press was vastly improved in 1455 with the development of movable type, and, with literacy expanding, books became important new vehicles for apocalyptic thoughts. Religious texts like the Gutenberg Bible were of great interest to Renaissance readers, and among the most popular was the book of Revelation, which appeared in print in over 750 different editions between 1498 and 1650.[6]

One edition of the book of Revelation featured woodcut illustrations by the gifted artist Albrecht Dürer. Among the sixteen drawings included in the book, the most evocative and powerful one depicted the four horsemen of the apocalypse. This picture of charging horses bearing ferocious riders and trampling bystanders seemed to represent the turmoil of the Reformation era itself, leading some Christians to associate real-life events with the visions depicted in the text. The white horse of the apocalypse was associated with the purifying theology of the Reformation, the red horse with war, the black with famine, and the pale horse with disease and death. On the lookout for signs of the onset of an apocalyptic purging of the church, many viewed the visions of John of Patmos as having prophesied a future that the religious turmoil of the Reformation was now fulfilling.[7]

With popular interest in the end times sparked by such publications, Italian preacher Girolamo Savonarola emerged as an important apocalyptic voice. Savonarola felt that the humanistic philosophy that was becoming so popular in the Italian court—advanced in particular by the Medici family, who were patrons of the arts as well as the church—was pagan and brought immorality into the church. In the late 1400s, he called for the reformation of the church, charging that it was marred by corruption at all levels, even within the papacy. Savonarola urged his followers to renounce luxury, and he delivered stirring apocalyptic sermons that vividly depicted the wrath of God descending to punish and cleanse the church and everyone else who was enamored of worldly goods and immoral ways. For a brief period he was quite popular in Florence, where many people attended his "bonfires of the vanities," pitching their books, jewels, playing cards, and dice into the fire. Not surprisingly, however, his critique of the church and the papacy brought a strong response, and he was excommunicated in 1497. A year later he was executed.

Critique of the church did not expire with Savonarola, however, nor did its expression in apocalyptic terms. Within two decades would emerge another leader who linked the corruption of the church with the end times. Martin Luther, leader of the Protestant Reformation, did not initially express his efforts to reform the church in apocalyptic language. With his excommunication in 1521, however, and his growing realization that a new religious perspective, a new respect for the gospel, would have to flourish outside of the Roman church, he gradually became convinced that the end times were imminent.

Eschatology lay at the heart of Luther's view of Christianity. His theme of salvation through faith alone focused Christian life on union with God after death. Only death, in his view, would unite the individual with God. Similarly, only the Day of the Lord, the Day of Redemption, would bring the reckoning of the world itself with God, eradicating evil and changing the very essence of earthly life. Luther was no millenarian, however. The idea of a peaceful, earthly millennium ruled by Christ was never a part of his thought. The Day of the Lord would be final, ending all time and place as we know it.

Luther's longing for the Day of the Lord was intensified by the growing corruption he saw on earth. Like the narrator of the book of Daniel, which he had studied thoroughly, he saw decline and desecration evident everywhere. People ignored the truth of the gospel. Evil, hate, and suffering were rampant. The only hope was to have faith in the coming judgment of the Lord. Faith would bring one through the catastrophe of this world and into the beauty of union with God. Thus, in tension with Luther's hope for salvation is a growing pessimism about the world's situation.

This pessimism infused Luther's analysis of the Bible, particularly his understanding of the prophesies of Daniel. In Daniel he saw a pattern of world decline that foretold the end times, and that same pattern, he felt, was all too evident in his own world. The beast with ten horns, Luther claimed, paralleled the many kingdoms of Christendom. The little horn, a particular threat to Christianity, he identified as the Turk—that is, the power of Islam against Christianity, a threat that also appeared in Ezekiel in the form of Gog. The antichrist, he reasoned, was an even more powerful threat to Christianity, due to its internal character. The antichrist had to be within the church; thus, it must be the papacy itself, he asserted.

Luther also saw other signs that indicated the imminence of the end times: earthquakes, eclipses, storms, floods, and plagues; scorn for the gospel, apparent, he felt in the Diet of Worms, which excommunicated him; and the turmoil of the Peasants' War. All of these situations, in a society seemingly out of control, indicated that God's judgment must be soon experienced. The only escape would be through faith.[8]

It should be noted here that the method Luther used to argue the imminence of the end times and to identify the major threats to Christianity is frequently referred to as the proof-text method. This method associates actual events, usually contemporary ones, with specific prophecies found in scripture. The Turkish invasion of eastern Europe in 1526, for instance, was seen by some as corresponding to the images of a war between mighty kingdoms described in Daniel. Similarly, Luther was not alone in identifying the Turks as Gog (Eze. 38, 39; Rev. 20:8) and the papacy as the antichrist (1–2 John). Natural events, such as a comet seen in 1532, also were associated with specific texts (Matt. 24:29; Rev. 6:13) as proof of their cosmic role.[9]

Millenarians and apocalyptic interpreters of every era have used the proof-text method, arguing that scripture communicates the divine plan for human history itself—and that this plan is rapidly approaching its culmination. This is also the method used by Tim LaHaye and Jerry Jenkins in the Left Behind series and the message they intend to convey. Whether employed in the early Christian period, in the medieval period, during the Reformation, or in the present day, the process of associating scriptural passages with current events expresses the human desire to know and understand the future while it also reveals the human need to believe that one's own time is, in fact, a key moment in all of history. Thus, the epoch in which one lives gives meaning not only to oneself but to all humanity and history as well.

Such views can, however, result in serious consequences. One radical reformer, Jan Bockelson, convinced himself and many followers that he was the messiah of the Last Days, who had come to lead the purification of the world. In order to accomplish this purification, Bockelson and his followers imposed a reign of terror on the German town of Münster in 1534. Protestants, particularly Lutherans, who did not follow his views were expelled from the city or executed for their beliefs, and the town was brought under siege as the group attempted to enact the end-times scenario they read in scripture.[10]

For Luther, Bockelson, and many others, then, being on the lookout for signs of the end times both grew out of the situations of their time and contributed to those situations. The result was a frame of mind that has been called a "Protestant apocalyptic tradition."[11] This perspective, however, was not without controversy, for it was rejected by major reform thinkers. John Calvin, for instance, urged his followers to focus on personal salvation and their own relationship with God. Rejecting historical understandings of prophecy, he felt that God's kingdom could be spread by believers who shared in God's glory by doing so. Christians themselves could assist in God's vanquishing of "the darkness and falsehoods of Satan's kingdom."[12] Like Luther's vision, Calvin's was not millenarian. He too felt that with God's final judgment, the entire world would change. Ulrich Zwingli, another Reformation leader, was little concerned with apocalyptic prophecy. He emphasized developing the Christian community in the here and now, a message that, like Calvin's, carried a hint of a progressive view of human improvement over time. Zwingli, in fact, addressed future generations in some of his writings, certain that the expansion of Christian truth would be carried on.[13]

Nevertheless, apocalyptic thought played a vital role in the critique of the Roman Catholic Church and in the Reformation itself. Being on the lookout for prophetic signs became deeply embedded in Protestant thought and action, and as Protestantism crossed the Atlantic, messianic ideas would continue to influence religion and society in the New World.

Biblical Prophesy and Millennialism in Early America

The extent to which millenarian ideas influenced the social, political, and religious development of America is hard to understate. European exploration of the Western Hemisphere itself seemed to verify that history was moving toward a divine culminating era. Christopher Columbus saw his voyages to the New World and his role in history as fulfillment of biblical prophesy. He wrote, "God made me the messenger of the new heaven and the new earth of which he spoke in the Apocalypse of St. John . . . and he showed me where to find it."[14] In Columbus's view not only did he play a role within divine history, but so did the American continents themselves.

Over a century later English Puritans establishing the Massachusetts Bay Colony similarly conceived of the New World as a fulfillment of part of God's divine plan. John Winthrop, first governor of the colony, asserted that if the new colony stayed true to its Puritan (Calvinist) beliefs, God would aid its members and make the colony as a "city upon a hill," a shining example of his own "elect" or sanctified nation (cf. Matt. 5:14). Having removed themselves from the corruption of England and Europe, the Puritans creating this purified new world would confidently greet the impending return of Christ.

Despite this initial hopefulness, what Winthrop and the Massachusetts Puritans ultimately experienced brought them little comfort. Their New World colony did not seem to be enjoying God's providence. Throughout the seventeenth century, the first and second generations of English colonizers looked for signs that God was aiding them, but what they saw were devastating wars with the Indians, starvation, hardship, and growing numbers of unchurched people arriving from England and Europe.

These realities transformed their outlook. Many people read them as signs of an impending climax or culmination of history, and they grew convinced that God would soon end human existence in a burst of wrath, judgment, and punishment. Here again we see social crises engendering apocalyptic thought. In the late 1600s poet Michael Wigglesworth published a highly popular poem, titled the "The Day of Doom," which warned of the apocalyptic conclusion that would soon beset humanity, and Calvinist ministers such as John Cotton and Increase Mather spoke frequently of the coming day when judgment would rain down.

For these seventeenth-century writers and theologians, the omniscient God had forewarned of this impending doom in the Bible, but they also reasoned that his foreknowledge extended beyond simply knowing when Christ would return. God, who knew all things, they asserted, also knew who would be saved and who would not. This belief in predestination went hand-in-hand with the understanding of biblical prophecy as a blueprint to human history. God's omniscient power extended to all things: He had foreordained not only the historical trajectory of human society but that of individuals as well. Puritans hoped for salvation and dreaded the opposite, but their fate would be revealed only upon death, just as the fate of the world would be culminated only in a climactic judgment.[15]

In the eighteenth century a more optimistic, Augustinian understanding of the overlapping character of the kingdom of God and the current world emerged among Protestant millenarians. Noted theologian and minister Jonathan Edwards exemplified this new approach. Edwards kept a journal in which he recorded "Notes on the Apocalypse," and he preached many sermons that used scripture and current events to point to the imminent consummation of history. He claimed that the central theme of the book of Revelation was the destruction of the antichrist, which he, like Luther, identified as the Roman papacy. Also like Luther, he felt that time was on the verge of its ultimate culmination. Unlike Luther's, however, Edwards's apocalyptic thought did not stem from despair over current events. Instead, Edwards was enormously heartened by the revival of religion that had taken place in the New England region in the 1730s. With conversions to Christianity growing and gospel truth spreading, Edwards saw a new day at hand, a new era of Christian faith centered in America. He wrote, "[We have] abundant reason to hope that what is now seen in America, and especially in New England, may prove the dawn of that glorious day; and the very uncommon and wonderful circumstances and events of this work, seem strongly to argue that God intends it as the beginning or forerunner of something vastly great."[16] This optimistic view harkened back to the Puritan idea of America as God's elect nation and anticipated a far different kind of end times than had Luther.

The religious revivals that gave Edwards such hope were grounded in a humanistically centered idea called Arminianism: the belief that individuals themselves could influence their salvation by placing their faith in Christ. This view had been challenging the Calvinist view of predestination for over a century, but it was only in the 1740s and 1750s that it gained wide currency as preachers like the British evangelists George Whitefield and John Wesley staged religious revivals aimed at gaining converts to Christianity. During revivals, ministers preached, faithful Christians told stories about their own conversions to Christianity, and large numbers of individuals experienced their own conversions (now more commonly known as being born again). As revivals spread, Edwards's belief that these public religious activities heralded a new day was echoed by many religious leaders, who similarly thought that not only was the end imminent but that the ultimate fulfillment of Christ and Revelation probably would begin in America. "The Kingdom of God is come to us at this Day," Whitefield proclaimed. A new age had arrived.

These evangelical revivalists shared an optimistic view of the progression of divine history toward the millennium. This perspective, called "postmillennialism," asserted that divine history was occurring in the present time and was working toward human perfection, which, when achieved, would prompt the return of Christ. In other words Christ, they thought, would return after society had achieved a period of peace and human perfection—that is, after the millennium was established.

Postmillennialism corresponded with other philosophical views popular during the eighteenth century. Enlightenment thinkers stressed human rationality, free will, and individual rights. In a political context, this perspective informed a growing dissatisfaction with colonial rule and contributed, by the 1770s, to the American war with England. The old authority of monarchs and aristocrats, many argued, could be challenged by the authority of the individual in whom God had vested certain inalienable rights. This philosophical position, like its religious counterpart in Arminianism, was profoundly optimistic. People could, indeed, change their situations; social and political oppression could be lessened or even overcome through human action.

Convinced that human faith and action could usher in the millennium, many Christians began to focus intently on the moral improvement of society. Particularly in the nineteenth century, Protestants who were caught up in postmillennial enthusiasm strove to curb alcohol consumption, end prostitution, establish democratic government, extend public education, and convert sinners to Christianity. Sunday schools, moral reform societies, tract and missionary societies, and the abolitionist movement all shared the belief that, with their efforts and the mass conversion of individuals to Christianity, society would flourish and the kingdom of God would emerge. In addition, a number of religious communitarian societies emerged, whose members were intent on living fully Christian lives in isolated communities in order to achieve a heavenly paradise on earth in anticipation of Christ's return. From the Shakers to the Oneidans to the Rappites and Harmonists, these communal experiments epitomized postmillennial thinking.

The Advent of Premillennial Dispensationalism

The particular scheme that forms the basis of the Left Behind series originally emerged in this context of optimistic postmillennialism. While most evangelicals in the nineteenth century held a generally postmillennial outlook, a handful of groups were not so sanguine about the future of humanity. These individuals asserted that no perfecting activities or good works could improve the world or usher in the millennium; rather, Christ must come in judgment to purge the world of immorality and evil and then remake it in the millennium. Individuals, replete with sin, had only one hope of avoiding damnation: to convert to Christianity as quickly as possible, before Christ's imminent return. Thus, while postmillennialists saw divine history as a process of improvement, these premillennialists, who felt that Christ's return must happen before the millennium, saw history as a struggle between good and evil in which human society was inherently corrupt and which only Christ could resolve.

As with Luther and other previous millenarians, early nineteenth-century premillennialists were on the lookout for signs that society had become so corrupt that Christ must surely appear soon to set things right. The atrocities of the French Revolution filled the bill perfectly. In addition, end-times thought also was fueled by feelings of religious persecution, particularly in Great Britain, where the state-sponsored Church of England ran roughshod over dissenting religious perspectives. British religious dissenters scoured the Bible for prophecies regarding the end times, and they came together to share their findings at several conferences in the 1820s and 1830s. It is with these meetings that the understanding articulated today in the Left Behind series—a position called premillennial dispensationalism—first began to take on its modern shape, though, to be sure, many of the ideas grew out of earlier interpretations.

The first steps toward systemizing premillennial dispensationalism occurred in England during conferences held in Albury Park from 1826 to 1829. Attended by English and Scottish Anglican clergy, these conferences were intended to establish a chronology of world events as described in scriptural texts, describe the events of the second coming, and discuss the possibility for the restoration of the Jews to Palestine, an event participants agreed would herald the onset of the end-times events. The only authority accepted by the conferees was the Bible, which was not to be read as allegorically or symbolically conveying its spiritual messages, the approach of the new "higher biblical criticism," but was to be read "literally"—that is, as a document describing literal events occurring either in the past, present, or the future.[17]

Among the tenets this conference endorsed was the view that human history will end in cataclysmic judgment and destruction and that the year-day system of using scripture to calculate the onset of these end times was appropriate. This system, first proposed in the early seventeenth century to explain why Christ had not returned centuries earlier, as a literal reading of the Bible suggested, substituted a year for every mention of a day in crucial biblical texts. Thus, when the Bible said "day," it really meant "year," in God's parlance. This strategy, of course, was a divergence from the conferees' desire for a fully literal approach to scripture. With regard to the passage of time, they agreed, God's language needed to be understood metaphorically.

Using the year-day system, the Albury Park conferences calculated that the vials of wrath described in Revelation 16 were just then being poured out and that the second advent or return of Christ would happen at any minute. They also pointed to the atrocities of the French Revolution and the social disorder caused by the Industrial Revolution as corroborating signs that Christ soon would reappear.

The notion that Christ would soon return was not limited to the Albury Park conferees, however. About the same time as the conferences, a small group of dissenters in Scotland, who were also concerned about what seemed like increasing corruption in the world, became convinced of the imminence of Christ's return when they began to have amazing, supernatural experiences of the Holy Spirit. Filled with the Spirit, James Macdonald of Glasgow seemed to have the power to heal the ill; his brother George spoke in tongues. More important for our inquiry, their sister, Mary Macdonald, had several wondrous visions of Christ. She described one in this way: "the awful state of the land . . . pressed upon me. I saw the blindness and infatuation of the people to be very great . . . but suddenly . . . I saw . . . the Lord himself descending from heaven with a shout."[18] Mary was convinced by her vision that the Spirit which filled true believers lent them a "spiritual eye" that would allow them to "see" Christ when he returned and thus be "caught up to meet him." The spiritual eye also would shield them from being deceived by wickedness and the "false Christ." Filled with the Spirit and the spiritual eye, true Christians would pass through the trials to "be counted worthy to stand before the Son of man."[19]

Although it is not likely that Macdonald's mystical vision was widely known, it did correspond with the perspectives on the end times being proposed at the Albury conferences and being discussed by others in Great Britain. In particular, Macdonald's vision correlated with ideas presented at another series of prophetic conferences held that same year by a group critical of the Church of Ireland. Among those who attended was John Nelson Darby, a former Church of Ireland priest who had joined a schismatic group called the Brethren, which had proclaimed the church corrupt and split from it in the late 1820s. Four years later Darby himself would become one of several leaders of a schism within the Brethren that would bring about the formation of the Plymouth Brethren, a group that would become widely associated with pretribulationist premillennial dispensationalism, the very view that now, over a century and half later, informs the Left Behind series.

As with Savonarola and Luther, Darby's concern about the end times was instigated by perceived corruption in the church. Darby felt that the Church of Ireland (and England) was false in its teachings and that its erroneousness contributed to a widespread lack of belief in the gospel. Darby, like many before him who despaired of ongoing cultural, social, and spiritual conditions, postulated that God soon would bring about the culmination of human history. Given the corruption of the church, however, it was not likely, in his opinion, that many of those who considered themselves Christians actually would be numbered among those to be selected for eternal salvation. Most would be damned. But, he asked, what would happen to the true Christians? Did they deserve to endure the punishing and apocalyptic events of the end times?

Attempting to answer these questions, Darby asserted that the true Christians would be spared the soon-to-commence horrors of an apocalyptic end times. Like Mary Macdonald, he claimed they would be lifted, or "caught up," into heaven, whisked away in a moment to dwell with Christ, before the onset of the dreadful events. Unlike Macdonald, who received her understanding though spiritual revelation in a vision, Darby based his view on a proof text, 1 Thessalonians 4:17. This "secret rapture," as he called it, would be brought about by Christ prior to the period of trials, the tribulation, and thus we call the position "pretribulationist."

The question of whether this secret rapture was essentially a new idea, unique to Darby and the Brethren's theology, or a refinement of earlier understandings has been vigorously debated by a variety of writers. A somewhat similar idea of a physical lifting of Christians into heaven had been suggested a century earlier by American Puritan leader Cotton Mather. Similarly, Mary Macdonald, as we have seen, talked about being lifted up by Christ, while some were left.[20] Tracing the exact origins of any idea is frequently an impossible task, particularly when, as in this case, the idea has its roots in centuries-old discussions. What can be said with some certainty is that it was with Darby and the Plymouth Brethren that the idea was given name, the rapture, and it became a cornerstone of a theological system that would resonate with many in the nineteenth and twentieth centuries.

In fact, more radical than the secret rapture idea was Darby's claim that it really had nothing to do with the second coming of Christ. Rather, he said, it was a means of reestablishing the prophetic progression or time line indicated in the Bible, which had been interrupted temporarily. Darby came to this conclusion in his attempt to understand why the Old Testament prophets had not specifically mentioned the Christian church. Given the importance of Christianity and the hope for salvation it offers humanity, why, he asked, had God not revealed its future formation to the Hebrew prophets? The realities of what had in fact transpired—the formation of the Christian church—seemed to give lie to the earlier prophecies. Yet this was impossible, in Darby's view, because the texts themselves were inspired by God and therefore infallible.

To solve this conundrum, Darby postulated that what earlier dispensationalist thinkers had called the "church era,"—that is, the period extending from the death of Jesus to the present day—was, in fact, a kind of pause or parentheses in the chronology of events presented in biblical text—a hiatus between dispensations—and that this pause had simply not been revealed to the ancient prophets. To end the pause or close the parentheses, Christ would eliminate the true church by calling it to heaven and thus restart the chronology and instigate the events described in the books of Daniel and Revelation. Thus, Darby reasoned, the events of the end times await the conclusion of this pause, and, along with all the other prophesied events, they remain in the future.[21]

Not surprisingly, Darby's ideas drew heavy fire, even from premillennialists. In particular, those millenarians who argued that current events like the French Revolution corresponded to biblical prophesies were outraged with the suggestion that the events of Revelation had not yet begun and in fact would not begin until after the true church had been called to heaven. Their more traditional "historicist" position, which sought proof texts to place ongoing events into the divine plan, was significantly threatened by Darby's "futurist" position, which located prophesied events in a future that would be launched only by Christ's return. Historicist millenarians as well as non-millennialists attacked Darby's ideas as nonbiblical, arguing that not only was a secret advent of Christ not literally described in the Bible but that it contradicted parts of scripture.[22]

Despite this opposition, Darby's futurist position was appealing for a number of reasons. It emphasized that the second coming could happen at any time, keeping imminence in place and, even more important, eliminating the need for humanity to wait for or identify any specific event or series of events as signs of Christ's return. Over the centuries historicists have been embarrassed again and again as Christ had not returned despite identification of events presumed to be scriptural signs of the impending event. Further, in a period of strong evangelicalism and revival-inspired religious enthusiasm, Darby's notion of being physically swept away in a dramatic moment carried great emotional appeal.

Despite sharp criticism, Darby continued to advance the idea of the secret rapture and the chronological parentheses throughout Great Britain and, during a series of visits between 1862 and 1877, throughout the United States as well. In America, Darby found receptive audiences, for as we have seen, millenarian ideas already had deep roots in American soil. At the turn of the twentieth century, many American evangelicals would embrace Darbyite pretribulationist premillennial dispensationalism.[23]

Premillennialism in the United States

At the time Darby was developing his ideas in England, postmillennial revivalists in the United States were in ascendancy, predicting that a glorious future was to be won through conversions, which would perfect human society and usher in the kingdom of God. Nevertheless, some Americans did find the premillennial position persuasive, most notably Vermont lay preacher William Miller and his followers. Miller had spent several years in Bible study, fascinated by the year-day system and attempting to predict the precise onset of the second coming. In the 1820s he became convinced that the Bible revealed that it would come sometime in the year 1843. Over the next several years Miller spread his message of the impending Advent to anyone who would listen, and by 1843 he had attracted several hundred (perhaps thousands of) followers. Believing that Christ was coming and would call them up to heaven, these "Millerites" sold their worldly possessions and assembled on hilltops in March 1843. When Christ did not appear, Miller did some recalculating and the groups reassembled in October 1844. Alas, again the moment did not come.[24] The dramatic and very public failure of the Millerites, along with the optimism of a new nation caught up in the new democratic national experiment, evangelical revivalism, and industrial development, relegated premillennialist warnings of impending apocalypse to the margins of society.

Two decades later, however, premillennial dispensationalism did gain followers in the United States, spurred in no small part by the national and spiritual crises caused by the slavery issue and resulting Civil War. These traumatic national events challenged the progressive postmillennial outlook shared by evangelicals. As the slavery debate raged between 1830 and 1861, Protestant congregations and denominations began to split apart over differing views of the role the church should play with respect to slavery and other controversial political issues. Working toward postmillennial reform, and particularly abolitionism, seemed to many to add to the nation's turmoil. Progressive notions seemed unrealistic to many who feared that Christianity itself would not survive the political situation. As a result, the premillennial idea that only the return of Jesus would bathe the world of sin gained stature.

Also influential in the growth of premillennialism was the horrible carnage of the war, which challenged postmillennialism by indicating to many that human progress toward a more perfect world was a pipe dream. One event in particular gave people pause—the battle of Gettysburg. Fought in early July 1863, the battle resulted in a horrible death toll of over 51,000 men. What was the meaning of such vast carnage? Could it be a punishment from God? Was it an indication of the growing sinfulness of humanity? The slaughter on this and other battle-fields, the sheer scale of death and impairment, the fact that no American family could avoid being touched by the war all suggested that America's divine mission as a prophetic leader nation had not been fulfilled. The nation had failed in its holy task to become a "city upon a hill." Addressing this loss of faith, Abraham Lincoln pointed out in his second inaugural address that to redeem the sin of slavery, God had exacted a heavy price from both the North and South. "The Almighty," he asserted, "has His own purposes."

For Lincoln, restoring the Union and ameliorating society would return the country to its divine course. But for others, the events lent themselves to a bleaker interpretation: Humanity was sinking rapidly into the abyss of sin that would bring about God's wrath, unleashing the apocalyptic scenarios by which he would exact retribution. One individual who was deeply changed during that horrible summer of 1863 was

James H. Brookes, a Presbyterian minister from St. Louis, who would become a nationally known leader of the premillennial dispensationalist movement in the next three decades. As historian Carl E. Sanders has noted, in 1863 the tone of Brookes's sermons shifted dramatically from a general tone of postmillennialism in the spring to a distinctive premillennial apocalypticism in the autumn.[25] The shocking events of Gettysburg seem to have transformed his view of God's plan for human history.

For Brookes and many like him, evil had proved far too powerful for humanity to overcome. Only Christ could eradicate it. The lyrics of Julia Ward Howe's poem "Battle Hymn of the Republic," written in 1861, eloquently, if violently, expressed this belief and helped to broadcast premillennialist belief in Jesus' imminent return and God's impending judgment.

Higher Criticism, Darwin, Fundamentalism, and Premillennialism in Late Nineteenth-Century America

Premillennialism was fostered by other events in American life besides the Civil War. Social transformations and new scientific strategies added to some people's fear that earthly life was bound for catastrophe and that only Christ's return would rectify the situation. Among those transformations was the development of an important new understanding of the Bible. Originating in Germany and growing out of Enlightenment ideas about rational methods of critical analysis, this new approach, called "higher biblical criticism," viewed the Bible as a collection of historical documents written by a variety of ancient and early Christian writers, from a variety of viewpoints. German scholars examined the texts in relation to the genres of writing popular at the time they were written and with an eye toward the ongoing historical and cultural situations that influenced their authors. As this approach was adopted in some American universities, opposition coalesced. In particular, opponents charged that the new scholarship questioned the divine origin of the texts. To people like Darby and Brookes, who believed that each word of the Bible should be read literally because it was God's inerrant word, the historical approach, which emphasized the human authorship of the texts, denied God's sovereignty and was tantamount to blasphemy.[26]

Some also saw transformations in science as attacking Christianity, the Bible, and even God. Dispensationalists like Darby felt that Charles Darwin's work indicating that the world was millions of years old challenged the divine time lines they found in the Bible. Many also felt that Darwin's notion of evolution—that creation itself and change over time were the results of biological processes and natural selection, not divine decree or instigation—threatened to displace God entirely.

Christians adopted a continuum of responses to the new critical and scientific perspectives. At one pole, religiously liberal Protestants embraced modernism and adopted the view that biblical and scientific research could be readily meshed with a belief in God because they were simply aspects of God's gifts to humanity. Theologically conservative Protestants, at the other pole, tended to condemn higher biblical criticism and inquiry into evolution. Most important for our purposes, the gradual coalescing of a conservative response to these situations brought about a significant new type of evangelicalism, called "fundamentalism," which itself grew out of and subsequently encompassed premillennial dispensationalism. Thus, it is to Christian fundamentalism that we must turn to fill in the final piece of the background of the Left Behind series.

The most influential responses to these scientific and philosophical challenges came from the Presbyterian Theological Seminary in Princeton, New Jersey, where scholars and clergy responded to the new methods of biblical exegesis and scientific attacks by systematizing and institutionalizing their own notions of biblical inerrancy and literal reading. These ideas remain at the heart of both fundamentalism and premillennial dispensationalism today. Called the Princeton theology, this perspective argued that the Bible could contain no errors because it was God's word.[27] Furthermore, it claimed, God gave his biblical messages to humankind in a manner that was readily understood. The stories and events in the Bible were not analogies or spiritual examples but literal truths, laws, and prophecies of coming events. This "literal" approach to the Bible had, of course, been the foundation of many eschatological ideas for centuries.

The Princeton theology gave premillennial dispensationalism a certain amount of intellectual credibility, and it contributed significantly to a series of summer conferences that began in 1876 and were intended to bring together religious leaders who shared premillennial views. Spearheaded by James Brookes and such well-known religious leaders as Dwight L. Moody, these Niagara Bible Conferences developed a distinctive creed that countered ideas of modern progress and emphasized biblical inerrancy and premillennial dispensationalism, tenets that would become the foundation of fundamentalism in the twentieth century.

Brookes, whose 1874 book, *Maranatha: Or the Lord Cometh*, presented a distinctive chronology for end-times events, emerged as a leader of the premillennial dispensationalists. Using the proof-text method, Brookes touted a time line quite similar to Darby's. The church age, he asserted, will terminate with the rapture of the true church, an event in which deceased Christians will be resurrected and they, along with living believers, will be "caught up to meet Christ in the air (I Thess. iv 17)." Then will begin the tribulation, during which time, he claimed, "God begins to deal with Israel again and will restore them to their own land (Isa. xi II; Acts xv 16), Antichrist will be revealed, (2 Thess. ii 8). The vials of God's wrath poured out (Rev. vi–xix). Israel accepts Christ and are [*sic*] brought through the fire, (Zech. xiii 9)." The tribulation, he argued, will be terminated in the Revelation, or the second coming, in which "Christ and His saints [come] in flaming fire to execute judgment on the earth (Matt. xxiv 24, 29, 30)." And at this point, the millennium will begin. At the end of Christ's thousand-year reign, Satan will be "loosed for a little season, and destroyed with Gog and Magog (Rev. xx 7–10)." And the final judgment of the dead will take place along with the destruction of death and hell. Eternity, then, will proceed.[28]

Paralleling Darby, Brookes advocated a pretribulation rapture. Many American dispensationalist leaders would come to share this view, including Cyrus I. Scofield, who incorporated it into the influential and still widely used *Scofield Reference Bible*, published in 1909. It would, however, instigate great controversy among American dispensationalists. Opposing the pretribulationist view was the idea that the church would remain on earth during the tribulation and that Christ would come after that period of suffering to rapture his church. This "posttribulationist" view stemmed from questions regarding the precise relationship between Israel—God's chosen people who will be saved during the tribulation—and the Christian church, a later institution.[29]

Tim LaHaye, co-author of the Left Behind series, has been a strong advocate of the pretribulationist view. The series itself begins with the rapture, suggesting that the church does not experience the tribulation. Yet unlike the beliefs of early pretribulationists like Brookes and Scofield, the series is based on the notion that conversions to Christianity will in fact still be possible during the tribulation. It is this refinement of the pretribulationist position that allows for the dramatic story told in the Left Behind series. If all true Christians were taken in the initial rapture, the story of the tribulation would simply be a tedious accounting of rampant evil. But with the conversion of the main characters, Cameron (Buck) Williams, Rayford Steele, and others, the story becomes one of good fighting against evil and gives readers likable, sympathetic characters for whom they can root. The series' pretribulationism, then, is somewhat modified. LaHaye and Jenkins even give a playful nod to the posttribulationists, naming their leading character, Cameron Williams, in a way that reminds insiders of posttribulationist advocates Robert Cameron, William Erdman, and William Moorehead.

However, at the turn of the twentieth century, despite the best efforts of both pretribulationist and posttribulationist dispensationalists, these views were not widely accepted by American Protestants. Religious conservatives interested in maintaining the voice of evangelical values in public policy and religious liberals interested in expanding social reform and humanitarian programs were suspicious of dispensationalism. One major criticism was that its pessimistic outlook encouraged withdrawal from the problems society faced. Premillennialists, they argued, tended to see political, social, or scientific efforts to improve conditions as futile; only Christ's return, which would happen very soon, would save the world. Many premillennialists further considered scientific efforts to learn more about the universe and human evolution as blasphemous, and some deemed missionary work, or the spreading of Christianity, unnecessary. Such beliefs marginalized the movement in a country where progress and modernism were widely embraced.

New "Signs of the Times" and America's Changing Role in the Divine Plan

While, as we have seen above, millenarianism always has been shaped by changing social and political events, the political character of premillennial dispensationalist thought is perhaps easier to grasp in the twentieth century. Premillennial beliefs have been fueled by a host of events that believers have pointed to as signs of the imminent return of Christ. The collapse of the Ottoman empire and the Allied occupation of Jerusalem in 1914 left many premillennialists convinced that Israel would soon be restored and the end times would soon begin. World War I itself, with its catastrophic devastation, seemed to threaten the entire globe, and dispensationalists believed that only God's intervention would bring it to an end. Because of this, some fundamentalists and premillennialists tended to view U.S. intervention into World War I negatively, arguing that no nation had the power to end a conflict that was part of God's divine plan.

The Russian Revolution in 1917 gave dispensationalists new identities for the antichrist: Bolshevism and Russia. As we have seen, dispensationalists earlier had identified the papacy and the Turks (Muslims), among others, as the antichrist, but through most of the twentieth century, American premillennial dispensationalists identified Russia and, later, the Soviet Union with that figure. With the Soviet Union's embracing of communism and repeated evidence of its military strength, many dispensationalists in the post–World War II period argued that the Soviet Union was the expansionist aggressor, the "evil from the north" (Jer. 4:6), that would bring destruction.

To be sure, dispensationalists suggested other identities for the antichrist during World War I—the most prominent being Benito Mussolini and Adolf Hitler—but their defeat at the hands of the Allies proved they did not wield the cosmic power of the antichrist. For dispensationalists, no nation could vanquish the antichrist; only God could accomplish this in accordance with biblical prophecy. Throughout the cold war period, the Soviet Union and, particularly, communism proved much more likely, seemingly invincible, candidates, as the United States failed to halt their advance in North Korea, Cuba, Vietnam, and later Latin America. Communism, many thought, was truly the enemy of God.[30]

In addition to the presence of this powerful antichrist, twentieth-century premillennialists found other signs of the imminent return of Christ. Among the most important of these was the formation of Israel in 1948, a political event that end-times believers had awaited for centuries. Only after the reunion of Israel, many believed, would Christ return, a topic discussed further in chapter 5 of this book. A further suggestion of the imminent advance of the end times was the development of the atomic bomb. Pointing to this weapon of mass destruction, which could readily rain fire down on humanity, premillennialists joined scriptural proof text with technological innovation, arguing that such an ultimate weapon of destruction fulfilled biblical prophecy. Nuclear power became the ultimate sign of the approaching end times and has been used to highly dramatic effect in such premillennial films as *Testament* and *A Thief in the Night*, as well as in the Left Behind series.

In addition to these signs of the end times, contemporary dispensationalists, like their predecessors, also have been interested in the role that America will play in the divine culmination of history. Although Columbus and Winthrop viewed America as holding out the promise of being God's exemplary nation, dispensationalists since the Civil War have lamented the failure of America to become that virtuous leader because of what they have considered to be its growing secularism, corruption, and sinfulness. Crime, poverty, women's rights (including reproductive rights), changing authorities, and scientific advancements all have been viewed as signs that, if America does hold a special role within the divine plan, it is as a failed example. Nevertheless, most American dispensationalists hold onto notions of America's and Americans' special role in the end times, a point made especially clear by LaHaye and Jenkins throughout the Left Behind series.

Contemporary Premillennial Dispensationalism

Of the many premillennial dispensationalist books that appeared during and after World War II, the most influential was Hal Lindsey's *The Late Great Planet Earth*, published in 1970. Taking a historicist position, this hugely popular work argued that key biblical prophecies already had been fulfilled, including the formation of Israel as a nation and the rise of Russia as Magog. In one chapter Lindsey correlated biblical texts with then-existing national powers to argue that an impending World War III, to be instigated by the Soviet Union in collaboration with China and other communist countries, would bring about a nuclear holocaust that will fulfill scriptural prophesies. He sternly warned people to look out for the impending rise of a charismatic "future fuehrer" as the antichrist, the development of a one-world religion that would dupe people away from true Christianity, increasing tensions in the Middle East, and a decline in U.S. power vis-à-vis Europe. Closer to home, "crime, riots, unemployment, poverty, illiteracy, mental illness, [and] illegitimacy," he predicted, would increase as would drug addiction and belief in "astrology, witchcraft and Oriental religions."[31] For Lindsey, individuals' only hope to avoid death and destruction lay in their immediate conversion to Christianity—conversion that must occur before the any-moment return of Christ.

The popularity of Lindsey's book spurred a host of premillennial works, in both the fiction and nonfiction categories. Among these, of course, are the books of the Left Behind series, in which many of Lindsey's themes are evident. For instance, LaHaye and Jenkins's fictional account echoes Lindsey's critique of political and social efforts to improve society through institutions like the United Nations and other peacemaking efforts. The political and social institutions described in Left Behind are inherently corrupt. The conversion of the main characters and their faith that they are fighting the Lord's fight are all that save them from annihilation. These themes and others are examined in chapter 6.

Political Consequences of the Dispensationalist View of History

What does it mean to ordinary people that history is controlled by God and inevitably will culminate in a series of apocalyptic events? How does this religious belief affect one's view of or role in social and political life?

The answers to these questions are complex. For those who believe that history is foreordained in the Bible and controlled by God, human action aimed at change may well seem futile. Sin is rampant and the horrible events of the end times will occur no matter how human society responds to evil. In some cases this view promotes quietism, or passivity in the face of conflict or challenge.

Despite such a tendency in the early twentieth century, premillennial dispensationalists more recently have joined other conservative Christians in taking public political stands on issues pertaining to the moral character of the nation. Such action arose dramatically in the 1970s, when fundamentalist Christians formed the Moral Majority and, later, the Christian Coalition, organizations intended to exert influence on the political front. This turn toward political activism was a distinctive shift for premillennialists, although it sometimes was seen to contradict their core belief that only God—certainly not government and often not individuals—can effect significant change.

Belief in the impending return of Christ and an ensuing period of divine punishment, tribulation, and judgment continues to influence responses to ongoing events, occasionally in ways decidedly contrary to the mainstream. In early responses to the terrorist attacks of September 11, 2001, some premillennial dispensationalists suggested they were a sign of God's retribution on a sinful nation—a view that was met with widespread outrage.[32] That interpretation, however, was a logical conclusion drawn from premillennial thought. Just as premillennialists viewed the horror of the battle of Gettysburg in 1863 as a divine act aimed at chastising America for its sin, some saw the carnage of September 11 in the same light. Some fundamentalists and premillennialists take this interpretation further, seeing these horrific events as indications that Christ's return is imminent.

Premillennialists also have criticized attempts to limit the production of nuclear weapons, efforts they deem futile at the very least. This line of argument suggests that because God allowed for the creation of nuclear weapon—and they so aptly correlate with biblical descriptions of destruction—they must have been a part of his divine plan. Attempts to hinder the production of such weapons, therefore, could actually hinder God, a course of action any true believer would avoid. Such thinking has influenced many premillennialists' support for nuclear weapons, including that of Jerry Falwell and Ronald Reagan. Some similarly view peace efforts as futile, if not obstructive, in a world that God is going to soon draw to an end. Here again, quietism is the result of premillennial dispensationalist thinking.[33]

Harking back to the radicalism of Jan Bockelson during the Reformation, some also fear that violence is an inherent threat within millenarian thought. In recent years the question has arisen whether extremist millenarians will attempt to hasten the arrival of the end times by committing some violent act, such as destroying the Dome of the Rock in Jerusalem, a Muslim shrine located on the site of the Jewish Second Temple, which was destroyed in 70 C.E. and which many dispensationalists believe will be reconstructed by the Jews just prior to Armageddon. Similarly, groups like the Branch Davidians, who traced their roots to Seventh-Day Adventism and attempted to retreat to their Mount Carmel compound to await the impending end-times events, have been widely considered—correctly or incorrectly— to be potentially dangerous. It is clear now that David Koresh and his followers viewed the attempts by the Federal Bureau of Investigation and the Bureau of Alcohol, Tobacco, and Firearms in 1993 initially to frighten and then to roust them from their compound through the lens of premillennial dispensationalism. They believed the siege was the onset of the end times, and much of Koresh's communication with the FBI during the siege consisted of scriptural proof texts he believed prophesied the ongoing military assault.[34] As it turned out, Koresh's belief in an imminent apocalypse proved to be a self-fulfilling prophecy.

The moral of this story is that one's view of history does indeed have consequences: It influences how one understands not only the past but the present and future as well. Millenarian thought always has provided means for people to deal with the events and ideas that affect their lives, from the power of the church to wars to scientific discoveries. In the nineteenth century, the refinement of premillennial dispensationalism was in many ways a product of the collision of Christianity with modernism. Its championing of biblical inerrancy and literal interpretation of prophetic texts countered Enlightenment-driven advancements in biblical criticism and scientific methods. Darby, Brookes, and many others looked to end-times prophecy as a means of making sense of such new developments. Under God's plan for the culmination of history, such threats would dissolve and the righteous would be vindicated.

In the twentieth century, the threats of war and technology combined, providing ever more indication that the world was moving toward some apocalyptic event. Left Behind imagines those events, describing at length the suffering and carnage they will bring. Culminating this tale of violence with the return of Jesus in what they call the "glorious appearing," LaHaye and Jenkins mirror those earlier messianic thinkers who similarly combined despair over the current situation with hope for a peaceful millennium led by Christ.

As we have seen, premillennial dispensationalism is not the only Christian understanding of history or biblical prophecy. Nor is it the only Christian response to unsettling world events. It does, however, have deep roots in both Christian and American history. With knowledge of those roots, readers are better prepared to understand and evaluate the millenarian thought of the Left Behind series.

Notes

1. John J. Collins, *The Apocalyptic Imagination: An Introduction to the Jewish Matrix of Christianity* (New York: Crossroad, 1984), 87–91. See also Norman Cohn, *The Pursuit of the Millennium: Revolutionary Millenarians and Mystical Anarchists of the Middle Ages*, rev. ed. (New York: Oxford University Press, 1970), 19–25. All biblical quotations are taken from the New Revised Standard Version unless noted.

2. Calvin J. Roetzel, *Paul: The Man and the Myth* (Columbia: University of South Carolina Press, 1998), 103–104. See also Cohn, *Pursuit of the Millennium*, 19–29.

3. Cohn, *Pursuit of the Millennium*, 29–36.

4. Ibid., 108–109. Eugen Weber, *Apocalypses: Prophesies, Cults, and Millennial Beliefs throughout the Ages* (Cambridge, Mass.: Harvard University Press, 1999), 52–54.

5. The phrase is from Bernard McGinn, ed. and trans., *Apocalyptic Spirituality: Treatises and Letters of Lanctantius, Adso of Montier-en-Der, Joachim of Fiore, the Franciscan Spirituals, Savonarola* (New York: Paulist Press, 1979), 14, as quoted in Robin Bruce Barnes, *Prophecy and Gnosis: Apocalypticism in the Wake of the Lutheran Reformation* (Stanford, Calif.: Stanford University Press, 1988), 19.

6. Andrew Cunningham and Ole Peter Grell, *The Four Horsemen of the Apocalypse: Religion, War, Famine, and Death in Reformation Europe* (Cambridge: Cambridge University Press, 2000), 4.

7. Ibid.

8. Martin Luther himself was seen as fulfilling a prophesy made a century earlier by John Hus, a Bohemian martyr, who, as he was burned at the stake as a heretic, predicted the rise of a new prophet one hundred years hence. Ibid., 20, 24–25.

9. It should be noted that millenarian and apocalyptic beliefs are no long held by most Lutherans.

10. Cohn, *Pursuit of the Millennium*, 267–280.

11. Katharine R. Firth, *The Apocalyptic Tradition in Reformation Britain, 1530–1645* (New York: Oxford University Press, 1979), 5.

12. Barnes, *Prophecy and Gnosis*, 33.

13. Ibid., 34–35.

14. The quote is from a letter written in 1500 by Columbus to "a member of the royal court," and appears in Christopher Columbus, *Memorials of Columbus: A Collection of Authentic Documents of that Celebrated Navigator*, compiled by Giovanni Battista Spotorno (London: Treuttel and Wurtz, Treuttel jun. [Jr.] and Richter, 1823), 224. See Pauline Moffitt Watts, "Prophecy and Discovery: On the Spiritual Origins of Christopher Columbus's 'Enterprise of the Indies,' " *American Historical Review* 90 (February 1985), 73–102.

15. On apocalyptic currents in American culture, see Charles H. Lippy, "Waiting for the End: The Social Context of American Apocalyptic Religion," in Lois Parkinson Zamora, *The Apocalyptic Vision in America: Interdisciplinary Essays on Myth and Culture* (Bowling Green, Ohio: Bowling Green University Popular Press, 1982), 37–43. See also Paul Boyer, *When Time Shall Be No More: Prophecy Belief in Modern American Culture* (Cambridge, Mass.: Harvard University Press, 1992), 68–79.

16. Jonathan Edwards, *Some Thoughts Concerning the Present Revival of Religion*, in the *Works of Jonathan Edwards*, ed. Perry Miller (New Haven, Conn.: Yale University Press, 1957), 4: 353–58, as quoted in George M. Marsden, *Jonathan Edwards: A Life* (New Haven, Conn.: Yale University Press, 2003), 264. On Edward's apocalyptic thought, see also Stephen J. Stein, "Editor's Introduction," *Jonathan Edwards: Apocalyptic Writings* (New Haven, Conn.: Yale University Press, 1977), 1–93.

17. On the Albury prophetic conferences, see Ernest R. Sandeen, *The Roots of Fundamentalism: British and American Millenarianism, 1800–1930* (Chicago: University of Chicago Press, 1970), 19–22.

18. Robert Norton, *Memoirs of James & George MacDonald of Port-Glasgow* (London: John F. Shaw, 1840), 171.

19. Ibid., 174. A similar account of Macdonald's visions also appears in Robert Norton, *The Restoration of Apostles and Prophets in the Catholic Apostolic Church* (London: Bosworth & Harrison, 1861), 15–18.

20. Although some have claimed that Mary Macdonald originated the pretribulationist position, Norton's account of her vision is somewhat unclear on the point. For instance, her emphasis on the idea that the spiritual eye will aid Christians in "seeing" the antichrist and understanding his deceit suggests that Christians will endure the end times. She also mentions, "The trial, through which those are to pass who will be counted worthy to stand before the Son of man." Norton, *Memoirs*, 175. On Macdonald as a pretribulationist, see Dave MacPherson, *The Incredible Cover-Up: The True Story of the Pre-Trib Rapture* (Plainfield, N.J.: Logos International, 1975), 49, 52. MacPherson's argument that the pretribulationist position has been based on a charismatic vision is meant as a means of discrediting what its defenders claim is scripturally based interpretation. Clearly, there are elements of this vision that correspond to later formalizations in the pretribulationist position, but this is hardly the smoking gun he claims. MacPherson's argument holds up better when he asserts acquaintances of the Macdonalds, particularly Francis Sitwell, articulated the pretribulationist position. See *The Incredible Cover-Up*, 59–60, where MacPherson quotes from an 1834 letter from Sitwell to his sister, published in Charles William Boase, *Supplementary Narrative to the Elijah Ministry* (printed privately and posthumously, 1868). [The author has not been able to corroborate quotations from Boase.]

21. On Darby and the Plymouth Brethren, see Sandeen, *Roots of Fundamentalism*, 31–34, 59–80. See also J. N. Darby, *Lectures on the Second Coming* (London: G. Morrish, 1909).

22. Sandeen, *Roots Of Fundamentalism*, 62–64.

23. It should be noted that the extent of Darby's influence in the United States has been debated by premillennialists and historians. See Carl E. Sanders II, *The Premillennial Faith of James Brookes: Reexamining the Roots of American Dispensationalism* (Lanham, Md.: University Press of America, 2001).

24. When Christ did not appear, a variety of responses ensued. Scoffers felt vindicated, some Millerites simply picked up and

carried on with their lives, and some developed theological explanations for why none of the Christians had been taken. Among
this latter group was Ellen G. White, who claimed that a new
dispensation had indeed begun in 1843, but that it consisted of
Christ moving into an antechamber in heaven to prepare for his
imminent return. White's interpretation inspired the formation of
a new religious group, the Seventh-Day Adventists, which continues to embrace belief in the imminent return. On the Millerites,
see *The Disappointed: Millerism and Millenarianism in the
Nineteenth Century*, ed. Ronald L. Numbers and Jonathan M.
Butler (Knoxville: University of Tennessee Press, 1993). On White,
see Ronald L. Numbers, *Prophetess of Health: A Study of Ellen G.
White* (New York: Harper & Row, 1976).

25. Sanders, *Premillennial Faith of James Brookes*, 12–14.
26. Although many biblical historians questioned scriptural inerrancy,
    not all dismissed the possibility of supernatural influence on the
    texts. Certainly many historians engaged in this type of examina-
    tion precisely out of their strong belief in Christianity.
27. Princeton Seminary no longer advocates this position. On funda-
    mentalism and Princeton theology, see George M. Marsden,
    Understanding Fundamentalism and Evangelicalism (Grand
    Rapids, Mich.: Eerdmans Publishing, 1991), 9–61.
28. All quotes appear in James H. Brookes, *Maranatha; Or, the Lord
    Cometh*, 3rd. ed. (St. Louis, Mo.: Edward Bredell, 1874), 546.
29. On these disputes, see Sandeen, *Roots of Fundamentalism*,
    162–187.
30. On premillennialism in the post–World War II period, see Boyer,
    When Time Shall Be No More, 115–224.
31. Hal Lindsey with Carole C. Carlson, *The Late Great Planet Earth*
    (Grand Rapids, Mich.: Zondervan, 1970; HarperCollins, 1977),
    174.
32. The statement was made by Jerry Falwell, who apologized for it
    shortly after.
33. Boyer, *When Time Shall Be No More*, 140–144.
34. James D. Tabor and Eugene V. Gallagher, *Why Waco: Cults and
    the Battle for Religious Freedom in America* (Berkeley: University
    of California Press, 1995), 76–79.

What Does the Bible Say About the End Times?

A Biblical Studies Discussion of Interpretive Methods

Mark Reasoner

The Left Behind series calls its readers to pay attention to the Bible. But does the Bible really say what the Left Behind authors suggest? Is the series trustworthy in its interpretation of the Bible? To answer these questions, this chapter considers the interpretive choices Tim LaHaye and Jerry Jenkins have made on a number of issues and compares them with some alternative viewpoints. My conclusion is that while the biblical views of the Left Behind authors may be legitimate readings, they are not mandated by the biblical text. The Left Behind scenario is not what many Christians believe will happen, nor is it the only picture of the end times that one might glean from the Bible.

The view of the end times that the Left Behind series offers is the result of five interpretive choices that Tim LaHaye and Jerry Jenkins make as they read the Bible. Of course, the authors also make interpretive choices as they approach social and political issues, but those are considered in another chapter in this volume. This chapter's task is to help explain how LaHaye and Jenkins move from the Bible to the plot of the Left Behind books and to discuss the interpretive decisions they make along the way.

What do we mean by the phrase "interpretive choices"? Consider an analogy. At some fast food restaurants, there are children's play areas that rise above the restaurant floor. A spiral stairway and a set of climbing shelves provide the routes up into the play area. High above the restaurant's tables, the stairway and shelves connect to a maze of tunnels, sometimes opening into wider areas with windows from which the exploring children can look down. And there are usually at least two slides down which children can descend, once their explorations through the tunnels and window rooms are concluded. Like a child climbing into this play area, all biblical interpreters have to make choices. They have to choose how to enter, and they choose among alternative tunnels and rooms along the way. Because of these choices, they may come to quite different conclusions.

To enter into the maze of tunnels and rooms, LaHaye and Jenkins insist on climbing only the stairs of literal interpretation. This decision is a very intentional one that they take pains to defend. The first interpretive choice we consider in this chapter is the claim by LaHaye and Jenkins that we should read the Bible literally whenever possible.

The second interpretive choice involves the emphasis on certain parts of the Bible in constructing a picture of the end times. Most biblical interpreters gravitate toward certain portions of the Bible to provide a lens through which they read everything else. Here we will discuss LaHaye's instinctive emphasis on the apocalyptic books of Daniel and Revelation and some of the basic disagreements about what those books mean.

On the basis of these first two general interpretive choices, we then turn to three major topics in the Left Behind scenario: the rapture, the tribulation, and the antichrist. Are they clearly in the Bible? With many other Christians, LaHaye and Jenkins argue that they are, although other biblical interpreters disagree. These next three interpretive choices are focused more on particular topics than on general approaches. The third interpretive choice therefore pertains to what the Bible says or does not say about the rapture. The fourth interpretive choice is about a period of tribulation. And the fifth interpretive choice is about the antichrist.

Once we consider the five interpretive choices, and some alternative views about each one, readers will be in a more informed position to decide whether to accept or modify the end-times scenario of the Left Behind series. My basic intention is not to persuade readers either to accept or reject the viewpoints of LaHaye and Jenkins. My goal is rather to lay out a variety of options, so that readers can understand some of the contrasting arguments and make their own decisions.

How Literally Can We Read the Bible?

His view, echoed dozens of times, was that the book of Revelation was "wonderful, archaic, beautiful literature, to be taken symbolically, figuratively, metaphorically. This earthquake," Mathews had told Buck by phone, a smile in his voice, "could refer to anything. It may have happened already. It may refer to something someone imagined going on in heaven. Who knows?"

—Tim LaHaye and Jerry B. Jenkins, *Nicolae*, p. 359

A major, basic division among Christians is whether the Bible should be read literally or symbolically. There are not simply two positions on this issue, but a great spectrum of variations, all held by sincere Christians. Yet for summary purposes, it is possible to sketch out two basic approaches in broad strokes: those who, like the authors of the Left Behind series, read the images in the Bible literally, and those who, like Pontifex Maximus Peter Mathews (referred to in the passage above)— the religious leader in the series who serves Nicolae Carpathia, the antichrist—understand them to be symbolic.

To take a very contentious example, consider the account of creation provided in the first three chapters of Genesis. Some Christians read it literally as a historical account of how things came to be. There is some disagreement about whether the seven days of creation refer to twenty-four-hour days or to longer periods of time, but the literal approach agrees that individual species were created, in the order described in Genesis, as intentional acts of God. There really was an Adam and an Eve, the literal first God-created human beings from whom all other humans descended. Those who read Genesis as a literal, scientific, historical account have become opponents of Darwin and theories of evolution, seeing those scientific views as rivals to the literal reading of the biblical narrative. Many Christians who take this position say that one has to accept all of the Bible as true; people are not justified in accepting parts of the Bible and rejecting other parts.

Other Christians see the creation account in Genesis as something like a parable, a story that communicates spiritual truth, not to be read as a literal, historical narrative. In this view, the first three chapters of Genesis provide a symbolic story that affirms certain truths: However the world came to be, God was behind it; God had good intentions for human beings, but humans have fallen short. This approach would argue that the Genesis creation story was never intended to be a scientific or historical account to be taken literally. In support, they claim that the first three chapters contain more than one creation story, and the stories vary in their details. If we were intended to take it literally, how do we explain what appear to be contradictory details?

Many persons think that this is a modern argument, but similar disagreements existed even in the early church. Scholars describe two "schools" of biblical interpretation associated with important Christian communities at Alexandria and Antioch, in the eastern part of the Roman empire in the first few centuries of Christian history. Representatives of the Alexandrian approach included Clement of Alexandria, Origen, and, later, Gregory of Nazianzus. Alexandrians advocated figurative interpretations of scripture when the literal meanings seemed impossible. Would God really "walk" in a garden? What about discrepancies between the gospels in describing Jesus' life? These must not be literal, historical passages, the Alexandrians said, but rather passages with metaphorical or spiritual meanings.

The Antiochene school (in other words, associated with Antioch) advocated a literal, historical approach and strongly opposed what they saw as the allegorical excesses arising from Alexandria. Prominent among the Antiochenes were Theodore of Mopsuestia, Diodorus of Tarsus, and John Chrysostom. Jerome, who produced the important Latin Vulgate version of the Bible, converted from one school to the other, leaving behind most of his allegorizing when he became convinced by Antioch's approach. The school of Antioch insisted that whenever there was a deeper spiritual meaning in scripture, it was built on the literal or historical meaning, not opposed to it or in place of it.[1]

This early disagreement about how literally to read the Bible is not exactly the same as more recent arguments, but there are interesting parallels. The reason for mentioning Antioch and Alexandria is to show that contention over the meaning of the Bible did not begin only a century or two ago; it arose in the early church and continued through medieval and Reformation periods down to the present. And just as there is disagreement in the example discussed above, about how literally to read the creation story, there also is significant disagreement about how to read passages about the end times.

In today's arguments about whether to read the Bible literally or not, I should note that each side sometimes oversimplifies the stand of the other. For example, it is not true that those who read the Genesis creation story symbolically wish to deny any literal meaning at all in the entire Bible. They accept much of the story of the Jewish people and the life of Jesus as historical, but they insist that *some* parts of the Bible are figurative and/or historically conditioned and should not be interpreted literally.

Similarly, most advocates of literal interpretation, including LaHaye, certainly acknowledge the presence of some symbolism in the Bible. Charles Ryrie, who would include himself in the literalist camp, describes how the principle of literal interpretation handles symbolism, writing: "the principle might also be called normal interpretation since the literal meaning of words is the normal approach to understanding in all languages. It might also be designated plain interpretation so that no one receives the mistaken notion that the literal principle rules out figures of speech. Symbols, figures of speech and types are all interpreted plainly in this method and are in no way contrary to literal interpretation."[2]

Thus, for all of the contrasts between the two general biblical approaches described here, they start to become somewhat ambiguous on further examination. Symbolic interpreters recognize historical and literal aspects of the Bible, and literalists accept some symbolism. The issue is how much, and in which passages, and here the differences remain sharp and wide.

Tim LaHaye, whose biblical approach guides the Left Behind books, clearly identifies himself as an advocate of the literal approach. Commenting on the success of the Left Behind series, LaHaye says that it "proves that laymen who take the Bible literally want to believe what it says. . . . And why shouldn't they believe it? It is what the New Testament clearly teaches if you consider all the prophecy passages about the Second Coming and take them literally (unless the immediate context indicates otherwise)."[3] In another passage, LaHaye indicates that one of the keys for properly understanding the end times "is taking the prophetic scriptures literally whenever possible."[4] LaHaye characterizes those who disagree with his views as "those who refuse to take prophecy as literally as they do other Scriptures."[5]

Of course, indicating that one should take the Bible literally "whenever possible" leaves open the question: Exactly when is it possible? That becomes especially complicated when one considers apocalyptic literature, especially the books of Daniel and Revelation, books that everyone acknowledges are filled with symbolic language. Anyone who has read the books of Daniel and Revelation can see that they are quite different in character from the rest of the Bible. They are filled with creatures and numbers, whose meanings are not obviously apparent, referring in some way to a conflict between good and evil. How are we supposed to read these parts of the Bible?

Do the Books of Daniel and Revelation Predict the Future?

If genesis meant beginning, maybe revelation had something to do with the end, even though it didn't mean that.
—Tim LaHaye and Jerry B. Jenkins, *Left Behind*, pp. 122–123

When Christians desire to learn about the end times, they usually gravitate to the biblical books of Daniel and Revelation. Daniel in the Jewish scriptures, or what Christians call the Old Testament, tells of Jewish youths who are taken into captivity in Babylon. In a time of insecurity, danger, and persecution, Daniel interpreted visions received by others and then received visions himself, all filled with symbolism. The visions expressed hope, prompting expectations that God would punish the wicked and save the faithful.

The book of Revelation in the New Testament is also known as the Apocalypse, from the Greek word meaning "disclosure," "unveiling," or "revelation."[6] The author identifies himself as John, and biblical interpreters have disagreed about whether he is the same person as the apostle John. John was exiled or imprisoned on the island of Patmos (Rev. 1:9), probably as a result of the Roman empire's persecution of Christians, and, like Daniel, he received visions filled with symbolism. Like Daniel's message, the message John received includes hope that God will triumph and evil will be defeated.

So, how should we read these books? What do they mean? LaHaye and Jenkins believe that Daniel and Revelation predict events that were future to the biblical authors and the original readers of these books, and that the events are still in the future for us as well.[7] This is an interpretive decision, and other approaches disagree. In general terms, what are the options?

Because of the brevity of this current discussion, let us focus on Revelation, although the same basic analytical approaches also could be applied to Daniel. Biblical interpreters have taken three general approaches to understanding Revelation.[8] One view is that the book refers to events in the first century, when Christians were persecuted by the Roman empire. (This view is sometimes called the "preterist" position.) The first major persecution of Christians took place about 64 C.E., under the emperor Nero, and a second time of persecution perhaps occurred in 90–91 C.E. under Domitian. Some biblical scholars are convinced that John's exile to the island of Patmos and his writing of the book of Revelation took place during the second persecution. Thus, according to this view, the visionary, symbolic references in Revelation refer to the persecution taking place at the time the book was written, events that are now in the past. The "beast" that persecutes Christians is the Roman emperor. The requirement to worship an image of the beast refers to forced participation in the imperial religious cult. "The harlot that rides upon the beast is the city set on seven hills—clearly Rome," which is called Babylon in the text.[9] Advocates of this position claim that the true "literal" or "plain" sense of the book of Revelation refers to first-century Rome, not to some events two thousand years later.

A second viewpoint (sometimes called the "idealist" position) argues that the message of Revelation is timeless, with teachings that apply to every generation. In this view, Revelation provides "a vision of the spiritual battles that Christians in all times and places" should wage against sin. Interpreting the symbols, some have suggested that the seven heads of the beast are the seven deadly sins, and the ten horns of the beast are violations of the Ten Commandments.[10] Others would emphasize the more general theme of an ongoing battle between good and evil. The visions of John advise people in all times and places to have courage, to maintain their faith in the midst of difficulties, and to trust in the promise that God will triumph in the end. These are seen as spiritual messages for all times, not specific predictions of literal events at some future date.

A third approach believes that God, through inspiration of the Bible, has provided clues about the future and, even more, a literal chronological outline of the events that will occur at the end of time. In this view, Revelation, along with Daniel and many other scriptural passages, provides coded predictions of what will happen in the future. The task is to properly decipher the codes and apply them to world events.

One version of this third approach (sometimes called the "historicist" position) believes that Revelation describes *all* of history from John's day until the new Jerusalem descends from heaven. Some historicists give great attention to the "seven churches that are in Asia" (Rev. 1:4), identified in Revelation 2–3 as Ephesus, Smyrna, Pergamum, Thyatira, Sardis, Philadelphia, and Laodicea. These are not only historical churches, they claim, but they symbolically represent seven ages of the church. Other historicists have other classifications of ages or "dispensations," outlining God's plan for human history from the beginning to the end, and they examine current events to discern where we are in the outline of sacred history.

Another version of this third approach (sometimes called the "futurist" position) sees all of Revelation, beginning with the fourth chapter, as referring to events in the future, not yet fulfilled. This is the position of LaHaye and Jenkins and of virtually all premillennial dispensationalists (i.e., those who hold a specific set of beliefs about the end times, described in chapter 2 of this volume). They believe that Revelation provides a script of the end times, describing events that will happen literally in the future in human history. They disagree with those who say that the prophecies already have been fulfilled in biblical times. To answer the suggestion that these events already have happened, futurists point to certain Bible passages to support their belief that they remain in the future. For instance, when Revelation 3:10 says "I will keep you from the hour of trial *that is coming on the whole world*" [italics added], LaHaye and others would argue that none of the times of trial humanity has experienced thus far have yet encompassed the whole world. This, they say, must be a reference to something that has not yet come to pass, an event that is still in the future.

Thus, there are three general approaches to the book of Revelation. One sees the visions of John as describing events in first-century Christianity, in the Roman empire, events that are now in the past. Another approach interprets the book as symbols that communicate timeless messages for every generation. And a third approach believes that Revelation provides a symbolic outline of human history and a coded prediction of literal events that will happen in the future, in the end times. Biblical interpreters may prefer or be convinced by one approach or another, and sometimes they combine them in various ways. Which approach or approaches a person chooses will make a *huge* difference in the conclusions reached about the topics to follow: rapture, tribulation, and the antichrist.

Does the Bible Teach That There Will Be a Rapture of True Christians?

"Our senior pastor loved to preach about the coming of Christ to rapture his church, to take believers, dead and alive, to heaven before a period of tribulation on the earth. He was particularly inspired once a couple of years ago." . . .

"Well," Barnes said, *"the pastor used that sermon and had himself videotaped in this office speaking directly to people who were left behind. He put it in the church library with instructions to get it out and play it if most everyone seemed to have disappeared."*
—Tim LaHaye and Jerry B. Jenkins, *Left Behind*, p. 194

First of all, here's a surprise: For all of the controversy about a rapture, the word itself never appears in most English translations of the Bible. The *idea* comes from 1 Thessalonians 4:17, which refers to those who "will be caught up in the clouds . . . to meet the Lord in the air." The key Greek word here usually is translated into English as "caught up" or "snatched." When the Bible was translated into the Latin of Jerome's Vulgate in the fourth and fifth centuries, the term "rapiemur" ("we will be snatched") was used in translating this verse, and from this Latin term the use of the English word "rapture" developed.

Tim LaHaye acknowledges that "some Christians are disappointed when they learn that the word *rapture* does not appear in the New Testament."[11] They should not be, he says, because the concept of the rapture is taught in the Bible, even if the term comes later, from Latin. Yet LaHaye also acknowledges that the rapture is a "mystery revealed" and thus somewhat hidden. He writes: "Eleven mysteries revealed in the New Testament were not known to Old Testament saints. They were not given to make Christianity mysterious, but to reveal things that had never before been announced. That is what Paul explains to us in 1 Corinthians 2: 7–10: 'We speak the wisdom of God in a mystery, the hidden wisdom which God ordained before the ages for our glory, which none of the rulers of this age knew. . . . but God has revealed them to us.' The greatest of these mysteries, in my opinion, is the rapture of the saints."[12] Thus, in LaHaye's view, the rapture is taught in the Bible, but in a somewhat hidden way, as a mystery revealed to those who can properly understand the appropriate biblical passages.

The three major New Testament passages on which Tim LaHaye and many others base their argument for a rapture are John 14:1–3, 1 Thessalonians 4:16–17, and 1 Corinthians 15:51–53. Here are the texts:

> Do not let your hearts be troubled. Believe in God, believe also in me. In my Father's house there are many dwelling places. If it were not so, would I have told you that I go to prepare a place for you? And if I go and prepare a place for you, I will come again and will take you to myself, so that where I am, there you may be also. (John 14:1–3, NRSV)[13]
>
> For the Lord himself, with a cry of command, with the archangel's call and with the sound of God's trumpet, will descend from heaven, and the dead in Christ will rise first. Then we who are alive, who are left, will be caught up in the clouds together with them to meet the Lord in the air; and so we will be with the Lord forever. (1 Thessalonians 4:16–17, NRSV)
>
> Listen, I will tell you a mystery! We will not all die, but we will all be changed, in a moment, in a twinkling of an eye, at the last trumpet. For the trumpet will sound, and the dead will be raised imperishable, and we will be changed. For this perishable body must put on imperishability, and this mortal body must put on immortality. (1 Corinthians 15:51–53, NRSV)

Many persons who read these passages might say, "I don't see a rapture here. I see a promise of resurrection for the faithful when Christ returns, but is that the same as people mysteriously disappearing while others continue their normal lives?" Premillennial dispensationalists (including LaHaye and Jenkins) believe in a chronology such as: (1) a rapture, in which true Christians are taken up to heaven; (2) a seven-year period of difficulties called the "tribulation" for all of the people who remain on earth; and (3) the glorious appearing of Jesus to defeat evil and initiate a thousand-year reign on earth called the "millennium." As discussed elsewhere in this book, some other persons who believe in a rapture place it in the middle or at the end of a period of tribulation, instead of before it. The question is, do the "three main Rapture passages" (LaHaye's phrase) really teach that kind of complicated scenario?[14] Don't they simply describe a resurrection at the time of Jesus' second coming?

For example, the noted biblical scholar N. T. Wright, a member of the evangelical wing of the Anglican church and now bishop of Durham, discusses the description of Christ's coming that Paul provides in 1 Thessalonians 4:16–17. He argues that Paul was using a mixed metaphor when describing Jesus' return to earth, adding: "Few in the U.K. hold the belief . . . that there will be a literal 'rapture" in which believers will be snatched up to heaven, leaving empty cars crashing on freeways."[15] His remark illustrates that widespread acceptance of a rapture may be culturally limited to North America.

Gary DeMar, author of an extensive biblical critique of Tim LaHaye's theology, also is convinced that there is no rapture in the Bible. He asserts: "LaHaye takes Bible passages that refer to the general resurrection and applies them to a pretrib [pretribulation] rapture of the church. The resurrection of the dead, not the rapture of the church, is the hope of the church."[16] Referring further to the issue of biblical support, Demar says: "There is no single verse or group of verses that specifically describes any of these . . . Rapture positions. In terms of pretribulationsim, since that's the Rapture position advocated by LaHaye, we should expect to find at least *one* verse that describes Jesus coming for His *church* to take Christians to heaven *prior* to a seven-year period of tribulation, and then Jesus returning with His church seven years after the Rapture to defeat Antichrist and set up a kingdom in Jerusalem that will last for a thousand years. Of course, there is no such verse or group of connected verses that mentions these very necessary doctrinal elements."[17] DeMar also wonders why Christians did not see the rapture in the Bible for seventeen centuries of Christian history although supposedly it is self-evident.[18]

How would LaHaye respond to claims like DeMar's, that the rapture is not in the Bible? I do not have the space to consider every argument he might raise, but I can summarize three of them. All three point to additional biblical passages and arguments that LaHaye then connects with the three main passages quoted above.

First, LaHaye is convinced that a rapture and Christ's glorious appearing are separate events, that they will not happen at the same time. Here he gives great emphasis to Titus 2:13, which appears in two major translations:

> . . . we wait for the blessed hope and the manifestation of the glory of our great God and Savior, Jesus Christ. (NRSV)
> . . . we wait for the blessed hope—the glorious appearing of our great God and Savior, Jesus Christ. (NIV)[19]

Many Christians interpret the verse to mean that the blessed hope is a hope for one event: the second coming or return of Jesus Christ. LaHaye, translating the verse as "looking for the *blessed hope* and *glorious appearing*," says that this verse refers to two separate events. The blessed hope is the rapture of the church, he claims, and the glorious appearing of Jesus Christ will happen separately, later. LaHaye's critics object that this interpretation stretches the plain sense of the passage.

It is easy for people excited about the Left Behind series to take such charts as the "Overview of the End Times" found in its Bible Study Guides, with separate sections for "Rapture Passages" and "Second Coming Passages," as gospel truth, but a chart such as this represents the end result of many choices that form the structure of premillennial dispensationalism, not a basic set of end times truths on which all Christians agree.[20]

Second, LaHaye is convinced that God has promised to protect true believers from the wrath to come, citing verses like 1 Thessalonians 1:10 ("Jesus, who rescues us from the wrath that is coming") and Revelation 3:10 ("I also will keep you from the hour of trial"). Some readers would say that these verses simply promise that the faithful will be saved from hell, from the wrath of a final eternal punishment. LaHaye interprets the verses as referring to the tribulation (discussed in the next section). He and others contend that God has promised to save true Christians from a predicted seven years of tribulation on the earth. To fulfill that promise, according to this viewpoint, it is a logical deduction that there must be a rapture, when the faithful are suddenly and unexpectedly lifted off the earth, even if it is not fully and explicitly described in scripture.

Third, LaHaye and many others also find evidence for a rapture of the church in a change in language that occurs in the book of Revelation. In Revelation 4:1–2, John writes:

> After this I looked, and there in heaven a door stood open! And the first voice, which I had heard speaking to me like a trumpet, said, "Come up here, and I will show you what must take place after this." At once I was in the spirit, and there in heaven stood a throne, with one seated on the throne. (NRSV)

Many readers understand this passage to be an invitation to John "to ascend to heaven, to behold visions of God."[21] It might be seen as John's temporary entrance into a spiritual ecstasy or trance to receive the visions he then recorded in the remainder of the book of Revelation.

Premillennial dispensationalists understand this passage differently. They see it as a reference to the rapture, not only of John but of the church. "Come up here" is a description of the rapture, they say, and John is a "symbol of the church."[22] They note that Revelation 1 to 3 mentions the church sixteen times, but from this passage on, in chapters 4 to 18 in Revelation, the term "church" does not appear. Instead, Revelation chapters 4 to 18 include mention of "saints." Thus, say LaHaye and other premillennial dispensationalists, the rapture of the church occurs in Revelation 4:1–2, and chapters 4 to 18 in Revelation tell the story of the tribulation when the church is no longer on the earth. The "church" is raptured, and the "saints" are people who convert to Christianity after the rapture.

John is a *symbol* of the church? Critics of premillennial dispensationalism say that this does not seem to be the kind of plain, literal reading of the Bible that LaHaye and others advocate. In addition, critics claim that this whole line of interpretation, drawing an artificial distinction between "church" and "saints," ignores the context of the verses. In the first three chapters of Revelation, John specifically addressed himself to "the seven churches that are in Asia" (Rev. 1:4), and he offered specific messages to each church, so of course he uses the word "church" frequently. Then, they say, in Revelation 4:1–2 John changed the subject and told about a series of visions he received, no longer addressing himself directly to the seven churches. Even Tim LaHaye acknowledges that "this passage alone would not establish the Rapture as a pre-Tribulation event," but he finds the case convincing when connected with other verses and arguments.[23]

Does the Bible teach its readers about a rapture? The views summarized here contrast dramatically. Although the term "rapture" technically does not appear in the biblical text, LaHaye and others believe they find extensive biblical support for a literal rapture of the church, prior to a period of tribulation and the glorious appearing of Christ. Others disagree about the timing of the rapture, expecting it in the middle of the tribulation or after it. Still others argue that there is no rapture at all in the Bible; they see it as a recent notion in Christian history, misrepresenting biblical passages that talk about resurrection.

Does the Bible Predict a Period of Tribulation?

What [Rayford] had been learning from Bruce and his own study of prophecy indicated that the day would come when the antichrist would no longer be a deceiver. He would show his colors and rule the world with an iron fist. He would smash his enemies and kill anyone disloyal to his regime. That would put every follower of Christ at risk of martyrdom. Rayford foresaw the day when he would have to leave Carpathia's employ and become a fugitive, merely to survive and help other believers do the same.

—Tim LaHaye and Jerry B. Jenkins,
Tribulation Force, p. 356

The Left Behind series is an extended story about people left behind at the rapture of the church, who then must live through "the tribulation." Premillennial dispensationalists believe that the tribulation will be an exact seven-year period, between the rapture and the glorious appearing when Jesus Christ returns to earth to reign. This is Tim LaHaye's description:

> This world only *thinks* it has seen tribulation.
> The day is coming when the worst traumas in history will be eclipsed by a seven-year period that will be far more terrifying than anything man can imagine. . . .
> Take the horror of every war since time began, throw in every natural disaster in recorded history, and cast off all restraints so that the unspeakable cruelty and hatred and injustice of man toward his fellow men can fully mature—then compress it all into a period of seven years. Even if you could imagine such a thing, it wouldn't approach the mind-boggling terror and turmoil of the Tribulation.[24]

What is the biblical basis for believing in this period of tribulation, and do all biblical interpreters agree with it?

Those who talk about the tribulation would focus especially on details in the symbolic narrative in the middle chapters of the book of Revelation, but in addition, they would say that almost the entire Bible offers predictions of the horrible time to come. LaHaye and Jenkins favorably quote evangelical writer Arnold Fruchtenbaum: "In every passage of the Scriptures that the term the 'Day of Jehovah' or the 'Day of the Lord' is found, it is always and without exception a reference to the tribulation period. This is the most common name for this period in the Old Testament, and it is also found in various passages of the New Testament."[25] Thus, they contend, every reference to either of those two phrases throughout the Bible is a reference to the tribulation at the end of time. "Jacob's distress" in Jeremiah 30:7 also is equated with this time period, as well as certain visions in Daniel. In addition, most references to "tribulation" or similar terms in the New Testament also are said to refer to this seven-year period after the rapture. Matthew 24 is an often-quoted chapter in this regard, in which Jesus discusses signs of the end of the age and says, "For then there will be great distress, unequaled from the beginning of the world until now— and never to be equaled again" (Matt. 24:21, NIV). And finally, Revelation chapters 6 through 18 contain an overwhelming number of symbolic descriptions of dramatic and frightening occurrences, including seven seals, seven trumpet blasts, and seven vials, plus plagues, earthquakes, wars, and "seven bowls of the wrath of God." All together, in this view, the numerous biblical allusions paint a consistent and terrifying picture of tribulation at the end of time.

The problem that other biblical interpreters have with this construction is that they contend the passages have all been wrenched out of their biblical and historical contexts in order to apply to one single period in the end times. For instance, does every reference to "Day of Jehovah" or "Day of the Lord" really refer to a future tribulation? When the phrases arise in texts such as Joel 1:15; 2:1; Amos 5:18–20; and Zephaniah 1:7, they appear to refer to the destruction of Israel and/or Judah at various times in Jewish history. When the phrase appears in Obadiah 15, it refers to Edomites, Israel's southeastern neighbor, and "all the nations" that have troubled Israel. Thus, they ask, are these really references to a future tribulation immediately prior to Jesus Christ's second coming?

In the New Testament, many uses of "tribulation" or equivalent terms appear to refer to more immediate situations. Paul claimed that he himself had gone through tribulations (2 Cor. 1:16; 4:8; 7:5; Col. 1:24). In 1 Thessalonians 3:4 (NRSV) Paul wrote, "In fact, when we were with you, we told you beforehand that we were to suffer persecution; so it turned out, as you know." In that instance, the reference to persecution or tribulation is about something in the past, not in the future. And when one moves to the extensive symbolic narrative in Revelation, we return to the basic question discussed earlier, about whether these symbolic passages refer to the suffering of Christians under Roman persecution, rather than a prediction of happenings far in the future. Thus, from this opposing viewpoint, it is not clear that the Bible says as much about a period of final tribulation as the pretribulation rapture position claims. In particular, it does not seem to those who hold the preterist view of Revelation that the many uses of the words "tribulation," "Day or the Lord," "Jacob's distress," and other expressions for times of trial all relate to the same period in history, a seven-year period in the future in which Christians will suffer profound persecution. Nations and individuals frequently suffer tragedies and challenges, and it makes sense that scripture would refer to such difficult times. All such references should not be seen as predictions of the future, according to LaHaye's critics.

A further issue is the length of time of the tribulation. Of course, people who do not expect a literal period of tribulation at the end of time are not terribly interested in this question, but those who expect a tribulation have engaged in vigorous debates about its length. The claim of seven years rests principally on one verse in the book of Daniel. In chapter 9, Daniel prayed to God confessing the wickedness and rebellion of the people of Israel and asking for God's mercy. The angel Gabriel then appeared before Daniel and interpreted some of the things that were to come, including a time line that gets confusing for many readers: seventy weeks to put an end to sin and anoint a holy place, including seven weeks between instructions to restore Jerusalem and the coming of an anointed prince, and then sixty-two weeks to build Jerusalem, followed by a final dramatic week described in Daniel 9:27.

> After the sixty-two weeks, an anointed one shall be cut off and shall have nothing, and the troops of the prince who is to come shall destroy the city and the sanctuary. Its end shall come with a flood, and to the end there shall be war. Desolations are decreed. He shall make a strong covenant with many for *one week*, and for half of the week he shall make sacrifice and offering cease; and in

their place shall be an abomination that desolates, until the decreed end is poured out upon the desolator. (Daniel 9:26–27, NRSV, italics added.)

In the premillennial dispensationalist view, this is a prediction of the tribulation at the end of time, and the period of desolation is said to last for "one week," divided into two halves. For LaHaye and others, the book of Revelation describes in more detail what will happen in that last "week," and they claim that each day is a symbol for a year, thus making the final tribulation seven years long (a "week" of years).

Interestingly, the book of Revelation never mentions a seven-year period, nor does it describe the final events as taking place in one week. The book of Revelation is filled with all kinds of references to sevens, but not to seven years. There are five references to some different time periods:

42 months (Rev. 11:2; 13:5)
1,260 days (Rev. 11:3; 12:6)
"a time, and times, and half a time" (Rev. 12:14)

If one does the calculations, 42 months equal three and a half years, and 1,260 days are *almost* the same length of time. If "a time" is one year, and "times" are two years, then that reference might equal three and a half years as well. Persons like LaHaye claim that the tribulation is divided into two halves, and these time periods refer to those halves, sometimes duplicating each other. Others argue, on the basis of these verses in Revelation, that the tribulation is really three and a half years long, not seven. And some persons find all of these numbers and symbols very obscure and believe it is foolish to attempt precise calculations.

This is indeed the complaint of many, who believe that too many people are too certain in trying to interpret all of these symbols. Evangelical commentator John Goldingay, writing about Daniel 9:24–27 (considered above), says that "the verses do not indicate that they are looking centuries or millennia beyond the period to which chapters. 8 and 10–12 refer. . . . It does not refer specifically to concrete persons and events in the way of historical narrative . . . but refers in terms of symbols to what those persons and events embodied, symbols such as sin, justice, an anointed prince, a flood, an abomination. Concrete events and persons are understood in light of such symbols, but the symbols transcend them. They are not limited in their reference to these particular concrete realities. They have other embodiments. What these other embodiments are is a matter of theological, not exegetical, judgment—a matter of faith, not of science."[26] Basically, Goldingay is saying that this particular passage in Daniel refers explicitly to a second-century B.C.E. situation, although the symbolism used to depict this situation in the Jews' past can be reapplied to other scenarios. By stating that such a reapplication is theological, not exegetical, Goldingay indicates that it is not finally demonstrated by biblical passages. Goldingay wants to put in perspective all of our attempts at constructing a specific outline of God's future work with the earth. Various theological reapplications of the biblical material may be legitimate, but none can be proven, and it is difficult to claim that the Bible clearly teaches exactly what will happen in the end, Goldingay argues.

Along the same line, Stephen Spencer, while still professor of systematic theology at Dallas Theological Seminary, a school known for its strong stance in favor of premillennial dispensationalism, wrote the following comments about the Left Behind series: "One of my biggest complaints about the series is that the extensiveness of the books requires them to go far beyond biblical doctrine. Pre-trib advocates acknowledge that there is very little information about human life and society during that period in Scripture. The books are more socio-cultural than theology, I would suggest, and at that, a very problematic socio-cultural perspective. I fear that the books, purportedly biblically based novels, actually inform the readers' socio-cultural outlook and mold an escapist stance toward contemporary culture."[27]

Thus, a swirl of disagreements surround discussion of the belief in a seven-year tribulation at the end of time. Some expect a literal time of extreme difficulties for those left behind after a rapture, for a seven year period, and they find much support for it in scripture. Some argue about the length of time of the tribulation. Others believe that most of the Bible verses being quoted actually refer to various historical time periods in the past, and they are not predictions of the future. Still others think that the symbolism in many of these passages is too obscure for us to claim certain knowledge.

Does the Bible Predict an Antichrist as Part of the End Times?

Let me warn you personally to beware of such a leader of humanity who may emerge from Europe. He will turn out to be a great deceiver who will step forward with signs and wonders that will be so impressive that many will believe he is of God. He will gain a great following among those who are left, and many will believe he is a miracle worker. . . . This person is known in the Bible as Antichrist. He will make many promises, but he will not keep them.

—Tim LaHaye and Jerry B. Jenkins,
Left Behind, pp. 212–213

Clearly, the central evil character in the Left Behind series is Nicolae Carpathia, a handsome, deceptively personable man who rises to become General Secretary of the United Nations and who eventually is indwelt by Satan and becomes the antichrist, inflicting unspeakable death and destruction on the world. Carpathia is a fictional character, but the belief in an antichrist who will play a major role in end time events is widespread among many Christians. So, is the antichrist really in the Bible, or is it yet another example of conflicting biblical interpretations?

First we need to examine the biblical roots of the term "antichrist." Indeed, this is one more case where the biblical references are not as clear as the general public expects. If we were to look up the term "antichrist" in a biblical concordance, we would find that the word occurs only five times, in four verses in the New Testament. Perhaps the biggest surprise is that it never occurs in the book of Revelation. Not once. All of the references are in the first and second letters of John. Christians often have identified the author of these letters as the same person who wrote the gospel of John, but many biblical scholars now believe that the letters were written a little later, about 100 C.E., by one or more people standing in the tradition of John. Thus, the gospel and letters of John all may not have been written by the same person, but they were at least written by persons who saw themselves representing a "Johannine tradition."[28]

It is important to note a few details about the references to antichrist in 1 and 2 John. In all of the major English translations—King James, New Revised Standard, New International, and others—the word "antichrist" is never capitalized. Sometimes the phrase "the antichrist" is used, but once it is simply "antichrist" and once it is plural ("antichrists"). For your examination, here are the full texts of the biblical references:

> Children, it is the last hour! As you have heard that *antichrist* is coming, so now many *antichrists* have come. From this we know that it is the last hour. They went out from us, but they did not belong to us; for if they had belonged to us, they would have remained with us. But by going out they made it plain that none of them belongs to us. But you have been anointed by the Holy One, and all of you have knowledge. I write to you, not because you do not know the truth, but because you know it, and you know that no lie comes from the truth. Who is the liar but the one who denies that Jesus is the Christ? This is the *antichrist*, the one who denies the Father and the Son. (1 John 2:18–22, NRSV, italics added.)
>
> Beloved, do not believe every spirit, but test the spirits to see whether they are from God; for many false prophets have gone out into the world. By this you know the Spirit of God; every spirit that confesses that Jesus Christ has come in the flesh is from God, and every spirit that does not confess Jesus is not from God. And this is the spirit of the *antichrist*, of which you have heard that it is coming; and now it is already in the world. (1 John 4:1–3, NRSV, italics added.)
>
> Many deceivers have gone out into the world, those who do not confess that Jesus Christ has come in the flesh; any such person is the deceiver and the *antichrist*! (2 John 1:7, NRSV, italics added.)

What do these passages mean? One viewpoint says that this is about a theological argument among people living in biblical times, and another viewpoint combines these passages with other Bible verses to see a prediction of an evil figure who will arise sometime in the future. Let's briefly summarize each view.

From the first perspective, many biblical scholars claim that the author or authors of the letters (I will call him John) was involved in early Christian disagreements about who Jesus was and how Christians ought to understand Jesus' divinity. Now that Jesus was no longer living among them, his followers discovered that they had different ways of describing Jesus and how he was related to God. For instance, some persons claimed that Jesus only *appeared* to be human. Others said that Jesus was born an ordinary human being and that the heavenly "Christ" later descended on Jesus at his baptism. The author of 1 and 2 John was outraged by claims like this, and he was very combative in opposing such teachings. More or less, the author of the letters is saying that if you do not believe the proper things about Jesus, you are "antichristos," or "against Christ." Anyone who "denies the Father and the Son" is "the antichrist," in other words, against Christ.

Further, when the term "antichrist" was used in its various forms (antichrist, the antichrist, antichrists), the verses in 1 and 2 John appear to apply the terms to ordinary men and women who held the wrong beliefs. Most important, they were people "already in the world" (1 John 4:3). Therefore, in this view, though 1 John 2:18 and 1 John 4:3 admit the teaching that antichrist is coming, the verses in their context do not emphasize a single powerful figure (the antichrist) who will arise far in the future. Instead, the verses refer to people living at the time the letters were written.

After Jesus' crucifixion, many Christians believed that he would return to earth at any moment, very soon, within their lifetimes. John believes that the rise of arguments about how to understand Jesus must be a sign that the expected return of Jesus is about to occur: "it is the last hour." Thus, the letters of 1 and 2 John are filled with passion and urgency, because the author believes that the theological disagreement is very important, and because he believes that Jesus will return at any moment. The letters were written to defend one view of Jesus, to condemn people who held other views as "antichristos," against Christ, all in a time when Jesus' second coming was expected at any moment.

Tim LaHaye, along with others, interprets the passages quite differently, because he links the idea of an antichrist who is to come in the future (see 1 John 2:18; 4:3) with other references in other books of the Bible: the "little horn" in Daniel 7:11; "man of lawlessness" in 2 Thessalonians 2:3; "evil man" of 2 Thessalonians 2:9; and "the beast" of Revelation 13:1–18, 14:9–11, 15:2.[29]

It is the vision of two beasts in Revelation 13 that provides the most specific details for LaHaye's scenario. Borrowing the term "antichrist" from 1 and 2 John, LaHaye and many others label one of these beasts as the antichrist. In Revelation, the biblical author describes a beast from the sea (Rev. 13:1–10) and a beast from the land (Rev. 13:11–18). The first beast appeared to receive a death blow but was healed, uttered blasphemies against God and made war on the saints. The second beast "uttered all the authority of the first beast on its behalf" and caused an image of the first beast to be created. It then killed those who would not worship the image of the beast. Some interpreters claim that the beast discussed here symbolizes Nero or Domitian, Roman emperors notorious for persecuting Christians. However, LaHaye combines the first beast in Revelation 13 with the "antichrist" expected in 1 John 2:18 and 4:3, the "little horn" of Daniel 7, and the "lawless one" of 2 Thessalonians 2 and sees all as coded predictions of "the antichrist," a horrible world leader who will come sometime in the future as a part of dramatic end-time events.[30] LaHaye follows the description of the second beast ("another beast") in Revelation 13:11 and calls it a "false prophet" for the antichrist and "the Antichrist's primary minister of propaganda."[31]

This returns us to the kind of arguments we have heard already. Is it "literal" (the "plain sense") of Revelation 13 to see it as a reference to Roman emperors, in the era when Revelation was written? Or is it "literal" to see it as a coded prediction of something two thousand years in the future? Also, which expresses the plain sense of the passages: viewing 1 and 2 John and Revelation 13 as referring to separate situations, or combining them as references to the same thing?

LaHaye draws additional scriptural passages together as well, stating that "many titles are given to Antichrist in the Scriptures—at least twenty in number."[32] These include Lucifer (Isa. 14:12), "the king of Babylon" (Isa. 14:4), "the prince who is to come" (Dan. 9:26), "the son of destruction" and "the man of lawlessness" (2 Thess. 2:3), among others. LaHaye sees this as putting together the pieces of a puzzle, all from the Bible, a source inspired by God. LaHaye's critics see it as indiscriminately lifting biblical passages out of their contexts and molding them into one.

Concluding Comments

Clearly, Christians offer some dramatically different biblical interpretations when they discuss the end times. On one hand, we have encountered a detailed, carefully articulated view of the end times that has been called "premillennial dispensationalism." Tim LaHaye has been a strong proponent of that view, and the Left Behind books are built on the premises of that view. It insists that prophetic passages of scripture (those that seem to talk about the end times) should be read as literally as other portions of scripture. In other words, LaHaye and others expect dramatic and literal historical events to happen in the end times, and they are very interested in learning as much as possible about those events by carefully examining the entire Bible. What they find there is a picture of a literal rapture, tribulation, and second coming of Jesus that is derived from elements of Daniel, Revelation, and many other books, extensively cross-referenced into a tightly argued system. Each event is repeatedly interlocked with the others. This approach has been meaningful for a great number of Christians, especially in the United States; it encourages close attention to details in the biblical text, and it has been an effective tool for evangelization.

Disagreements with the premillennial dispensationalist view come from many directions, but in the preceding discussions two complaints seemed common. One is that the cross-referencing of scripture passages from throughout the Bible ignored the particular contexts of each passage, assuming that all refer to the same thing. Does it make a difference that portions of scripture were written in different historical circumstances, to different people, with different concerns? Many people would say yes, it does. The second complaint is related: Critics repeatedly charge that LaHaye and others are not as literal in their biblical interpretations as they claim. Wouldn't a literal reading of scripture pay more attention to the contexts of particular verses? Also, when a week is interpreted as seven years, or when an invitation to John to "come up here" is said to symbolize the rapture of the entire church, is that really a literal or plain reading of these passages? Many feel that LaHaye and others turn the plain sense of some biblical passages into symbols, in order to make a case for literal end-time events.

In the end, the problem is that Revelation does not come with its own glossary or interpretation manual. All interpretations of this book and the other passages discussed above seem to involve guesswork, a point well illustrated by the wide variety of interpretations throughout Christian history and today. So how can we come to terms with the texts and debates? I would recommend that instead of claiming that there is only one way to read the Bible on these topics, one should recognize that sincere Christians hold a number of differing viewpoints. As we try to sort them out and reach our own conclusions regarding what the Bible says about the end times, I would recommend that we do so humbly, hesitant to claim that we have the final answer.

Notes

1. Robert M. Grant with David Tracy, *A Short History of the Interpretation of the Bible*, 2d. ed. (Philadelphia: Fortress Press, 1984), chapters 6–7.
2. Charles Caldwell Ryrie, *Dispensationalism Today* (Chicago: Moody, 1965), 87.

3. Tim LaHaye, *Rapture Under Attack: Will You Escape the Tribulation?* (Sisters, Ore.: Multnomah Publishers, 1998), 11.

4. Ibid., 44.

5. Ibid., 12.

6. Michael D. Coogan, ed., *The New Oxford Annotated Bible*, 3rd. ed., New Revised Standard Version (New York: Oxford University Press, 2001), New Testament 420.

7. For example, LaHaye and Jenkins write, "we are indebted to Daniel, the great Hebrew prophet, who asked the same questions we would ask about spiritual conditions during the end times." Tim LaHaye and Jerry B. Jenkins, *Are We Living in the End Times?* (Wheaton, Ill.: Tyndale House, 1999), 309.

8. A helpful discussion of the three approaches can be found in Craig R. Koester, *Revelation and the End of All Things* (Grand Rapids, Mich.: Eerdmans, 2001), pp. 1–40. Alternatively, a description of four views, preterist, historicist, futurist, and idealist, can be found in Merrill C. Tenney, *Interpreting Revelation* (Grand Rapids, Mich.: Eerdmans, 1957), 135–146.

9. Koester, *Revelation*, 31.

10. Ibid., 6. Koester refers to Origen and to Arthur W. Wainwright, *Mysterious Apocalypse: Interpreting the Book of Revelation* (Nashville, Tenn.: Abingdon, 1993), 203.

11. LaHaye, *Rapture Under Attack*, 33.

12. Ibid.

13. NRSV refers to the New Revised Standard Version of the Bible.

14. LaHaye refers to the three as "three main Rapture passages" in *Rapture Under Attack*, 75.

15. N. T. Wright, "Farewell to the Rapture," *Bible Review* 17 (August 2001), 8. Compare this to Tim LaHaye's rejoinder in his *The Merciful God of Prophecy: His Loving Plan for You in the End Times* (n.p.: Warner Books, 2002), 57–58, 73. LaHaye does not address Wright's use of Old Testament imagery to explain 1 Thessalonians 4:17 nor, in my view, does he seek to represent Wright's position accurately in his rejection of it.

16. Gary DeMar, *End Times Fiction: A Biblical Consideration of the Left Behind Theology* (Nashville, Tenn.: Thomas Nelson, 2001), 36. Both quotations from DeMar in this paragraph mention "pre-trib Rapture" or "pretribulationism." This refers to the belief that a rapture will occur before the period of tribulation. Others believe that a rapture will occur in the middle of the tribulation ("midtrib") or at the end of the tribulation ("posttrib").

17. Ibid., 18.

18. Ibid., 19.

19. NIV refers to the New International Version.

20. Neil Wilson and Len Woods, *Left Behind Bible Study Guide #1: The Rapture* (Chicago: Moody Press, 2003), 12; Wilson and Woods, *Left Behind Bible Study Guide #2: The Antichrist* (Chicago: Moody Press, 2003), 13.

21. Coogan, ed., *New Oxford Annotated Bible*, New Testament 427, note attached to Revelation 4:1.

22. LaHaye, *Rapture Under Attack*, 58.

23. Ibid., 80.

24. Ibid., 55–56.

25. LaHaye and Jenkins, *Are We Living in the End Times?* 147, quoting Arnold Fruchtenbaum, *The Footsteps of the Messiah: A Study of the Sequence of Prophetic Events* (San Antonio, Texas: Ariel Press, 1982), 121–122.

26. John E. Goldingay, *Daniel*, Word Biblical Commentary 30 (Dallas: Word, 1989), 257.

27. Stephen Spencer, e-mail communication to Mark Reasoner, April 20, 2001. The "escapist stance" mentioned in Spencer's quotation is sometimes held by premillennial dispensationalists who accept LaHaye's scenario, for if they are convinced that the rapture will happen very soon, they will apply all efforts toward getting non-Christians to believe in Jesus and exert little or no effort in the arena of social justice on this earth.

28. Raymond Brown, *The Epistles of John: A New Translation with Introduction and Commentary*, Anchor Bible 30 (Garden City, N.Y.: Doubleday, 1982), 14–35, 69–115.

29. Wilson and Woods, *The Antichrist*, 33 and passim; LaHaye and Jenkins, *Are We Living in the End Times?* 271–282.

30. LaHaye and Jenkins, *Are We Living in the End Times?* 271–282.

31. Ibid., 285.

32. Tim LaHaye, *Revelation Unveiled*, rev. ed. (Grand Rapids, Mich.: Zondervan, 1999), 207, as quoted in DeMar, *End Times Fiction*, 135.

4

When Do Christians Think the End Times Will Happen?

A Comparative Theologies Discussion of the Second Coming

STANLEY J. GRENZ

"When will this happen?" asked the astonished disciples in response to Jesus' prediction that the beautiful temple in Jerusalem would one day be destroyed. Convinced that such a catastrophic event would by necessity mark the end of the world as they knew it, they added, "and what will be the sign of your coming and of the end of the age?" (Matt. 24:3 New International Version). According to Matthew's narrative, what followed was Jesus' lengthy depiction of the end times, which is often termed the Mount Olivet discourse because of the location where the gospel writer places it. The disciples' query has been raised by Christians at nearly every turn in church history. Indeed, concern for this perennial question—"When will this happen?"—accounts in part for the popularity of the Left Behind series. In these books, Tim LaHaye and Jerry Jenkins present in fictional form one widely propagated interpretation of the end-times scenario that Jesus outlined in his conversation with his disciples on the Mount of Olives nearly two thousand years ago.

Of course, not everybody anticipates a catastrophic end to human history in the not-too-distant future. Even many Christians today give no credence to the idea that Jesus might actually return sometime soon. In the opinion of some, such language is merely a holdover from a pre-modern era when myths and superstitions held sway. We might say that the eschatology (the understanding of the "end times") most widespread in the church in America today focuses on personal death, rather than human history, as the ultimate human encounter with Christ and hence as the true scene of whatever "second coming" might legitimately be anticipated. In the eyes of many people, the assumption that Jesus comes for the believer at death leaves little need for antiquated and seemingly unscientific expectations of a cataclysmic return of a divine Lord of the cosmos from a heavenly realm above the earth.

The long-standing absence in many churches of any talk about a future end of the age has served to increase the appeal of the Left Behind series. When encountered by Christians nurtured in a community in which such texts as Jesus' Mount Olivet discourse have been routinely ignored or "demythologized," fantastic renditions of a soon-arriving future replete with Christians being snatched away to heaven, evil rulers taking control of world governments, and good people engaging in surreptitious political intrigue often ignite the imagination and provide a welcome, plausible explanation of current world conditions. Yet expectations clustered around two poles—the wholesale dismissal of every expectation regarding the end of the age or the unqualified acceptance of the LaHaye-Jenkins rendition—do not exhaust the options. On the contrary, four general eschatological views can be found among contemporary Christians who anticipate a literal return of Christ at some future point.

The names of these views derive from the perspective each offers regarding the timing of Jesus' return with respect to the millennium, or the thousand-year period of peace and righteousness mentioned in Revelation 20:1–6. Advocates of *postmillennialism* look for the return of Jesus *after* the earthly "kingdom of God." Proponents of *premillennialism* expect Christ's second coming to occur *prior to* the millennium, and therefore anticipate that the Lord will be physically present on the earth to exercise dominion during what will be his thousand-year reign. In contrast to millenarians of either persuasion, *amillennialists* do not anticipate that an earthly golden age will occur at some particular point in human history, but believe that the thousand-year reign mentioned in Revelation 20 carries symbolic significance.

Contemporary adherents of the second perspective are further divided into two groups. *Historic premillennialists* anticipate a time of tribulation directed against the church that will climax in Christ's coming to rescue the community of his disciples from the forces of evil. The millennium, in turn, will occasion God's blessing of Christ's faithful followers. *Dispensational premillennialists*, in contrast, believe that the future tribulation and the millennium are part of God's program for the nation of Israel. Insofar as the tribulation will be God's opportunity to prepare the Jewish people to accept the messiah, dispensationalists theorize, the church will be raptured out of the world immediately before the tribulation begins. As readers of the Left Behind novels can easily guess, this latter perspective is set forth in the series.

The following paragraphs present a synopsis of the main features of these four major answers to the question, "When will this happen?" together with the biblical and theological arguments offered by proponents of each. In so doing, the chapter indicates that the perspective presented in the Left Behind series is not the only alternative to the wholesale dismissal of the expectation of the return of Christ, which has become the "default position" in so many churches today.

The Dawning of the Kingdom: Postmillennialism

Although postmillennialism may be the least familiar—and least understood—eschatological proposal today, it was the preeminent perspective in the United States from the colonial period to the early twentieth century. In fact, so dominant was postmillennialism within nineteenth-century American Christianity that in 1859, the *American Theological Review* could speak of it as the "commonly received doctrine" among American Protestants.[1] Lyrical expression was given to the postmillennial ethos in many of the hymns of the day. Christians set forth to conquer their spiritual foes singing "Lead On, O King Eternal," which couched the conflict and its resolution in postmillennial terms: "For not with swords loud clashing, Nor roll of stirring drums; With deeds of love and mercy, The heav'nly kingdom comes."[2] The postmillennial vision spawned a great worldwide missionary effort that was encapsulated by the writer of the hymn "O Zion Haste, Thy Mission High Fulfilling." Christian evangelists crisscrossed the globe confident that "the darkness shall turn to dawning, And the dawning to noonday bright, And Christ's great kingdom shall come to earth, The kingdom of love and light."[3]

The Central Features of Postmillennialism
In the eyes of many, postmillennialism is linked with the social gospel movement, and its central focus often is deemed to be the quest for social transformation. Many of the activities of churches in the United States from food bank drives to work in prisons can be traced to this movement and its attempt to improve society in anticipation of the coming of Christ. Yet at the heart of postmillennialism is not just social transformation but the spread of the gospel and the conversion of a great number of persons, leading to an era of peace and righteousness on the earth prior to Christ's return. Postmillennialists anticipate that the kingdom of God will gradually expand until it encompasses the whole earth.

Postmillennialists, therefore, view the millennium as a long era of universal peace and righteousness that arises as the result of the preaching of the gospel, the saving work of the Holy Spirit in the hearts of individuals, and the Christianization of the world. They anticipate a golden age of spiritual prosperity for the entire world that will occur at the end of our own era.

The millennium is, in the words of one postmillennial theologian, "the culmination of the work of the Holy Spirit," and as such it will be characterized by "a universal revival of religion" with "the kings of the earth bringing their glory and honor into the city of God."[4]

Both premillennialism and postmillennialism anticipate an earthly golden age, a future era in which the reign of Christ (the "kingdom of God") will be present on this earth. In this sense, the two views share what is known as a millenarian outlook. Nevertheless, postmillennialists differ from premillennialists regarding the exact nature of the relationship between the present and the anticipated kingdom age. One point of difference focuses on the transition between the two eras. In contrast to the catastrophic beginning of the millennium anticipated by premillennialists, according to postmillennialism the progression to the kingdom era is smooth. Like the coming of summer or the beginning of any historical epoch, the advent of the millennium cannot be pinpointed, for it arises as the result of a slow process, although the long preparation may be followed by a sudden consummation. Because the future arrives as the outworking of forces that are already active in the world, the millennium may dawn without its inauguration being perceived. And given the symbolic nature of the time span in Revelation 20, its duration may exceed a literal thousand years.

The two eschatologies also differ regarding the nature of the millennium. In contrast to the discontinuity that premillennialists tend to emphasize, the postmillennial vision of the thousand years focuses on the continuity of the future epoch with the present era. In many ways, life in the golden age will be quite similar to life in the present. Marriage and the natural process of birth, for example, will continue. Most important, the church will keep its place in the program of God as the outward, visible expression of the inward presence of God's Spirit. We might say that the changes that will emerge in the future age will be differences of *extent*, not *content*. The gospel will continue to be preached as it is now. Yet the millennial era will be characterized by a heightened influence of Christian principles in human society.

Moreover, people living in the golden age will enjoy the blessings that flow from the worldwide spread of the gospel and the waning of the influence of evil. As the Holy Spirit regenerates human beings, their changed character will lead to reforms in the social, economic, political, and cultural spheres. This heightened spirituality will open the way to the great material prosperity promised in both the Old and New Testaments. Furthermore, as humans engage in the task of proper management of the earth assigned to them before the fall, a marvelous transformation will occur in nature.

Because the postmillennial ethos focuses on the anticipation of the dawning of the glorious kingdom of God, advocates give little place to the kind of political intrigue and doomsday expectations that are so prominent in the Left Behind novels. The fuller postmillennial end-times scenario could be summarized as follows: As the gospel spreads throughout the earth and brings its divinely intended and Spirit-energized results, evil (and perhaps its personal representation in the form of the antichrist) is eventually routed, and the millennium arrives. During this era the nations live in peace, for Satan is "bound," meaning that evil is temporarily restrained. After the thousand years have ended, Satan is loosed to lead a short-lived rebellion, the final conflict of evil with righteousness, whether this takes the form of a spiritual battle of truth against error or political persecution. Satan's rebellion is ended by the triumphal return of Jesus (the second coming), followed by the general resurrection, the judgment, and the entrance into the eternal state (i.e., heaven or hell).

The Case for Postmillennialism

Postmillennialists believe that their eschatology sets forth the correct understanding of the vision of the thousand-year reign disclosed in Revelation 20:1–8, which they are convinced will follow chronologically after the subjection of the world by the rider on the white horse depicted in Revelation 19:11–21. In a sense, their interpretation of the rider forms the heart of the biblical case for postmillennialism. Loraine Boettner speaks for many postmillennialists, when he declares that this text presents "a vision setting forth in figurative language the age-long struggle between the forces of good and the forces of evil in the world, with its promise of complete victory."[5] According to the post-millennialist interpretation, therefore, the rider represents the victorious Lord not in his coming at the end of the age (as pre-millennialists believe), but in the process of gaining the victory over his enemies through the preaching of the gospel within the era of the Christian church on earth.[6]

This crucial conclusion arises out of one particular feature that postmillennialists see in the text, the presence of a sword coming out of the mouth of the rider. To understand the significance of this aspect of John's vision, postmillennialists point to a declaration found elsewhere in the Bible: "For the word of God is living and active. Sharper than any double-edged sword" (Heb. 4:12). Postmillennialists conclude that John is envisioning the advancing victory of Christ, the Word of God, that is accomplished by the proclamation of the gospel throughout the church age and will inaugurate the thousand-year era of Revelation 20.

According to postmillennialists, the vision of the rider presents in symbolic form the great New Testament teaching regarding the progress of the gospel that Jesus himself presents in the parables of the kingdom in Matthew 13. Especially important are the four parables that compare the kingdom of heaven to growth processes.[7] The parables of the mustard seed and the yeast (Matt. 13:31–33) teach that the gospel influence begins small, but spreads progressively until it is found throughout the world. The presence of the gospel in human hearts results in the influence of Christian principles in society, which in turn brings about the long-expected era of peace and righteousness. The parables of the weeds and the net (13:24–30, 47–50) indicate the mixed nature of the growth of the kingdom. In this age the world will never be without the presence of evil; yet as the kingdom advances, the weeds and the bad fish eventually diminish in relative numerical strength until they constitute a comparatively small part of the whole. The parables of the weeds and the mustard seed, on one hand, and the yeast, on the other, indicate that kingdom growth occurs both within a specific believer or location (intensively) and from individual to individual or throughout society and its institutions and activities (extensively).

This crucial theme of the progress of the gospel that postmillennialists find in Mathew 13 and Revelation 19 is paralleled by the New Testament declaration of the absolute power of Christ. According to Matthew's account of the great commission, the risen Lord based the sending of the disciples—and, by extension, his commissioning of the church throughout the age—on his own reception of authority: "All authority in heaven and on earth has been given to me. Therefore go" (Matt. 28:18). Not only do postmillenialists desire to take this command seriously, they believe that the church possesses all the resources necessary to fulfill its mandate. In the words of James Snowden, "All authority includes all power of every kind that is applicable to this task. Jesus Christ can never have any more power than He has now, for He now has all there is."[8] Consequently, postmillenialists argue, Christ's millennial rule will begin in this age as the church is successful in fulfilling its mandate.

Postmillennialists find the basis for their eschatological perspective in the pages of the Old Testament as well. They point out that one of the most pervasive themes of the Hebrew scriptures is that the glory of the Lord will fill the earth and the nations will worship Yahweh (e.g., Num. 14:21; Psa. 86:9, 97:5; Isa. 2:2–3; Zech. 9:10 and messianic texts such as Psa. 47, 72, and 110). Thus, the great nineteenth-century Princeton theologian Charles Hodge argues from Isaiah 45:22–23 that "the true religion shall prevail over the whole earth. Jehovah shall everywhere be recognized and worshipped as the only true God."[9] Texts such as this, Hodge notes, were applied by the New Testament writers to the era of the church's existence on earth. As a result, he concludes, the conversion of the gentile world is assured. The mandate of proclamation has been assigned to the church; under the authority of Christ and by the power of the Holy Spirit, the church can be successful in its assigned task.

Postmillennialists likewise point out that the Old Testament prophets anticipated a time of global peace and righteousness

within history. One crucial text that articulates this is Isaiah's vision of a new heaven and a new earth (Isa. 65:17–25), which the writer of the book of Revelation later expanded. In contrast to premillennialists, who anticipate a new physical universe inaugurated by Jesus at his return, postmillennialists see this vision as referring to a moral and spiritual revolution in human society fostered by the gospel.

We might summarize the postmillennialist perspective by concluding that advocates pour the prophetic expectations of a future golden age into the mold provided by the millennial vision of Revelation 20. On the basis of their conviction that the goal of God's work in the Old Testament is attained in the church, postmillennialists conclude that the anticipated blessed era comes as the culmination of the church age and forms the era of the victory of the church in the world.

The case for postmillennialism moves beyond the biblical texts to human history. Advocates note that great advances have been made since the first coming of Christ, and these, in turn, spark hope for a Christianization of the world prior to the Lord's return. Postmillennialists readily admit that there have been times of apparent setback and that great problems continue to exist. At the same time, they claim that when viewed as a whole, the conditions of human existence have improved since the first century, when the world at large was "groping helplessly in pagan darkness."[10] They also point out that the gospel is now being proclaimed around the globe to a degree unparalleled in past eras. In short, although world conditions may not be improving daily, the general direction of history since the Christ's advent and the inauguration of the church has been upward, thereby offering tangible confirmation that the golden age will indeed arrive in its fullness in the not-too-distant future.

A Future Kingdom for Israel: Dispensational Premillennialism

If the nineteenth century was the heyday of postmillennialism, the twentieth belonged to dispensational premillennialism. By

the midpoint of the century this eschatological system had become the most widely held view among fundamentalists and evangelicals in America, even if it was largely unknown within mainline churches. In fact, in many conservative circles the dispensational scheme of biblical interpretation and its chronology of the end times became the standard of right belief, so much so that any move away from this eschatology was seen as an attack on the doctrine of Christ's second coming itself.[11]

Since midcentury, adherents have been tinkering with the system. In fact, contemporary "progressive dispensationalists" have revised this eschatological outlook so drastically that it barely resembles the perspective reflected in the Left Behind series. In the interest of simplicity, however, the following paragraphs will ignore the differences that divide dispensationalists today, as well as the revisions offered in recent years, and concentrate instead on the older, more widely known variety that continues to enjoy wide influence in part through the writings of LaHaye and Jenkins. Moreover, my presentation will focus on the underlying dispensationalist system as a whole, rather than the particular details of the tribulation period that are so prominent in the novels. Readers of this chapter who are also readers of Left Behind may find themselves surprised by the complexity of the system on which the novels are based. Dispensationalists like LaHaye and Jenkins base their interpretation of the Bible on somewhat complicated concepts that are not immediately obvious. At the same, Jenkins and LaHaye, like most dispensationalists, strongly believe that their reading of the Bible is the truest to common sense. As you read what follows, keep in mind that dispensationalists believe that their understanding of the text is in fact the most "literal."

The Central Features of Dispensational Premillennialism

The term "dispensation" is used in the King James Version of the Bible to refer to the administration of God's earthly household (1 Cor. 9:17; Eph. 1:10, 3:2; Col. 1:25). Drawing from this biblical term, dispensationalists divide the history of salvation into distinct epochs, in order to distinguish the unique ways in which

God has been at work in different eras in directing human history to its divine goal. Although dispensationalists were not the first to propose such an approach, the nineteenth-century architects of this theological system emphasized the differences among the successive divisions of history in a manner unparalleled by their predecessors. C. I. Scofield, the compiler of the famous *Scofield Reference Bible*, found seven such epochs in the biblical narrative: innocence, conscience, human government, promise, law, grace, and kingdom.[12] In each successive epoch, dispensationalists theorize, God reveals a specific aspect of his will for human beings. But because humans fail to live in obedience to the divine will, each epoch climaxes in judgment.

To understand the way that dispensationalists read the Bible, we must first understand that, for them, there are two peoples of God: God's Old Testament, earthly people (the nation of Israel) and his New Testament, spiritual or heavenly people (the church). This distinction between Israel and the church corresponds to a distinction between two phases of God's program for salvation history. The first focuses on the land of Palestine and involves God's promise to bestow material blessings on the physical descendants of Abraham. The second centers on heaven and the spiritual blessings God has for those from every nation who acknowledge Jesus as savior and thereby become Abraham's spiritual children.[13] According to the dispensationalist reading of the Bible, neither phase of God's program is yet complete. The Israel phase, which began with Abraham, was delayed when the Jews rejected Jesus as their messiah. This opened the way for the church phase, begun at Pentecost, which acts like a parenthesis in God's "Israel program." The beginning of the church was not the end of God's plans for Israel. Once the task of the church has been completed, God will return to the unfinished, divine program for Israel. This is one of the reasons dispensationalists give for the rapture followed by the tribulation. The rapture is the culmination of God's plan for the church; during the tribulation God focuses once again on Israel. God will use the tribulation to prepare the Jews to receive their messiah, Jesus, at his return. The millennium, in turn, will provide the occasion for God to honor the Old Testament promises to bless Israel.

Dispensationalists anticipate that the current age will soon be brought to a close by the rapture of the (true) church. This will occur as Christ appears in the sky, Christians who have died and believers who are living meet the Lord above the earth, and together they ascend into heaven to celebrate "the marriage supper of the Lamb" (Rev. 19). Meanwhile on earth, the appearance of a political tyrant, the antichrist, will mark the beginning of the seven-year tribulation, during which time the antichrist rules over the nations, and God's wrath is poured out on the earth. By suffering under the political treachery of the antichrist, Israel will be prepared to be converted back to God. The tribulation period will climax with a military conflagration in Palestine. In the midst of this event, known as the battle of Armageddon, Jesus will return with the armies of heaven and rout the enemies of Israel. In this one battle, "the Lord destroys every hostile force that would challenge His right to rule as Messiah over the earth," to quote Dwight Pentecost's description.

According to the dispensationalist scenario, Israel will acknowledge Jesus as messiah at his return, and the thousand-year kingdom will be established on the earth. During this time Christ will be physically present on earth, ruling over the nations from Jerusalem. Humankind will live together in peace and safety, because Satan will have been bound and cast into the bottomless pit. Most important, Israel will enjoy presence in the land of Palestine and prominence among the nations. At the close of the millennial era, Satan will be freed from his prison to gather the unbelieving nations in a rebellion against Christ's government. His rebellion will be short-lived, however, for it will be squelched by fire from heaven. Then will occur the general resurrection (including the resurrection of the unrighteous), the judgment, and the inauguration of eternity (i.e., heaven and hell).[14]

The Case for Dispensationalism Premillennial
Once it was introduced into American Christianity, dispensational premillennialism spread quickly. Although various sociological

explanations could be cited, ultimately its phenomenal rise to prominence came about because its account of the world seemed both biblical and plausible. Its apparent correctness was greatly enhanced by global political developments that seemed to lend verification to this interpretation of Bible prophecy. The "rebirth of the state of Israel" in 1948 and the subsequent military victories that led to the capture of Jerusalem seemed to follow precisely the dispensationalist script. Similarly, the tendency among dispensationalists during the cold war to identify the Soviet Union as the evil kingdom of the north as depicted in the book of Daniel seemed to add credibility to the dispensational claim that the Bible predicted a worldwide military conflict in the Middle East immediately prior to the return of Christ. Such events have greatly supported the dispensationalist admonition to read the newspaper in one hand and the Bible in the other.

More important to dispensationalists than the apparent confirmation of their viewpoint by current world events is their conviction that it reflects the correct interpretation of the Bible itself, when scripture is read literally. In fact, proponents tend to elevate the literal approach as the central principle of correct biblical interpretation. As theologian Charles Ryrie asserts, the primary goal of dispensationalist expositors is to accept the text of scripture "at its face value," that is, to give to every word "the same meaning it would have in normal usage, whether employed in writing, speaking or thinking."[15]

Their desire to be consistent in reading the Bible literally leads dispensationalists to conclude that the promises of Israel's eschatological renewal—including their future possession of the land of Palestine and their enjoyment of physical blessing—that God spoke through the Old Testament prophets will be fulfilled as they were given. For this reason, dispensationalists reject the belief, common throughout most of church history, that the church is the New Israel, the culmination of God's activity in the Old Testament era. Moreover, the absence of references to the church in the description of the tribulation era found in Revelation (specifically, chapters 4 to 18) suggests to them that the church is not on earth during this period of time. Because the church is present neither in the Old Testament nor in the tribulation—that is, during those periods when God is working specifically with Israel—dispensationalists conclude that the church is a "mystery," a plan of God not revealed to the Old Testament prophets, and as such it is an interruption or "parenthesis" in the divine program for Israel.

The axiom that the church is a parenthesis in God's Israel program arises especially from the older dispensationalist understanding of one crucial Old Testament text, Daniel's vision of the "seventy sevens" (9:20–27). The Christian interpretive tradition generally has understood the sevens as prophetic years that climax in the first advent of Christ and his accomplishment of the messianic vocation. The architects of dispensationalism, however, proposed an innovative alternative: The sixty-nine weeks ended at the point when Jesus offered the kingdom to Israel and himself as their messiah (e.g., Palm Sunday), an offer that the nation rejected, resulting in the postponement of the coming of the kingdom as Jesus went instead to the cross. When this occurred, the seventieth prophetic week was delayed, "God's prophetic clock was stopped," and the church age began. One future day, however, the church phase of God's program will be completed, and the church will be raptured. This event will commence the seventieth week of Daniel's prophecy, the seven-year tribulation period, during which time the kingdom will once again be offered to Israel, leading to the millennium, the era in which God pours out material blessings on the nation of Israel.

If there are two peoples of God and two phases of God's program in the world, and if the Israel phase has been delayed during the church age, the pretribulation rapture follows logically. God's program for the church must be brought to completion (which will occur by means of the rapture) before God's program for Israel can continue. Dispensationalists offer four additional biblical arguments for this aspect of their eschatological system. First, the pretribulation rapture is demanded by the nature or purposes of the tribulation. This seven-year period is the time of "Jacob's trouble" (Jer. 30:7), that is, a latter-day trial during which Israel will turn to the Lord (Deut. 4:27–30). Furthermore, during the tribulation God's wrath is poured out on the world (1 Thess. 5:9; Rev. 6:17, 11:18). Because the church is not the object of God's wrath (1 Thess. 5:9), the church simply cannot experience the horrors of those years. On the contrary, dispensationalists say, God has promised to exempt the church from both the future eschatological divine wrath (1 Thess. 1:10; 5:9) and the time of wrath (Rev. 3:10).

A second argument supporting the pretribulation rapture arises from Paul's encouragement of Christian living during this age on the basis of a "blessed hope" that can occur at any moment (Titus 2:11–13; 1 Thess. 1:9–10). Dispensationalists interpret this hope to be the rapture of the church. The "imminence" of the rapture (the blessed hope) implies that no other event in "God's prophetic timetable," and hence no tribulation period, can occur before the rapture. Indeed, dispensationalists believe passionately in the rapture of the church as the very next prophetic event.

Third, dispensationalists assert that the pretribulation rapture is demanded by the book of Revelation. They point out that after having been dominant in the first three chapters, the church is completely absent in Revelation 4 to 18, which describes the tribulation period. Instead of the church, the people of God mentioned in these chapters as being on earth are the 144,000 chosen and sealed from among the tribes of Israel, in contrast to the twenty-four elders standing before God's throne who represent the church raptured, rewarded, and present in heaven while the tribulation rages on earth. This interpretation is confirmed by the significance many adherents find in the promise given to the Philadelphian church (Rev. 3:10), that it will be "kept from the hour" of trial. Dispensationalists argue that this church symbolizes the godly, pure, separated church of the end times that will be rewarded for its faithfulness by being raptured out of the world prior to the tribulation.

Finally, dispensationalists argue that the pretribulation rapture arises from Paul's somewhat mysterious declaration that the "restrainer" must be removed before the revelation of the "man of sin" (2 Thess. 2:6–8). Although the apostle does not identify the restrainer, on the basis of Jesus' declaration that his disciples are salt and light in the world, dispensationalists conclude that it can only be the church. As salt and light, the church exerts a preservative force in society, preventing evil from becoming as widespread and intense as it potentially could be. Once the church is removed from the world, however, the way is open for the full development of evil and hence for the reign of the antichrist that will mark the tribulation.

Millennial Blessings for the Church: Historic Premillennialism

The early Christians sensed that they were living in the final days before the consummation of God's plan for humanity. They expected that the current era would climax with a time of trial when the forces of evil would run rampant, followed by God's intervention on behalf of the saints (e.g., 2 Thess. 2:1–12). In the vicinity of Ephesus, the location of the seven churches addressed by the book of Revelation (now western Turkey), this chronology came to be expanded under the influence of the prediction of a thousand-year reign mentioned in Revelation 20:1–6. The premillennial tradition that ensued focused on the material blessings that will accompany the future rule of Christ over the renewed physical earth following the resurrection at the end of this age. The second-century church father Justin Martyr encapsulated this anticipation when he declared, "I and others who are right-minded Christians at all points, are assured that there will be a resurrection of the dead, and a thousand years in Jerusalem, which will then be built, adorned, and enlarged as the prophets and Ezekiel and Isaiah and others declare."[16]

In the twentieth century, dispensationalism emerged as the dominant eschatology among conservative Christians in America. Nevertheless, the century also witnessed the renaissance of another variety of premillennialism. Adherents of this perspective term their view "historic premillennialism," to signal their claim that they stand in the lineage of an eschatological tradition dating to Justin and other early church leaders. As a consequence, this perspective provides a third major contemporary understanding of the correct response to the disciples' question, "When will this happen?"

The Central Features of Historic Premillennialism

Like dispensational premillennialists, historic premillennialists believe that Jesus' second coming will occur prior to the thousand-year golden age. They anticipate that the current age will climax with a period of tribulation, leading to the return of Christ to establish his reign. The second coming will bring the defeat of the antichrist and the resurrection of the righteous. At this point, Satan will be bound, and the era of peace and righteousness will commence, when Christ will be physically present on the earth.[17] Thus, rather than arising as the result of a gradual process of progressive growth, as postmillennialists assert, the millennium (the "kingdom of God") will be inaugurated cata-strophically, dramatically, and visibly. For the first time in human history, universal peace will encircle the globe. The harmony within the human family will spill over to all of creation, for the effects of the fall that are now experienced by nature will be lifted. As a result, hostilities among the animals and between humans and animals will cease (Isa. 11:8–9, 65:25). After the millennium, Satan will be loosed to lead a brief rebellion that will be squelched by divine intervention. This will be followed by the general resurrection, the judgment, and the inauguration of the eternal state.

Despite the many expectations that advocates of both escha-tologies share, historic premillennialists differ from their dispen-sationalist cousins at several significant points. In the eyes of many people, the chief distinction concerns the time of the rap-ture of the church. Historic premillennialists believe that the rap-ture is posttribulational (i.e., it will occur after the tribulation), rather than pretribulational. This means, of course, that historic premillennialists are certain that the church will be present on earth during the tribulation period, the duration of which may or may not be seven years. Yet the differences between the two views go deeper. Historic premillennialists reject the two central tenets of dispensationalism together with the strict attention to a literal approach to scripture on which these are based. Rather than concluding that Israel and the church comprise two distinct peoples of God, historic premillennialists view the church as the fulfillment of God's work in the Old Testament. Consequently, they do not believe that the tribulation and the millennium belong to the Israel phase of God's program, but claim that both—but especially the millennium—must be understood within God's purposes for human history, the focus of which is ultimately the church. More specifically, historic premillennialists argue that the thousand years will mark a further stage in God's redemptive purpose in Jesus, who is the Lord of history. Although Christ's reign began at his ascension when he was enthroned at the right hand of the Father, his triumph over his foes is not yet complete (1 Cor. 15:25). Nor is his reign apparent to all, for it is visible only to the eyes of faith. At his second coming, however, Christ's lordship will become public, complete, and universal. Then everyone will pay homage to him (Phil. 2:10–11). Furthermore, the millennium is the time in which the church reigns with Christ. Beginning with Irenaeus in the second century, premillennialists have argued that it is only proper that those who have been faithful to Christ should participate in his rule. The millennium offers the opportunity for the Lord to reward believers for their steadfast service.[18]

The Case for Historic Premillennialism

Historical premillennialists are convinced that the demonstration of Christ's glory and sovereignty cannot be relegated completely to the new heaven and the new earth beyond history. Rather, Christ's lordship must be demonstrated to *this* world, if Christ is indeed ruler of history. And this universal reign of Christ, which entails the fullness of the kingdom of God, will occur on earth during the millennium. During this time, historic premillennialists conclude, God will demonstrate his faithfulness to his creative purposes by completing his plan of salvation.

For a thousand years all creation will enjoy the idyllic, peaceful conditions God intended at the completion of the six days of Genesis 1.

Although premillennialism is based on this kind of lofty theological thinking, the linchpin of the case for premillennialism in general is the claim that this view best accords with the prophecy of the millennium (Rev. 20:1–10). Premillennialists argue that the key to understanding this prophecy is to read it as a central aspect of Christ's final victory over Satan, the chronology of which is presented in the final four chapters of the book of Revelation. According to what George Eldon Ladd calls "the most natural reading" of Revelation 20:1–10, the destruction of Satan occurs in two stages separated by the millennial era. Christ's cosmic opponent is incarcerated for a thousand years, and then following the final eschatological battle that this archenemy inspires, Satan is banished to the lake of fire.

Crucial to this understanding of the millennium is the interpretation of the two resurrections noted in Revelation 20. On the basis of the use of the Greek word (*ezesan*) that means "they came to life" in both references, premillennialists conclude that the author had in view two physical, bodily events that are separated by a thousand-year interval. They argue that there is no reason why the first reference should be "spiritual" and the second literal. Ladd speaks for all premillennialists when he declares that the meaning of the text is quite straightforward: "At the beginning of the millennial period, part of the dead come to life; at its conclusion, the rest of the dead come to life."[19] To interpret the text in any other manner, adherents add, is to violate a fundamental principle of biblical interpretation.

Premillennialists find their understanding of Revelation 20 confirmed by several additional New Testament texts that they believe implicitly imply two resurrections. In one text, Paul speaks of an "out-resurrection out from among dead ones," an indication that he anticipated that he would participate in a resurrection that would separate him from other dead persons (Phil. 3:11; cf. Luke 20:35). Other texts imply a partial resurrection (1 Thess. 4:16), a distinction between a resurrection of the righteous and a resurrection of the wicked (Luke 14:14), or a two-part resurrection (Dan. 12:2; John 5:29). Yet the most significant confirmatory text is 1 Corinthians 15:23–26. Premillennialists see in Paul's words an indication that Christ's triumph over death comes in three stages. The first, Jesus' own resurrection as "the firstfruits," has already occurred (v. 23). The second, the resurrection of "those who belong to him," will occur "when he comes" (v. 23). Not until a millennium later will the third stage occur, the grand event when Jesus "hands over the kingdom to God the Father" (v. 24). Premillennial apologists claim that the interjection of "then" between verses 23 and 24, which word separates the apostle's reference to the resurrection of the righteous from his mention of "the end," indicates that Paul anticipated an era of undefined duration between Christ's return and the final consummation of history.

Into the framework of the premillennial scenario deduced from Revelation 20:1–10 and confirmed by other biblical texts, adherents pour the various Old Testament prophecies of a future golden age. However, as noted earlier, the content of the millennial reign contemporary historic premillennialists find in such promises leads them to a parting of ways with their dispensationalist cousins. According to historic premillennialists, the object of the prophesies of a golden age is not the nation of Israel itself, as in the dispensational understanding, but "spiritual Israel"—that is, the church. In making this claim, historic premillennialists appeal to what they see as the practice of the New Testament authors in reinterpreting Old Testament prophecies in the light of the advent of Christ. By applying prophecies regarding the future of Israel to the church, the New Testament writers identify the church as "spiritual Israel" (see, e.g., Paul's use of Hosea in Rom. 9:24–26). Consequently, according to New Testament teaching, there is only one "church of the firstborn" (cf. Heb. 12:23) that encompasses Old Testament saints and New Testament believers (Heb. 11:40). The "bride" of Christ, which consists of the entire company of the redeemed, and not national Israel, will participate in the rule of the bridegroom during the thousand years, historic premillennialists believe.

To substantiate their claim that the church will be present on earth during the tribulation, historic premillennialists appeal to what they perceive to be the general teaching of the Bible regarding the tribulation, the specific teaching of the New Testament about the time of Christ's return, and the images that the biblical writers use to describe this glorious event. Historic premillennialists point out that the authors of scripture repeatedly assert that the saints of God should expect to undergo tribulation (e.g., John 16:33; Acts 14:22; Rom. 5:3; Rev. 1:9; 1 Thess. 3:3; 1 John 2:18, 22, 4:3). The trials endured by the people of God reach their climax in the eschatological tribulation, which, posttribulationists argue, the Bible presents as a period of great persecution of the saints on the earth and a time of God's judgment on the unbelieving world. Even in the midst of the tribulation, however, believers are shielded by the guarding hand of God (e.g., Rev. 3:10, 7:14).

Posttribulationists note as well that the return of Jesus, which comprises the "blessed hope" of believers (1 Thess. 2:19, 3:13; James 5:7–8; 1 John 2:28), is consistently presented in the New Testament as occurring after the tribulation (e.g., Matt. 24:3, 27, 37, 39; 2 Thess. 2:8). Furthermore, they assert that the three principle texts that describe the rapture (John 14:3; 1 Cor. 15:51–52; 1 Thess. 4:13–18) give no indication that this event can be separated from Christ's actual return to the earth, but instead favor locating the rapture after the tribulation and simultaneous with the second coming, a perspective that historic premillennialists find explicitly taught in other New Testament texts (e.g., 1 Thess. 5:1–11; 2 Thess. 1–2; Matt. 24). Hence, New Testament scholar Douglas Moo concludes, "a study of the vocabulary employed in describing the return of Christ paints a uniform picture: believers are exhorted to look for and to live in the light of this glorious event. And, while some texts obviously place this coming *after* the Tribulation, there are *none* which equally obviously place it before the Tribulation."[20]

Posttribulationists point out that of the several Greek terms that the biblical writers use to describe Christ's return, one word (parousia) is especially vivid. This term is best translated "presence," and therefore it emphasizes the final coming of Christ to be present with his people. The New Testament focus on Christ coming to be present with his people leads historic premillennialists to view this event in the light of several social practices prominent in the ancient Near East. In the story of the ten virgins (Matt. 25:6), Jesus draws from a custom associated with Eastern weddings. At the announcement that the bridegroom is coming, the wise virgins are a part of the welcoming party that goes out to meet him and then to accompany him to the wedding feast. Likewise, when Paul was en route to Rome, Luke reports, he was met by the believers from that city at the town of Three Taverns, who then accompanied him to their locale (Acts 28:15–16). Posttribulationists picture the rapture as the church forming a great welcoming party for the returning Lord, in a manner that emulates not only the ten virgins and the Roman Christians, but also the subjects of a king going out to meet their sovereign as he returns to his domain.

A Golden Age Beyond Time: Amillennialism

After declaring his own preference for premillennialism, Justin Martyr added, "Many who belong to the pure and pious faith and are Christians think other wise."[21] By this remark, the second-century Christian leader indicated the presence in the church of yet another perspective on eschatology—another answer to the question "When will this happen?"—that generally goes by the name "amillennialism." Although premillennialists likely outnumbered amillennialists in the second century, around the time of Augustine the fortunes of the two perspectives reversed dramatically. In fact, from the fourth century to the present, amillennialism in some form or another has reigned as the quasi-official teaching of most mainline Christian traditions, whether Orthodox, Roman Catholic, or Protestant.

The Central Features of Amillennialism

Basically, the term "amillennial" means "no millennium." The designation is appropriate insofar as amillennialists reject the idea that the millennial references in Revelation 20 refer to a distinct era of history that will occur between the present age and the advent of eternity. In this sense, amillennialism denotes the eschatological perspective that anticipates no future earthly golden age. Instead, amillennialists believe that this era will be followed by the eternal kingdom of God, not by any intermediary stage. Many amillennialists, however, contend that the term is not completely appropriate, but is a misnomer that is open to misunderstanding. "Amillennial" all too readily implies that proponents ignore Revelation 20:1–6. Contrary to what their critics delight to suggest, however, amillennialists do not deny the importance of the vision of the millennium in this text of the Bible. What they do deny is that the inspired seer intended this symbol to be interpreted as a literal earthly era prior to the final judgment. Rather than an intervening period that separates the current age from the dawning of eternity, proponents claim that the millennium pictured in Revelation 20 is a symbolic description of the church age. It represents the theological truths related to the current rule of Christ: Satan is in some sense already bound, and the saints are already reigning with Christ.

Despite their agreement on this general principle, amillennialists are divided regarding the exact meaning of the symbol of the thousand years. What today is perhaps the most widely held view interprets the millennium as the spiritual blessedness enjoyed by the saints in heaven during the time between death and final resurrection. Old Testament scholar Oswald T. Allis suggests that this view represents amillennialism in the strictest sense, for it denies that the symbol of the thousand years refers in any way to an actual period of time. In contrast to this interpretation, which Allis claims was first proposed in the nineteenth century, an alternative understanding that dates at least to Augustine sees in Revelation 20 a reference to the spiritual reign of believers on the earth. It is a symbolic description of conversion and the victorious life enjoyed now by believers.[22] A third perspective, which has been championed by the Dutch theologian G. C. Berkouwer, emphasizes that the intention of the book of Revelation is not to provide a chronology of the end, but what he calls "apocalyptic comfort." The symbol of the millennium, Berkouwer explains, refers to glorious truth that in the midst of tribulation the people of God experience triumph within the time of the "not yet."[23]

Despite variations regarding its exact nature, amillennialists are in agreement that whatever the symbol of the thousand years is meant to depict transpires during the era of the church on earth. Consequently, of the major eschatological chronologies, theirs is the simplest. The time between the two advents will be characterized by a mixture of good and evil until the end. At the close of the age, this conflict will intensify as the church completes its mandate of evangelism and the forces of evil coalesce in the appearance of the antichrist. In the midst of a final, intense time of persecution of the church, Christ will appear in the fullness of his glory. At the Lord's return a conglomeration of events will occur that bring his redemptive work to completion. These include Christ's victory over the forces of the antichrist, the general resurrection, the judgment, and the inauguration of eternity. For the saints of all ages resurrection will mean that they, together with believers on the earth, meet the descending Lord and enter into the eternal kingdom of God. For the wicked, resurrection facilitates their appearance before their judge, followed by banishment into eternal condemnation. The summarization of William E. Cox typifies the amillennial expectations regarding the conjunction of the events surrounding the Lord's return: "When the trumpet sounds, things will take place simultaneously. Our Lord will begin his descent to the earth, the brightness of this event will put down Satan, and all the graves will be opened . . . all the saints together will go out to meet the Lord and to escort him to the earth. . . . the unsaved . . . will be forced to bow the knee and acknowledge that this is of a certainty the Christ. . . . They will see the suffering Servant of the cross reigning now as Judge of the quick and the dead, and they will seek a place of hiding but will find none (Rev. 1:7)."[24]

The Case for Amillennialism
Like proponents of the other answers to the question, "When will this occur?" amillennialists believe that their perspective

reflects the view of the biblical writers themselves. In their estimation, the task of understanding the Bible rightly is facilitated by two principles of interpretation. The first of these, which amillennialists share with historic premillennialists and postmillennialists, has been a standard interpretive axiom throughout church history: The Old Testament must be understood in the light of the New Testament, and the New Testament writers themselves interpret the ancient Hebrew prophets in terms of Christ. This principle leads proponents of all three nondispensationalist views to conclude that the New Testament church is "spiritual Israel" and hence that Christians are heirs to the privileges and blessings that God promised to Israel through the Old Testament prophets. Amillennialists take the matter a step further, however, pointing out that this principle undercuts the need of a future earthly golden age for God to fulfill any of the promises given through the Old Testament prophets.

Even more central to the case for amillennialism is a second interpretive principle, namely that the clear teaching of the New Testament as a whole must form the basis for understanding highly symbolic texts, such as Revelation 20. As Floyd Hamilton states, "The clearest New Testament passages in nonsymbolic books are to be the norm for the interpretation of prophecy. . . . In other words, we should accept the clear and plain parts of Scripture as a basis for getting the true meaning of the more difficult parts of Scripture."[25] Amillennialists are convinced that the New Testament writers present a simple, straightforward eschatological chronology (e.g., 2 Pet. 3:10–13): The present age will climax in the return of the Lord in triumph and judgment, followed immediately by the inauguration of eternity. Whatever conclusions are to be gleaned from Revelation 20, amillennialists add, can neither contradict nor supersede but rather must be understood in light of this general New Testament eschatological expectation.

The simple chronology taught by the Bible entails, for example, only one rising of humankind from the grave. Amillennialists glean this conclusion from several types of biblical texts. Some texts represent the resurrection of believers and unbelievers as occurring together (e.g., Dan. 12:2; John 5:28–29; Acts 24:14–15). Others indicate that the righteous and the wicked remain together throughout the age until they are separated at the judgment (Matt. 13:30, 39, 49, 50), at which time death itself will be abolished (1 Cor. 15:26). A third group of biblical texts declares that this judgment will occur at Christ's second coming, which time is called "the last day" (John 6:40; Matt. 25:31; 2 Thess. 1:7–10). Amillennialists are convinced that the first resurrection envisioned in Revelation 20:4–5 must be understood in a manner that harmonizes with this general New Testament teaching.

But what is the first resurrection? Most amillennialists assert that the coming to life following the millennium (v. 5) refers to the general, physical resurrection, whereas the first resurrection is spiritual in nature. Proponents claim that the text itself indicates this. In their estimation, the interpretive key lies in the crisscrossing pattern of two pairs present or implied in the text, most significantly the link the seer makes between the first resurrection and the second death (v. 6). Most Bible interpreters are in agreement that the second death is spiritual, rather than physical; it refers to the eternal punishment of the wicked. In the same way, amillennialists add, the first resurrection, which frees an individual from the power of the second death (i.e., which frees the believer from eternal damnation), also must be spiritual.

Amillennialist interpreters are divided, however, as to what this spiritual event actually is. Some believe that it is a reference to the new birth or perhaps to the experience of baptism as it relates to conversion. The validity of this view, advocates argue, is indicated by New Testament texts that refer to conversion as a rising from death (e.g., Eph. 2:5–6; Col. 2:13; 3:1; Rom. 6:4, 5, 13), as well as the contrast Jesus draws in the Fourth Gospel between two resurrections (John 5:24–29; see also John 11:25–26). According to Jesus, one is present, the other future; one is spiritual, the other physical; one is restricted to believers, the other inclusive of all humankind. The first resurrection, adherents of this interpretation conclude, is conversion resulting in spiritual life for those who are dead in sin; the second is the eschatological physical resurrection of all humankind. Revelation 20:4–6, in turn, presents in symbolic form these truths about the new birth and eternal life.

Perhaps more popular among amillennialists today, however, is a second proposal: The first resurrection refers to the spiritual coming to life of faithful Christians at the time of their death, which "resurrection" results in their translation to heaven where they reign with Christ throughout the remainder of the travail that characterizes the church age.[26] The nineteenth-century Princeton theologian Benjamin Warfield explains: "The picture that is brought before us here is, in fine, the picture of the 'intermediate state' of the saints of God gathered in heaven away from the confused noise and garments bathed in blood that characterized the war upon earth, in order that they may securely await the end."[27]

Proponents claim that this interpretation arises both from the broader context of the book of Revelation as a whole and from certain clues in the text itself. The argument from the broader context focuses on one of the central purposes of the book, namely, to give assurance to believers who are facing the onslaught of Satan. Consequently, the imagery of the first resurrection intends to encourage the Lord's people to be "overcomers" by reminding them that faithfulness to the end is not in vain, but brings victory and blessedness. The vision, therefore, is in keeping with the emphasis of the entire book, which focuses on faithfulness. Viewed from this perspective, Revelation 20:4 forms a striking parallel to the vision of the cry of the martyrs under the altar that God avenge their blood (Rev. 6:9–11), but who in response are given white robes and told to rest a little longer. Revelation 20 is intended to assure the church that these resting martyrs are also reigning with Christ in heaven.

The internal argument builds from the language of the text itself, especially the seer's report that he saw the souls (rather than the bodies) of the martyrs. This, coupled with the limited length of their reign (a thousand years), indicates that the first resurrection cannot refer to a physical coming to life. In contrast to the blessedness that the dead in Christ enjoy as disembodied souls during the thousand years, in eternity the righteous will reign in their resurrected bodies forever. Proponents believe that their case is strengthened by the precise verb form that John the Seer uses in the text. Both verbs in verse 4 ("lived" and "reigned") are in what is known in the Greek language in which the New Testament was written as the aorist tense. Because both verbs are in the same tense, both must be translated in a parallel manner. And because they are aorist, a verb form that rarely refers to the inception of an action, they do not speak of an action that occurs at the beginning of the thousand years. Rather, the entire period is in view. Consequently, it is incorrect to interpret the first verb as indicating an event occurring at the beginning of the millennium and the second as a state of being throughout the era, as demanded by the premillennial eschatology. The best translation of the text, proponents conclude, is simply "they lived and reigned with Christ a thousand years."[28]

The principle that Revelation 20 must be understood in accordance with the plain teaching of the New Testament is evident as well in the amillennial interpretation of the symbol of the binding of Satan. The proper understanding of the vision of the thousand years, amillennialists claim, demands a return to the declaration found elsewhere in the New Testament that in his ministry Jesus bound his enemy. The Lord himself indicated that such an act was necessary for him to release Satan's captives (Matt. 12:24–29). This claim, in turn, forms the basis for the theme found repeatedly in the New Testament that in his life, death, and resurrection Jesus has triumphed over the power of evil (e.g., Matt. 4:1–11; Luke 9:1, 10:17–20; John 12:31–33; Col. 2:14–15; Heb. 2:14; 1 John 4:8). Even the book of Revelation gives evidence to the correctness of this interpretation, adherents assert, for the twelfth chapter, which forms the center of the book, depicts Christ's coronation as bringing about the ejection of Satan from heaven.

Premillennialists argue that the binding of Satan must be future because the devil is obviously active in the world (e.g., 1 Pet. 5:8). In response, amillennialists join postmillennialists in pointing out that the imagery of Satan's binding does not mean total powerlessness, but refers to the divine restriction of the devil's activities so that he is not able to thwart the advance of God's program. To illustrate this point, proponents appeal to Jude's declaration that the fallen angels are kept in chains awaiting the judgment (Jude 6). Even though the demons have been defeated by Christ and are therefore now under his control, they are not completely powerless in the world. Just as the chaining of the demons has restricted but not eliminated their activity, so also the binding of Satan has placed limits on what he is able to do. More specifically, the binding of Satan has rendered him unable to deceive the nations. In contrast to the Old Testament era, when the nations were under the dominance of Satan and ignorant of the truth (e.g., Eph. 2:11–12), the church age is the time of the worldwide proclamation of the gospel, the time when the devil is unable to prevent people everywhere from receiving the good news. In this manner, amillennialists (like postmillennialists) view Revelation 20:1–2 as a symbolic commentary on the great commission (Matt. 28:19–20).

At the heart of amillennialism is the belief that Revelation 20 is a vision of the present age, the time between Christ's two advents, not some future era. The opening verses of the chapter picture the cosmic victory won by Christ at his first advent. Verses 4–6 speak of the resultant victory of his faithful witnesses, despite apparent defeat, whether that victory be in the heavenly realm of the intermediate state or the earthly realm of Christian living. As a vision of the age between Christ's two advents, the thousand years are a symbolic presentation of the great New Testament declaration that the risen Lord is reigning now (e.g., Rev. 1:6, 9; 3:21; 5:10; 1 Cor. 15:24–28). His rule constitutes a present reality that believers enter at the time of conversion (Col. 1:13; Mark 1:15; Luke 17:20–21). Because Christ reigns throughout the church age, the biblical declaration of his rule does not necessitate that a future millennial era be inserted between the present and the eternal state. Despite the roar of the devil who seeks to intimidate the believers through deceit and persecution, Christ is reigning over history, and he has given his church the mandate to preach the gospel throughout the world. Their faithfulness is rewarded beyond death, and one day it will be rewarded as the king returns in vindication and judgment to inaugurate the eternal state. This is the message of the Bible as read by amillennialists.

Concluding Comments

The Left Behind series uses the literary form of the fictional narrative to paint a picture of a catastrophic end of the age that its authors believe is in keeping with what the Bible itself teaches. We might say that the novels offer an extended response to the question that was posed by Jesus' disciples two thousand years ago: "When will this happen?" By raising in the minds of many people this question, which in many mainline congregations has lain dormant for too long, LaHaye and Jenkins have done the church a great service. Yet the end-times scenario that is so vividly presented in the novels is not the only perspective on the events that will surround the return of Jesus. Nor is it, in my estimation, the best perspective. For this reason, despite the impression that they might leave with the reader, the volumes of the series are appropriately located on the fiction shelves of bookstores. They ought to be similarly cataloged in the personal libraries of their purchasers as well.

Notes

The material in this chapter is adapted from Stanley J. Grenz, *The Millennial Maze: Sorting Out Evangelical Options* © 1992 by Stanley J. Grenz, and is used with permission from InterVarsity Press, Downers Grove, Illinois.

1. "History of Opinions Respecting the Millennium," *American Theological Review* 1 (1859), 655, as cited in James H. Moorhead, "The Erosion of Postmillennialism in American Religious Thought, 1865–1925," *Church History* 53 (March 1984), 61.
2. Ernest W. Shurtleff, "Lead On, O King Eternal" (1887), in *The Hymnal for Worship and Celebration*, ed. Tom Fettke and Ken Barker (Waco, Tex.: Word Music, 1986), #483.

3. H. Ernest Nichol, "We've a Story to Tell to the Nations" (1896), in *The Hymnal for Worship and Celebration*, ed. Tom Fettke and Ken Barker (Waco, Tex.: Word Music, 1986), #296.

4. Augustus Hopkins Strong, *Systematic Theology*, 3 vols. (Philadelphia: Griffith and Rowland, 1909), 3:1014. See also Loraine Boettner, "Postmillennialism," in *The Meaning of the Millennium: Four Views*, ed. Robert G. Clouse (Downers Grove, Ill.: InterVarsity, 1977), 117.

5. Loraine Boettner, *The Millennium* (Philadelphia: Reformed Publishing Co., 1957), 30.

6. Benjamin B. Warfield, *Biblical Doctrines*, Banner of Truth ed. (Edinburgh: Banner of Truth, 1988), 647–648, 662, see also Boettner, *Millennium*, 31–34.

7. For a treatment of these parables, see James H. Snowden, *The Coming of the Lord: Will It Be Premillennial?* (New York: Macmillan, 1919), 72–84.

8. Ibid., 98.

9. Charles Hodge, *Systematic Theology*, 3 vols. (New York: Scribner, Armstrong, and Co., 1872), 3:800.

10. Boettner, "Postmillennialism," 126.

11. For example, see Herman Hoyt, "Current Trends in Eschatological Beliefs," in *Understanding the Times*, ed. William Culbertson and Herman B. Centz (Grand Rapids, Mich.: Zondervan, 1952), 147–51.

12. See *The Scofield Reference Bible*, ed. C. I. Scofield (New York: Oxford, 1909), note to Genesis 1:28. For an earlier alternative enumeration, see, C. I. Scofield, *Rightly Dividing the Word of Truth* (New York: Loizeaux Brothers, 1896), 12–16. Scofield's followers eventually renamed the dispensation of grace, preferring to call it the dispensation of the church, in that grace was not limited to the present era but was available in all dispensations. See *The New Scofield Reference Bible*, ed. E. Schuyler English et al. (New York: Oxford, 1967), note to Genesis 1:27. Ryrie, however, continued the older nomenclature. Charles C. Ryrie, *Dispensationalism Today* (Chicago: Moody, 1965), 50–52.

13. This distinction was set forth already at the end of the nineteenth century in Scofield, *Rightly Dividing the Word of Truth*, 5–12.

14. J. Dwight Pentecost, *Things to Come* (Findlay, OH: Dunham, 1958), 219–228.

15. Ryrie, *Dispensationalism Today*, 86, 96.

16. Justin Martyr, *Dialogue with Trypho, A Jew*, LXXX, in *The Ante-Nicene Fathers: Translation of the Fathers down to AD 325*,

American ed., ed. by A. Roberts and J. Donaldson (Grand Rapids, Mich.: Eerdmans, 1975), 1:239.

17. Millard Erickson, *Contemporary Options in Eschatology* (Grand Rapids, Mich.: Baker, 1977), 91–92.

18. D. H. Kromminga, *The Millennium* (Grand Rapids, Mich.: Eerdmans, 1948), 48.

19. George Eldon Ladd, *Critical Questions about the Kingdom of God* (Grand Rapids, Mich.: Eerdmans, 1952), 146.

20. Douglas J. Moo, "The Posttribulation Rapture Position," in *The Rapture: Pre-, Mid-, or Post-Tribulational*, ed. Richard R. Reiter et al. (Grand Rapids, Mich.: Academie, 1984), 177–178.

21. Justin Martyr, *Dialogue with Trypho*, 1:239.

22. Oswald T. Allis, *Prophecy and the Church* (Grand Rapids, Mich.: Baker, 1972), 5.

23. G. C. Berkhouwer, *The Return of Christ* (Grand Rapids, Mich.: Eerdmans, 1972), 314–315.

24. William E. Cox, *In These Last Days* (Philadelphia: Presbyterian and Reformed, 1964), 80–81.

25. Floyd Hamilton, *The Basis of Millennial Faith* (Grand Rapids, Mich.: Eerdmans, 1952), 53–54.

26. The location of the reign is the subject of the short study by Roman Catholic scholar Michel Gourgues, "The Thousand Year Reign (Rev. 20:1–6): Terrestrial or Celestial," *Catholic Biblical Quarterly* 47, no. 4 (October 1985): 676–681.

27. Warfield, *Biblical Doctrines*, 649.

28. See James A. Hughes, "Revelation 20:4–6 and the Question of the Millennium," *Westminster Theological Journal* 35, no. 3 (Spring 1973), 289–291.

5

How Are Jews and Israel Portrayed in the Left Behind Series?

A Historical Discussion of Jewish–Christian Relations

Yaakov Ariel

Page 6 of *Left Behind* introduces the readers to the first Jewish character in the novel and in the series at large: Chosen by a major journal as its "man of the year," Chaim Rosenzweig is a scientist-wizard whose secret formula has helped turn Israel into a thriving nation.[1] When a journalist for the *Global Weekly* interviews Rosenzweig, a major Russian attack on Israel takes place. Jews and Israel loom large in the novel and its sequels, and one cannot but notice their important role. Jews are neither ordinary figures nor incidental characters in the novel; nor is the State of Israel just one commonwealth among many. The Jews in the Left Behind series come to represent something much larger than their individual selves, just as their country plays a crucial role in the unfolding of the eschatological drama.

The representations of the Jews in the novels gives evidence to the expectations and hopes that the conservative evangelical theology has stirred among its adherents in relation to the Jews, as well as the frustrations evangelicals have developed in dealing with the Jewish people. Being an evangelical best-seller, the series popularizes and shapes the views on Jews among a new generation of conservative American Christians. Although Left Behind represents conservative evangelical premillennialist convictions regarding the Jews and their role in history, the series of novels also introduces some changes in the image of the Jews. Maintaining some standard evangelical stereotypes of Jews, it attempts, nonetheless, to present a more sympathetic picture of Jews than previously portrayed by evangelical writers. In general, Jews in the novels are shown as an errant but not evil people, and as righteous and constructive beings when they finally discover the truth and recognize their savior. The first step in analyzing the place of the Jews in the novel is to examine the role of the Jews in evangelical messianic theology.

Left Behind, Evangelical Messianic Theology, and the Jews

The evangelical theological standing toward the Jews as expressed in Left Behind seems at first glance to be ambivalent, if not outright self-contradictory. Adhering to a messianic premillennialist faith, evangelical Christians view the Jews as the children of Israel, the Chosen People, heirs to the covenant between God and Israel, and the object of biblical prophecies about a restored Davidic kingdom in the messianic times. At the same time, evangelical Christians have expressed disappointment over what they have seen as the Jewish unwillingness to recognize Jesus as Lord and savior, and the Jews' refusal to understand their role and mission in God's plans for redemption.

In the evangelical dispensationalist messianic theology that LaHaye and Jenkins promote, God has different plans for three categories of human beings: the Jews, the church, and the rest of humanity. Premillennialist evangelicals define the church not as a specific denomination, but rather as the body of the true Christians believers, an invisible entity composed of those who have undergone a conversion experience, have accepted Jesus as their personal savior, and have taken it on themselves to live perfect Christian lives. Those true believers will be saved and spared the turmoils and sufferings that will precede the arrival of the messiah. The apocalypse will begin with a dramatic, watershed event, the rapture of the church, in which the true Christian believers will be snatched from earth and meet Jesus in the air. They will remain in heaven for seven years and thus be spared the turmoils of the "great tribulation," the seven years that stand between this era and the messianic times. The events described in Left Behind are expected to take place in those yet-to-materialize years, after the rapture takes place and the true believers "disappear," and before Jesus comes back to earth to defeat the antichrist and establish his kingdom on earth.[2]

Premillennial dispensationalism, the specific school of messianic faith that the novels follow and promote, crystallized in Britain in the early decades of the nineteenth century and gained prominence in America at the turn of the twentieth century.[3] Premillennial dispensationalist writers and preachers were successful in turning this messianic faith into an acceptable creed to which millions of Protestants adhere. It became part and parcel of the conservative evangelical "fundamentalist" faith, meshing well with critical outlooks of conservatives on contemporary culture. Dispensationalism has served, since the late nineteenth century, as a conservative Christian philosophy of history, providing an outline of where history is heading and offering hope and reassurance in the face of uncertainty.[4] LaHaye and Jenkins should be viewed as heirs and continuers of a long chain of evangelists and writers who have promoted the dispensationalist messianic faith, connecting it with a larger evangelical worldview, a critique of culture, and a more literal reading of the Bible, as well as using it as an effective tool for evangelism. A century before LaHaye and Jenkins began writing the Left Behind series, evangelical premillennialists promoted views similar to theirs, albeit in the form of theological tracts. The dispensationalist messianic faith has provided its adherents with a clear vision of the meaning of current political, economic, social, and cultural developments and an assurance that true Christian believers will survive the turmoils and not be "left behind."

In the dispensationalist messianic faith, the Jewish people play a leading role as those who prepare the ground for the return of the messiah and the building of the kingdom of God on earth. As the Left Behind novels demonstrate, Jews, who have not converted to Christianity, remain on earth when the rapture takes place and become major participants in the events of the great tribulation. For the Jews, this period will be "the time of Jacob's trouble" prophesized in Jeremiah 30:7. This will be an unprecedentedly traumatic period for the Jews, involving natural disasters, political turmoils, and human cruelty. The Jews will stand in the center of the stormy developments, with many of the significant political and social events of the apocalyptic era taking place in the Holy Land.

Amazingly, premillennialist Christians anticipated the Jewish national restoration, before the rise of political Zionism. Propagators of the messianic premillennialist faith expected that the Jews would return to their ancient homeland "in unbelief," that is, without accepting Jesus as their savior. The Jews, according to that faith, will establish a political commonwealth in Palestine, which will be a major stepping-stone in the advancement of the messianic timetable. After the rapture takes place, some Jews will be enchanted by the antichrist and will help him rise to power, while other Jews, Left Behind scenarios predict, will become the antichrist's enemies and will take part in clandestine operations to curtail the dictatorship. In the Left Behind novels, while Chaim Rosenzweig initially finds Nicolae Carpathia, the antichrist, admirable, and Orthodox Jews look on Carpathia's international government as an ally in building the desired Temple, Jewish evangelists appear near the Wailing Wall and preach the Christian message relentlessly to the people of Israel. The antichrist eventually will show his real intentions and, as the Left Behind series indicates, inflict a reign of terror.

The arrival of Jesus at the end of the great tribulation, accompanied by the true Christian believers, will end the antichrist's rule, and Jesus will crush this evil tyrant and establish the kingdom of God on earth. The Jews, who will survive the turmoils and terror of the great tribulation, will accept Jesus as their savior. There will follow a period of a thousand years of a righteous rule of Christ on earth, with Jerusalem as the capital of the entire world. The Jews will again inhabit David's ancient kingdom, serving as Jesus' right-hand people, assisting the righteous world leader in administering the earth.

Left Behind and the Return of the Jews to Zion

It is not difficult to see how the premillennialist faith would motivate the interest of premillennialist evangelicals in the actual Jews of the current period and stir efforts to bring the Jews to fulfill their role in history. The new messianic school has inspired interest in the prospect of the Jewish conversion to Christianity as well as in the possibility of Jewish national restoration in Palestine. By the late nineteenth century, American evangelists came out with proto-Zionist initiatives and created extensive networks of missionary activity among the Jews.[5] Like LaHaye and Jenkins, evangelical writers promoted the idea that a Jewish commonwealth in the Holy Land is a crucial development toward the advancement of the messianic times. Evangelical initiatives to bring about the restoration of the Jews to Zion can be traced to attempts by British evangelicals, as early as the 1840s, to persuade the British government to propose the creation of a Jewish state in Palestine. The leader of the evangelical party in Britain at the time, the seventh Earl of Shaftesberry, sought ways to promote the return of the Jews to Palestine, rationalizing his quest with the claim that a Jewish state there could serve as a buffer against future Egyptian aggression and expansion.[6] Evangelical support played a key role in the rise of the Zionist movement in the later decades of the nineteenth century. William Hechler, a British German evangelical preacher, for example, became an advisor and confidant of Theodor Herzl, the founder of political Zionism. Hechler, who saw in Zionism the beginning of the fulfillment of prophecy, tried to help the Zionist movement by courting the support of influential European statesmen.

Although the influence of the evangelical movement and of premillennialist thinking weakened in Britain toward the end of the nineteenth century, in America the premillennialist faith had a growing influence on conservative members of Protestant churches. Influenced by premillennialist-dispensationalist thinking, many conservative American Protestant evangelists and theologians adopted the view that the Jews were heirs to the biblical promises God made to Abraham, Moses, and David and, as such, destined to resume their place as God's first nation and inhabitants of the Promised Land.

One evangelical best-seller of the turn of the twentieth century was *Jesus Is Coming*, which, like the turn of the twenty-first century Left Behind series, sold millions of copies and was translated into dozens of languages. The author, William Blackstone, an American evangelist and promoter of the dispensationalist messianic faith, militated in his book both the imminent arrival of Jews and the centrality of the Jewish people for the materialization of that faith's conception of the end times. Blackstone visited Palestine in 1889 and was deeply impressed by the developments that the first wave of Zionist immigration had brought about in a country that he had considered to be a deserted land. He viewed the agricultural settlements and the new neighborhoods in Jerusalem as "signs of the time," indicating that an era was ending and the great events of the apocalypse were to occur soon.[7] Blackstone decided to take an active line and bring about Jewish national restoration in Palestine. In 1891 he organized a petition urging the president of the United States to convene an international conference of the world powers that would decide on giving Palestine back to the Jews. More than four hundred prominent Americans signed Blackstone's petition—congressmen, governors, mayors, publishers of major newspapers, leading business people, and prominent clergymen. Although it failed to cause the American government to take any meaningful action toward the goal of establishing a Jewish commonwealth in Palestine, the petition reflected warm support for the idea among American Protestants.[8]

Blackstone devised a theory that has become a cornerstone of American evangelical attitudes toward Zionism and Israel. The evangelical leader asserted that the United States had a special role and mission in God's plans for humanity, that of a modern Cyrus, assigned the task of restoring the Jews to Zion and thus helping to advance the messianic timetable. Its imperfect cultural climate notwithstanding, America was chosen by God for that noble mission on account of its relative moral superiority in comparison to other nations.[9] This vision of America as an international advocate of righteous causes, and a vehicle toward the realization of the kingdom of God on earth, enabled American evangelicals to combine their messianic belief and understanding of the course of human history with their sense of American patriotism. Although premillennialist evangelicals often have criticized contemporary American culture, they have remained loyal citizens of the United States. In this respect, evangelicals have been significantly different from other American religious groups that have held intense messianic beliefs, such as Jehovah's Witnesses, who have developed opposition to the values and goals of the American polity.

In 1916 Blackstone organized a second petition calling on the president of the United States to help restore Palestine to the Jews. This time his efforts were coordinated with the American Zionist leadership. American Jewish leaders, such as Louis Brandeis, Steven Wise, and Nathan Straus, saw Blackstone's efforts as beneficial to the Zionist cause and encouraged him to pursue his plan. The Zionist leaders did not take the premillennialist doctrine seriously, dismissing it as an eccentric conviction, focusing instead on the support that those holding such beliefs could provide the Zionist agenda.[10] They were not bothered, therefore, by Blackstone's predictions that great turmoils were awaiting the Jews when the rapture would take place and the events of the end times would begin. Neither were they taken aback by Blackstone's assertion that the Jews would accept Jesus as their messiah by the time Christ would arrive to establish his kingdom. On their part, premillennialist evangelicals such as Blackstone criticized the secular character of the Zionist movement and were disappointed that the Zionists were unaware of what premillenialists felt was the real significance of their movement and its role in history.

The events of World War I, with its unprecedented killing and destruction, fueled premillennialist evangelicals such as Blackstone with apocalyptic anticipations. They were convinced that the war pointed to the beginning of the end times, interpreting the Balfour Declaration and the British takeover of Palestine as further indications that the ground was being prepared for the arrival of the messiah. Premillennialist joy and anticipation over these developments dominated two evangelical prophetic conferences that took place in Philadelphia and New York in 1918.[11]

Premillennialist evangelicals were further encouraged by the new wave of Zionist immigration to Palestine in the early years of the British administration of the country, and publicized in their periodicals events such as the opening of the Hebrew University in 1925 and the new seaport in Haifa in 1932. Premillennialist evangelicals interpreted these developments as signs that the Jews were energetically building a commonwealth in their ancient homeland and that the great events of the end times were to occur very soon.[12] Leading evangelical journals, such as *Our Hope, The King's Business, The Moody Monthly*, and the Pentecostal *Evangel*, regularly published news on the Zionist movement and the Jewish community in Palestine. Excited by hopes of the second coming, they lashed out at the British for putting restrictions on Jewish immigration and settlement and criticized the Arabs for their hostility toward the Zionist endeavor and for their violence against the Jews. They saw attempts at blocking the building of a Jewish commonwealth in Palestine as equivalent to putting obstacles in the way of God's plans for the future of humankind. Such attempts, they asserted, were futile, and the Arabs would pay dearly for their rebellious acts.[13]

Few evangelical activists, however, pressed their protest against British policy beyond the pages of their own journals. During the 1920s to the 1940s, conservative evangelicals were not very active politically as a group, withdrawing, to a large degree, from the American public arena. Their political influence, both in Britain and in America, weakened considerably.

Evangelical journals published sympathetic articles about the Zionist struggle for a Jewish state and supported the Zionist cause in the political struggles that preceded the birth in 1948 of Israel, but no particular pro-Zionist evangelical lobby developed at that time.[14]

While premillennialist evangelicals were not happy about the secular character of the Israeli government and society, the developments they saw in Israel of the 1950s and1960s filled them with enthusiasm and enhanced their messianic hopes.[15] The mass emigration of Jews to Israel from Asian, African, and East European countries was one cause for encouragement. This was undoubtedly a significant development, they felt, one that had been prophesied in the Bible, and a clear indication that the current era was terminating and the events of the end times were beginning to occur. Evangelical journals and books have reported on Israeli successes in turning desolate land into fertile agricultural ground. Echoes of such understanding of Israel's achievements play a part in the Left Behind series.

Contrary to popular myth, evangelical writers did take notice of, and showed concern over, the fate of hundreds of thousands of Palestinian Arabs who lost their homes in 1948. Although they criticized the Arab hostility against Israel and supported the Israeli state in its struggles with its Arab neighbors, evangelicals also expressed their belief that the land of Israel could maintain an Arab population alongside its Jewish one and that Israel had an obligation to respect human rights and treat the Arabs with fairness.[16] A few conservative evangelical churches, such as the Southern Baptists, the Christian and Missionary Alliance, the Assemblies of God, and the Church of God, have worked among Palestinians, offering relief and educational services. In striving to reconcile premillennialist teachings with the hopes and fears of the Arab congregants, a number of evangelical writers emphasized that the ingathering of the Jews in the land of Israel and the eventual reestablishment of the Davidic kingdom would not necessitate the banishment of Arabs from that land.

This attitude, too, is reflected in the Left Behind series, where a Jordanian is featured as an ardent Christian believer. The choice of a Jordanian is not accidental. Jordan sits on lands that, according to biblical narrative, were part of David's kingdom, but it is not the heart of the land of Israel, the Promised Land, thus signaling that Jordan is a legitimate Arab country, while Israel and its territories are first and foremost Jewish. Left Behind's scenarios reflect, as do other evangelical tracts and novels, the dramatic effect the Six-Day War had on American evangelical attitudes toward Israel. In fact, since the French Revolution and the Napoleonic Wars in the last years of the eighteenth century and the beginning of the nineteenth century, probably no political–military event has provided so much fuel for the engine of prophecy as the short war between Israel and its neighbors in June 1967, a war that led to the Jews taking over the historical sections of Jerusalem. The dramatic and unexpected Israeli victory, and the territorial gains it brought with it, strengthened the premillennialists' conviction that the State of Israel was created for an important mission in history and that the Jewish commonwealth was to play an important role in the process that would precede the arrival of the messiah.[17]

Since the Six-Day War, conservative evangelicals have been counted among Israel's most ardent supporters in the American public arena and often voiced their approval of American political and economic aid for Israel.[18] The decades following the Six-Day War were marked by massive American support for Israel in terms of money, arms, and diplomatic backing. Many conservative Christians saw support for Israel as going hand-in-hand with American interests. A pro-Israeli policy was, at the same time, a fulfillment of America's historical role and its immediate interests. The late 1960s, 1970s, and 1980s were years of the cold war. America and the Soviet Union were competing over world hegemony. Evangelical Christians saw the struggle as holding a messianic, cosmic significance, and as the battle between the Children of Light and the Children of Darkness. American policymakers often saw Israel as playing an important role in the world struggle, serving as a buffer against Soviet aggression and expansionist policies and winning battles against the political clients of the Soviets. Under such circumstances, it was easy for evangelicals to develop a supportive attitude toward Israel.[19] Although the Soviet Union has collapsed, cold war attitudes can be found in the Left Behind series, where Russia is identified with the evil Northern Empire, launching a potentially deadly (but futile) attack against Israel.

The evangelical premillennialist outlook influenced American policymakers. Although not devoid of prejudices against Jews, President Harry Truman saw himself as a modern Cyrus who had helped secure the reestablishment of the Jewish state.[20] The Eisenhower administration did not look on Israel through the prism of a biblical messianic faith, but matters changed in the 1960s. Conservative evangelicals might not have counted the liberal Lyndon Johnson as one of them, yet Johnson's views of the Jewish state were influenced by his biblical Texan-Christian upbringing.[21] His attitude was unmistakably very supportive. The pro-Israel policy was continued by the administration of the conservative, nonevangelical Richard Nixon. Jimmy Carter, who became president in 1977, combined an evangelical Christian concern over the unfolding of history with a pragmatic role of an American statesman, bringing Egypt and Israel together to sign a peace treaty.

Ronald Reagan, who followed Carter and became president in 1981, also was influenced, in his Middle East policies, by a premillennialist understanding of the course of history.[22] Reagan's friendly policy toward Israel was continued by his successor, George Bush, who depended heavily on evangelical support. While cold war considerations also determined Reagan's and Bush's policy toward Israel, favorable evangelical attitudes toward that country played an important part.[23]

His evangelical Christian affiliation notwithstanding, the liberal Bill Clinton did not receive much support from conservative evangelicals, who did not consider him to be one of them. Yet, while in Arkansas, Clinton was a member of a Southern Baptist church, where his pastor preached sermons on Israel's role in history and on America's (and Clinton's) obligation to protect Israel. Indeed, Clinton showed deep concern over the well-being of Israel and saw it as his personal mission to bring peace to the Middle East. Evangelical influence on American policy has also characterized the administration of George W. Bush, himself a devout born-again Christian.

The evangelical premillennialist understanding of Israel also has influenced the attitudes of other prominent American public figures toward Israel. One noted example of an influential, pro-Israel, evangelical, premillennialist politician who openly identified with the messages of Left Behind was Jesse Helms, a United States Senator from North Carolina during the 1980s, 1990s, and early 2000s. As the powerful chair of the Senate's Foreign Affairs Committee, Helms labored to limit American financial support abroad. A deeply convinced premillennialist, he, at the same time, approved of the extensive financial support that the United States was offering Israel.

Helms's supportive attitude toward Israel was not unique. In the 1970s, 1980s, and 1990s, dozens of pro-Israel evangelical organizations emerged in the United States. In addition to mustering political support for Israel in the American public arena, such organizations also have distributed material on Israel and its historical role in the evangelical community, organized lectures on Israel and its role in history, and conducted tours to the Holy Land.

One of the best known among evangelical pro-Israel organizations has been the International Christian Embassy in Jerusalem (ICEJ), which has seen its mission as mustering evangelical support for Israel on a global scale. The ICEJ was established by evangelical residents in Jerusalem who in the late 1970s came up with the idea of organizing large annual gatherings of Christian supporters of Israel during Sukkoth, the Jewish harvest festival commemorating the tent sanctuaries, or tabernacles, used during the Exodus. The theological rationale was that, according to the Bible (Zech. 14:15), gentiles were commanded to gather in Jerusalem during the festival. The ICEJ's Feast of Tabernacles includes major convocations of thousands of supporters from around the world. Activities include tours of the country for the "pilgrims," a march through Jerusalem's main streets, a "biblical meal" served and celebrated on the shore of the Dead Sea, and assemblies in Jerusalem.

In 1980 almost all countries with embassies and consulates in Jerusalem moved their diplomatic staffs to Tel Aviv. This evacuation provided a dramatic point at which the Jerusalemite evangelical group announced the creation of the International Christian Embassy.[24] In its effort to become an international organization, mustering support for Israel all around the Christian evangelical globe, the ICEJ opened branches in the United States, Europe, Latin America, East Asia, the former Soviet Union, and South Africa. The embassy chose as its logo two olive branches hovering over a globe with Jerusalem at its center. "This symbolizes the great day when Zechariah's prophecy will be fulfilled, and all nations will come up to Jerusalem to keep the Feast of Tabernacles during messiah's reign on earth," the group's leaders announced.[25]

In addition to sparking interest in Israel among evangelicals worldwide, the embassy has promoted various philanthropic programs in Israel, such as providing welfare services in Jerusalem and distributing money and goods to new Jewish immigrants as well as other needy Israelis. Aware that many Jews are suspicious of Christian charitable enterprises, ICEJ often has distributed its parcels through Israeli public agencies.[26]

The embassy's international work focuses on lecturing, mostly in churches, about Israel's role in history and the work of the embassy on behalf of Jewish immigration and settlement in the Holy Land. The embassy's branches distribute ICEJ journals, brochures, leaflets, and cassettes of "Davidic music" and sermons. Embassy representatives also recruit pilgrims for the annual Tabernacles gathering and collect money for the embassy's philanthropic enterprises in Israel. The day-to-day work of the embassy in Israel is devoted to this international mission. The Jerusalem headquarters supervises the work of the representatives in various countries, administers the finances, maintains public relations and publications departments, and oversees the production of videocassettes and audiocassettes in a number of languages. The radio department prepares a special program, *A Word from Jerusalem*, which is broadcast to evangelical radio stations, mostly in North America.

Another major evangelical, pro-Israel organization of special importance has been the Christians' Israel Public Action Campaign (CIPAC), established in the 1980s as a Christian counterpart to AIPAC (America Israel Public Affairs Committee, the pro-Israel lobby in Washington). This group serves as an evangelical lobby that channels Christian pro-Israel sentiments into political support for Israel in America. While Tim LaHaye or Jerry Jenkins have not been among the ICEJ or CIPAC leaders, they have been counted as pro-Israel supporters. ICEJ and CIPAC people have fully approved of the Left Behind series, its narrative and agenda.

From the 1970s to the 2000s, major evangelical organizations, including those that were not created for the purpose of aiding Israel, saw it as their aim to promote pro-Israel stands. The Reverend Tim LaHaye was an executive of such groups, including the Moral Majority, which played an important role in advocating conservative causes in America in the 1970s and 1980s. Jewish and Israeli leaders have considered the leader of the group, Jerry Falwell, as one of Israel's most ardent supporters.[27] LaHaye was also a founder in 1981 of the conservative evangelical Council for National Policy, and served as its first president. Almost needless to say, this organization, too, has viewed development in the Middle East in ways similar to those advocated in Left Behind.[28]

The years following the Six-Day War also saw an increase in the actual presence of evangelical Christians in Israel. Thousands of evangelical Christians have settled in Israel, turning the Jewish state into their permanent or temporary home. Attracted to the land of the Bible, evangelical Christians from all around the globe have built congregations in Israel. Many have joined or helped form congregations of Jewish Believers in Jesus.[29] Others have established "gentile" congregations such as the King of Kings in Jerusalem. Founded in the early 1980s by American and Canadian Pentecostals, the King of Kings is a vibrant congregation consisting of hundreds of charismatic Christians from all around the world, and is one of the largest and most dynamic religious communities in the city. Evangelicals also established institutions of higher learning in Israel, such as the Holy-Land Institute, which was set up by Douglas Young, an American pre-millennialist Christian with a pro-Zionist orientation.

Tours of evangelicals to Israel dramatically increased, turning evangelical tourism into the largest component of tourism to Israel worldwide. One can examine advertisements in evangelical journals to appreciate the scope of evangelical interest in touring the Holy Land. Churches, Bible schools, Christian colleges, missionary groups, and archeological publications routinely organize tours to Israel. Evangelists and premillennialist writers, such as Tim LaHaye, habitually visit the country. Indeed, one cannot think of the Left Behind series without the growing familiarity of evangelical Christians with Israel, the land, its people, and its issues. The book series conveys a good working knowledge of the land, its topography, and its social structure.[30]

Evangelists such as Tim LaHaye have been welcomed guests in Israel.[31] Israeli officials have not always comprehended the full nature of the special attitudes of conservative evangelicals toward the Jewish state and certainly have been unaware of the details of the Christian eschatological hopes, having never heard such terms as "the great tribulation" or the "Time of Jacob's Trouble."[32] Even if they have been aware of missionary intentions, secular Israeli leaders have not been particularly bothered, viewing the benefits of evangelical friendship and support for Israel as over-shadowing the setbacks of (unsolicited) evangelism.[33]

The Israeli government tried from its inception to build good relations with Christian groups and considered it essential to assure them that the new country would respect the status quo ante bellum in religious matters, allowing evangelical groups with missionary agendas to continue their operations in Israel without interruption.[34] Orthodox Jewish activists protested, at times, against the missionaries' work in Israel, and occasionally some Jews attempted to harass missions, but the government refused to change its policy, giving the police the task of protecting missionary centers.[35]

In the late 1970s, as the evangelical influence on American political life became more and more apparent, the Israeli government took more notice of this segment of Christianity and became more active in establishing a warm relationship with the evangelical community.[36] Israeli officials have spoken at evangelical conferences and invited evangelists to meet with Israeli leaders as part of their touring schedules in Israel. After the Israeli bombing of the Iraqi atomic plant in 1981, for example, Menachem Begin, then Israel's prime minister, called Jerry Falwell, one of America's better-known evangelists at the time and leader of the Moral Majority, and asked him to back Israel on the issue. Acquaintance with Israeli officials is reflected in the Left Behind series. Not only has Tim LaHaye visited Israel frequently, but he has met with public figures and government representatives.

Left Behind and Evangelical Criticism of the Jews

Evangelical premillennialist attitudes toward the Jewish people do not translate only into support and philanthropy. Their pro-Zionist sentiments notwithstanding, many conservative evangelicals have had mixed and ambivalent feelings toward Jews. For example, while believing the Jewish people to be central in God's plans for humanity, evangelical Christian simultaneously have maintained prejudicial stereotypes of Jews as greedy, shrewd businesspersons. In addition, there is anger at what many of them have seen as Jewish spiritual blindness, resulting from Jewish stubborn unwillingness to see the truth of Jesus' messiahship. The authors of Left Behind have put this idea in striking terms, making the claim that Jews hate Jesus.[37] Many evangelical writers have seen secular, "modern" Jews as fallen people who have allowed themselves to be seduced by harmful teachings and ideologies, such as secular humanism or socialism. Abandoning traditional Judaism, which had kept them praying for the arrival of the messiah and the rebuilding of the Temple and thus, unwittingly, prepared for them their heroic tasks in history, they were left with no moral guidelines. They had let themselves become instruments of Satan. During the first half of the twentieth century, many evangelical writers accepted as authentic the

Protocols of the Elders of Zion, a fabricated document produced by anti-semites at the turn of the twentieth century that claimed that the Jews were conspiring to overtake the entire world.[38]

In evangelical eyes, Jews have been responsible, at least partially, for their own misery. Had they been willing to accept their true savior, they would have been spared the turmoils that they have undergone throughout history. Evangelical writers, at the same time, have exonerated themselves from any maltreatment of Jews. True Christians—those who had undergone a genuine experience of conversion and have accepted Jesus as their savior—have not harmed Jews. Even if the perpetrators of acts against Jews were nominally members of Christian churches, they were non-Christians. This outlook has been adopted by the authors of Left Behind. In the narrative, those adopting the Christian faith after the rapture treat Jews with goodwill, creating alliances with Jews, who have come, as they have, to understand the true meaning of the natural and political developments around them. Those who attempt to harm Jews in the series are non-Christian, including misguided Jews who have not yet seen the light.

Along this line of thinking, the suffering, misery, and mass murder that at times characterized Jewish existence during the Middle Ages and the modern era did not derive from Christian anti-semitism instigated by theological factors, but rather has been the outcome of a rebellion against God. For example, Nazism, as described in evangelical writings, manifested an alienation from the knowledge of God, a state of being that most of the Jewish victims shared.[39] In evangelical eyes, the Holocaust is thus not merely an unfortunate chapter in Jewish and European history, or a chapter in the history of Christian–Jewish relationships. It is rather a chapter in the Jewish and non-Jewish encounter with, or alienation from, Christ. The more Jews and non-Jews accept the values of evangelical Christianity, the less chance there is of such brutalities repeating themselves.

As a rule, evangelical Christians did not join in the movement of interfaith dialogue. Left Behind offers striking evidence of evangelical disdain of the idea of treating all religions as equals and creating institutions of Christian unity or interfaith cooperation. Evangelicals have occasionally held conversations with Jews[40] but have refused to reexamine their faith, its theological premises in relation to the Jews, or its theological tracts and textbooks. Evangelical theology has insisted that the only means toward salvation is the acceptance of Jesus of Nazareth as Lord and savior. All religious systems that are advocating anything else are misleading their followers and depriving them of eternal life. Creating a nonevangelical universal religion, as indeed the antichrist attempts to do in the Left Behind series, is diabolical. The rightful "dialogue" with Jews, or for that matter with any other group, is the mission.

Since the rise of the evangelical movement in Britain at the turn of the nineteenth century, missions to the Jews have occupied an important place on the evangelical missionary agenda and have come to characterize the evangelical interaction with the Jews no less than evangelical pro-Zionist activity. For evangelicals, the importance of evangelizing the Jews is far beyond missionizing. Evangelicals see the propagation of Christianity among the Jews as part of the divine drama of salvation. Evangelizing the Jews means teaching the people of God about their role and purpose in history as well as saving some of them from the turmoils of the great tribulation.

Missions to the Jews have been on the forefront of promoting the messianic faith, emphasizing the centrality of the Jews in the apocalyptic times.[41] When propagating Christianity among the Jews, missions were careful to include the messianic premillennialist faith, including translations into Hebrew of major messianic evangelical tracts, such as *Jesus Is Coming*, *The Late Great Planet Earth*, and the Left Behind series.

The best known of the contemporary missions to the Jews has been Jews for Jesus. Established in 1970 and known for its innovative and confrontational style, Jews for Jesus became in the later decades of the twentieth century the largest mission to the Jews, opening branches all over the world where there are sizable Jewish communities.[42]

Evangelization of Jews is important for premillennialist evangelicals, not only in order to increase the number of Jews who will then enjoy, as Christian believers, the benefit of being snatched from earth during the rapture, stay with Jesus in the air, and be spared the turmoils of the great tribulation. It is perhaps even more important for the benefit of those "left behind," those who have not converted before the rapture and find themselves bewildered and frightened after other humans have disappeared from earth. Some of them will recognize the unprecedented developments as correlating with the predicted scenarios they have heard from Christian evangelists, whom previously they had not taken very seriously. *Left Behind* points to the special importance of evangelizing the Jews, drawing upon an interpretation of Revelation, chapter 7:4 and 14:1, 3. During the great tribulation, premillenialists believe, 144,000 Jews will become evangelists and spread the knowledge of God among the people of the earth.[43] The novel and its sequels offer lively descriptions of post-tribulation Jewish evangelists, their determination, and their superhuman power to carry out their mission against all odds.

The first Jewish character in the book, Chaim Rosenzweig, is a case in point. Chaim Rosenzweig echoes in name and occupation the figure of Chaim Wiseman, a Zionist statesman and scientist who served as Israel's first president and, among other things, invented a synthetic fertilizer. Rosenzweig, the scientist-wizard, is inherently a decent and pleasant person, but he becomes enchanted by Nicolae Carpathia and serves the ascending antichrist. As evangelical perceptions have it, Rosenzweig, a secular Jew, is destined to become an instrument of the antichrist, as he cannot differentiate between the real savior, Jesus of Nazareth, and the imposter, Nicolae Carpathia. Although Rosenzweig is portrayed sympathetically, ultimately he is a victim of his own inability to accept Jesus and the truth of the gospel, and by extension, he characterizes what the authors view as the unfortunate consequences of the Jewish refusal to accept Jesus.

LaHaye and Jenkins make an attempt not to repeat defamatory stereotypes of Jews, but Jews in the novel serve as archetypes.

They stand for entire groups of Jews and come to represent the different roles and expectations of premillennialist evangelicals for Jews once the rapture takes place and, by extension, point to the image of Jews in general among evangelical writers, such as the authors of *Left Behind*.

The choice of the names Moshe and Eli for the Wailing Wall evangelists, two miraculous preachers protected by God while passing the word of the true savior to the people of Israel, is not accidental. Moshe and Eli follow in the footsteps of two central biblical prophets: Moses and Elijah. Both prophets fought against idolatrous tendencies among the Israelites. Moses reintroduced the children of Israel to their God, serving as an intermediary between God and his people. Elijah is the great "crusader" against the Baal and his worshipers as well as a forerunner of the messiah.

Tsion Ben-Judah also carries a significant name: Zion, Son of Judah. Ben-Judah is a rabbinical scholar who interprets correctly the developments of the great tribulation and turns into a Christian underground leader and preacher.[44] Tsion exemplifies the Jews who see the light, accept Jesus, and turn into the most virtuous of Christian believers and the most admirable and articulate evangelists. Zion, Son of Judah signifies the "completed" Jews who have discovered their true role and mission in history. Now he is a true son of Judah, fulfilling the mission that originally had been entrusted to the Jews, but which they have rejected and are about to claim back. David Hasid's name and character also follow in this vein. Hasid means "pious" and "a follower of the rightful path." Some groups of ultra-Orthodox Jews call themselves "hasids." But LaHaye and Jenkins assert that the Orthodox "hasids" are not really the pious ones—rather, the pious are those who follow Jesus and dedicate themselves to his mission. In drawing the character of Tsion Ben-Judah as well as that of David Hasid, LaHaye and Jenkins have revealed the evangelical understanding of Jewish converts to Christianity as "fulfilled" or "completed" Jews, as Jews who have not only obtained salvation, inner peace, and eternal life but also have understood that the Christian faith has turned them into full, real Jews.

Left Behind and the Building of the Temple

At the center of evangelical interest in Israel, as demonstrated in the Left Behind series, is the prospect of the rebuilt Temple. The Temple has come to symbolize the end times. Premillennialist evangelicals such as LaHaye and Jenkins have predicted the rebuilding of the Temple by the antichrist and the Jews, and, in their eyes, its rebuilding correlates with major apocalyptic events. The yearning to see the apocalypse come true stood at the background of the excitement and hope that characterized evangelical reaction to the Six-Day War. After the war, it occurred to evangelical Christians who were waiting for the second coming of Jesus that Israel held the territory on which the Temple could be rebuilt and so the dramatic developments of the end times could unfold and lead humanity into the messianic age.[45] The Temple, or rather the prospect of its building, received great attention among premillennialist Christians as a watershed development standing between this era and the next. Evangelical tracts and novels published since the late 1960s, such as Hal Lindsey's (with Carole C. Carlson) *The Late Great Planet Earth*, a best-seller that sold about 30 million copies, anticipated the rebuilding of the Temple as a central event of the end times and the fulfillment of biblical prophecies. Lindsey, like other premillennialist evangelicals, was strongly impressed by the Six-Day War and its consequences and placed Israel at the heart of the eschatological drama.[46] For him, the rebuilding of the Temple and the rise of the antichrist to power were major components of the great tribulation, the period between this era and the next, without which the coming of the messiah cannot take place. Left Behind follows in that line, the rebuilding of the Temple becoming a mutual interest of the antichrist and Orthodox Jews. LaHaye and Jenkins have been well aware of both Jewish Orthodox and Christian premillennialist interest in rebuilding the Temple. Yet the authors have projected the yearning for such a move on Orthodox Jews and the antichrist and placed the orchestration of the removal of the Temple Mount mosques and the building of the holy house of worship in the antichrist's hands.

Christian promoters of the idea of rebuilding the Temple in the late 1960s noticed the obstacles on the way toward the advancement of the prophetic timetable. There was the unavoidable reality that the Temple Mount was a Muslim site, complete with magnificent mosques and administered by the Muslim *Waqf* charitable foundation. In addition, although many Israelis understood the outcome of the Six-Day War in messianic terms, most of them did not wish to rebuild the Temple.[47]

The Israeli minister of defense at the time, Moshe Dayan, designed a policy, which the Israeli government has upheld since 1967, that insisted on maintaining the status quo on the Temple Mount as well as in other Muslim and Christian sites. This meant that the Israeli government was committed to protecting the mosques and preventing attempts at destroying them and building anything else instead. In addition, prestigious rabbis declared that Jews were forbidden to enter the Temple Mount. Most rabbinical authorities have viewed the Temple Mount as being as sacred as it was when the Temple was standing.[48] All Jews had been required to purify themselves with the ashes of the red heifer before entering the Mount, and there was no red heifer to be found.[49] The rabbis also feared that Jews might step on restricted sacred ground, such as the Holy of Holies, onto which ordinary Jews (and even ordinary priests) were not allowed to enter. Most observant Jews at the time accepted the rabbinical ban and saw entrance to the Temple Mount as taboo.[50] In sum, as far as the majority of Jews since the late 1960s were concerned, the rebuilding of the Temple was either to be avoided altogether or postponed.

Premillennialist Christians were waiting for the Jews to build the Temple and were impatient with the status quo. One such person, Michael Rohan, a young Australian holding to a dispensationalist premillennialist conviction, decided to change the existing reality. Rohan visited Jerusalem in July 1969 and there, convinced that God had designated him for that task, planned and executed the burning of the El-Aksa Mosque on the Temple Mount in an attempt to secure the necessary ground for the building of the

Temple.[51] The mosque was damaged and Arabs in Jerusalem rioted. Rohan was arrested, put to trial, found insane, and sent back to Australia to spend his life in a mental institution.[52]

Since the 1970s, a number of Christian premillennialist organizations, groups, and individuals have taken active steps intended toward the building of the holy Jewish shrine. Most of them centered on helping Jews, who like them refused to accept the Israeli policy and the status quo, to prepare for the building of the Temple. Some of these groups were advocating their agenda publicly, while others were preparing more quietly for the reinstatement of the sacrificial system in a rebuilt Temple.[53] Such Jews were studying the Temple rituals, manufacturing utensils to be used for sacrificial purposes according to biblical or Talmudic measures, or trying to develop a new breed of heifers. Christian premillennialists marveled at such groups and their activities, viewing them as "signs of the time," indications that the current era was ending and the apocalyptic events of the end times were coming near.[54] The Temple Institute, a museum and workshop in the Old City of Jerusalem that has housed utensils and artifacts and was reconstructed since the 1970s by Jewish advocates of the building of the Temple, has become a site of pilgrimage for Christian advocates of the second coming. Christians expecting the second coming have been encouraged by the sight of Jews conscientiously preparing the implements for use in the Third Temple, and the visits have served to enhance the messianic faith.[55]

One of the Jewish groups that have established a working relationship with premillennialist Christians over the mutual agenda of rebuilding the Temple is the Temple Mount Faithful. Led by Gershon Solomon, a Jerusalem lawyer, the Temple Mount Faithful has been, since its inception in the 1970s, the best known of all the Jewish groups aiming at building the Temple. Its periodic attempts to organize prayers on the Temple Mount, not to mention its plans to install a cornerstone for the rebuilt Temple, have enjoyed much media coverage. Pat Robertson, the renowned leader of the 700 Club, a premillennialist evangelical charismatic group, and a one-time presidential hopeful, offered his support and hospitality to the Jerusalemite group. In August 1991 the 700 Club aired an interview with Solomon. Introducing his guest, Robertson described Solomon's group as struggling to gain their rightful place on the Temple Mount. "We will never have peace," Robertson declared, "until the Mount of the House of the Lord is restored."[56] Solomon, for his part, described his mission as embodying the promise for a universal redemption of humanity. "It's not just a struggle for the Temple Mount, it's a struggle for the . . . redemption of the world," he declared.[57]

The relationship between Christian evangelicals and Jewish groups over the prospect of rebuilding the Temple has been one of the most unexpected, if not bizarre, developments in the long history of Jewish–Christian relations. For both parties, it has been a marriage of convenience. Christian supporters have perceived the Jewish groups as instrumental to the realization of the messianic age. In their vision, the rebuilt Temple is a necessary stage toward that goal. Similarly, Jewish groups do not care for the Christian messianic faith any more than Christian premillennialist groups appreciate the Jewish faith, but they see such details as being beside the point. The important thing for them has been the Christian willingness to support their work.

Chuck Smith, founder and leader of Calvary Chapel, a chain of large and vibrant charismatic churches in America and Canada, secured financial support for the exploration of the exact site of the Temple.[58] A premillennialist associate of Smith's, Lambert Dolphin, a California physicist and archeologist who has led the Science and Archeology Team, took it upon himself to explore the Temple Mount.[59] Dolphin was ready to use sophisticated technological devices and methods, such as wall-penetrating radar and seismic sounding, in his search for the ruins of the previous Temples. Dolphin worked in cooperation with and received help from Stanley Goldfoot, an Israeli Jewish advocate of the rebuilding of the Temple. His attempts to research the Temple Mount to find conclusive evidence regarding the Temple's exact location had been frustrated by the Israeli police, who refused to allow the use of such devices on or under the Mount.[60] Many premillennialists, such as Texan Oz Hawkins, have not waited for conclusive findings by archeologists and have embraced the theory that the location of the Temple was between the two major mosques, El-Aksa and the Dome of the Rock. The Temple, they have concluded, could therefore be rebuilt without destroying the existing mosques, thus providing a "peaceful solution" to the problem of how to build the Temple at a site that is holy to the Muslims.[61]

Christian proponents of building the Temple have not limited their efforts to finding its exact site. Some have searched for the lost Ark of the Covenant, adding a touch of adventure to a potentially explosive topic. The search for the "lost ark" has inspired a number of novels and a movie, based in part on a real-life figure.[62] Some premillennialists also have searched for the ashes of the red heifer, which would allow Jews to enter the Temple Mount, while others have supported Jewish attempts at breeding red heifers.[63] A new interest has arisen in Christian evangelical conservative circles in the Temple building, its interior plan, and its sacrificial works as well as in the priestly garments and utensils. A number of books on these subjects have enjoyed popularity in Christian premillennialist circles.[64] The rebuilt Temple has played an important role in evangelical novels and fictions. The growing importance of the building of the Temple in evangelical eyes demonstrates itself clearly in the Left Behind series. The novel and its sequels promote the premillennialist understanding that the rebuilt Jewish Temple stands at the center of the events that were to precede the arrival of the messiah[65] and describes one of the antichrist's "schemes" as orchestrating the removal of the mosques and their transfer to New Babylon.[66] The novel, however, is oblivious to the history of Christian evangelical–Jewish Orthodox cooperation over the prospect of rebuilding the Temple and the proactive attitude that many evangelical Christians have shown toward the idea that Jews prepare for, and build, the Temple. The building of the Temple in the Left Behind series becomes a Jewish cause, one that brings Jews to support the energetic and charming Nicolae Carpathian, the antichrist.

Although Tim LaHaye and Jerry Jenkins have placed eagerness to build the Temple on the doorsteps of Jews, they have made a gesture toward Jews in their choice of antichrist, departing from the traditional dispensationalist identification of the antichrist as a Jewish leader. Since the early nineteenth century, and until the publication of *Left Behind*, dispensationalist writers have routinely characterized the antichrist as a Jew. The rationale for a Jewish antichrist had been the claim that since Jesus was a Jew, so the antichrist, impostering as much as possible, also will be a Jew. Trying to appease the Jews and reassure them that they were not identified with the antichrist, and at the same time wishing not to give rise to a Catholic–Protestant polemic, they did not repeat the old Protestant claim that the pope was the antichrist. Such an attitude would have offended Roman Catholics, would have rekindled old Protestant–Catholic antagonisms, and would have scared away potential Roman Catholic readers. Some awkward qualifications notwithstanding, evangelical Christians in the past generation avoided attacking Roman Catholicism or describing Roman Catholics as non–Christians. Following in that line, LaHaye and Jenkins made a gesture toward Roman Catholics, declaring the pope among the missing, the true Christians snatched from earth. LaHaye and Jenkins have skillfully come up with an antichrist who is nominally non–Roman Catholic but is still a Roman: a Romanian. Orthodox Christians, LaHaye and Jenkins concluded, would not be very offended, as a Romanian antichrist would not touch on sensitive historical nerves, as Protestants had not pointed historically to an Orthodox Christian leader as the antichrist. At the same time, Carpathia still serves his purpose: The antichrist, LaHaye and Jenkins were careful to point out, was a Romanian of Roman descent.[67]

LaHaye and Jenkins were not the only ones who modified the classical dispensationalist scheme in deference to the new atmosphere of evangelical–Jewish leadership. The close relationship between Christian and Jewish proponents of the Temple building has brought other evangelical Christians to rewrite the details of the role of the Jews in the rebuilding of the Temple.

Responding to input from Jewish activists who had been working, together with Christians, toward the rebuilding of the Temple, and who wondered about their dubious role as laborers in the service of the antichrist, evangelical writers such as Randall Price have reassured them that premillennialist Christians expected the Temple to survive the rule of the antichrist and to function gloriously in the millennial kingdom and not only in the period that preceded it.[68]

The building of the Temple has brought evangelical Christians to form historically unprecedented friendships and alliances with Jews that would have been difficult to imagine at other times and places. There is something surreal about the Christian and Jewish advocates of the building of the Temple, as their actions transcend the historical dynamics of Christian–Jewish interaction. The unique relationship that has developed between Jews and evangelical Christians over the prospect of the building of the Temple has brought about scenes that are almost unbelievable, including Christians marveling at and receiving reassurance for their messianic faith from Jews studying the priestly codex in preparation for reinstating the sacrificial system. Something of a symbiosis has developed between conservative evangelical Christians and Orthodox nationalist Jews over the building of the Temple. Although each of the groups has had a different vision for the messianic times, they all have shared the same agenda for the near future.

Left Behind came about after a generation of evangelical fascination with the idea of rebuilding the Temple, and just a short time before the Israeli government found the idea of evangelical interest in building the Temple rather scary. As the year 2000 approached, journalists, scholars, and government officials alike became preoccupied with the possible risks and dangers this seemingly outstanding year might bring. The year 2000 stirred the messianic imagination. Many Americans looked upon a technological breakdown as a possible potential catalyst of the apocalypse. Israelis, on their part, were concerned over the fate of the Temple Mount mosques. Should the mosques be bombed or seriously damaged through other means, all hell might break loose,

causing a Muslim–Israeli war to begin. In April 1999 Israeli security rounded up members of a Christian evangelical messianic
group called Concerned Christians that had come to Jerusalem to
take part in the events of the end times and, according to official
Israeli reports, to commit mass suicide or perhaps to damage the
mosques on the Temple Mount. Members of the group subsequently were deported. Toward the latter months of 1999, Israeli
fear that premillennialist Christians might try to blow up the
mosques bordered on hysteria. Israeli security forces arrested and
deported dozens of Christians who resided in Jerusalem and were
hoping to witness the second coming of Jesus, most of them
harmless persons.[69] Likewise, the Israelis refused entrance to the
country to "suspicious" Christians.

Left Behind is an antithesis to the Israeli and American official
attitudes at the turn of the twenty-first century. In the Left
Behind series, Christian believers who expect the rapture and
the apocalyptic events to begin are the wise ones, taking the
right steps toward the end times. Such figures as Irene Steele,
Rayford Steele's missing wife, a dedicated spouse and citizen,
are the sane, moderate persons. Although nonbelieving friends
and family members, not to mention other members of society,
do not take their theological views very seriously, they regret
their attitude when the rapture takes place. The Israeli and even
the American understanding of such events in 1999–2000 was
somewhat different: Those waiting too anxiously for the events
of the end times to take place were dangerous and were understood by the authorities to be less-than-reliable citizens.

Conclusion

The novel Left Behind and its sequels come to promote the idea
of the imminent apocalypse and the need to accept Jesus before
the rapture takes place. Israel nonetheless looms large in the
series, and the novel demonstrates the centrality of the Jewish
people and Israel in the evangelical eschatological faith. The
book points to the complex and ambivalent attitudes of the
authors and, by extension, of evangelical premillennialists in

general toward the Jews and Israel both in their current situation and in a prophesized future when Jews are "left behind." The attitudes of evangelical Christians toward the Jews, as LaHaye and Jenkins demonstrate, have been extraordinary in the history of relationships between religious communities. In no other case has one religious community assigned a special role in God's plans for human redemption to members of another religious group. Nor have thinkers and leaders of one religious group been concerned with the role and mission of another group as evangelical Christians have been over the Jews. Evangelical writers have turned their understanding of the historical mission of the Jews into their evangelization message, seeing it as an inherent part of their messianic faith. No wonder the authors of *Left Behind* have given so much thought to the subject, at times making their own choices as to how to present the Jews and their special mission in history. It is also not surprising that scholars of American policy toward the Middle East have taken great interest in the novel.[70] Likewise, right-wing Christian groups that do not share the authors' views of Israel and the Jews also have reacted strongly to the novel, offering alternative interpretations that suggest that Jews are not central to the end-times developments.[71]

While premillennialist evangelical writers have promoted the importance of Jews and Israel for the arrival of the messianic age, at the same time they have insisted on the exclusivity of their faith as the only true fulfillment of God's commands and as the only means to reach God and assure salvation. Judaism, the faith of the Jews, could not offer redemption to the Jews. This view has been just as crucial to shaping the evangelical relation to the Jews, which therefore has been marked by an amazing paradox: a vision of a deprived, crippled, yet chosen and essential people. The paradox has made it into the Left Behind series, where Jews stand at the forefront, helping the antichrist to power and at the same time resisting his rule. Jews create a formula that makes deserts blossom yet cannot tell, at least not initially, who their real savior is and attempt to lynch preachers promoting the true messiah. Although, according to

LaHaye and Jenkins, Jews hate Jesus, 144,400 Jews become, during the great tribulation, the most dedicated and relentlessly effective promoters of Jesus' messiahship.

Premillennialist evangelists such as LaHaye and Jenkins have taken a great interest in the realities of Jewish existence. In the latter decades of the twentieth century, they became Israel's most eager tourists and the religious cultural group that interacts more than any other with the Jews. Such growing intimacy has modified evangelical views and improved evangelical opinions on Jews. A survey conducted in the early 1960s discovered that conservative Protestants were more likely to hold prejudices against Jews than more liberal Protestants or Roman Catholics.[72] A similar survey, conducted by the Anti-Defamation League in the mid-1980s, discovered, however, a remarkable decline in evangelical negative opinions on Jews.[73] This has been due, in no small measure, to the dramatic growth in evangelical Christian encounters with Israel and with Jews in the wake of the 1967 war. The growth of the Jewish community in the American Bible Belt since the 1970s also has contributed to that trend. Although previously evangelicals read about Jews in the New Testament or heard about them in sermons, between the 1970s and the 2000s millions of evangelicals have met Jewish friends or colleagues, have taken tours to Israel, have met with Israeli officials, and many have spent time in kibbutzim or in evangelical educational programs in Israel.

The theme of the novel notwithstanding, *Left Behind* is not necessarily about the future; it is very much about the present and serves as an excellent source to reveal the evangelical attitudes toward almost all aspects of contemporary culture and world order: from married life to the United Nations. The series reveals the evangelical understanding toward Israel and the Jews, as a misguided nation, yet one that is destined to return to its biblically promised position as God's first nation. The Jewish characters in the novel and its sequels, from Chaim Rosenzweig to Moshe and Eli, the Wailing Wall preachers, to Rabbi Tsion Ben-Judah, a leader of Tribulation Force, come to convey the different aspects of the evangelical understanding of the Jews, their merits and limitations.

The Left Behind series has been marked by the deliberate wish of the authors to convey a sympathetic evangelical understanding of the Jews, avoiding bitter or defamatory representations that have characterized, often unwittingly, evangelical writings on Jews, yet they would not compromise evangelical premillennialist faith, and so theirs is an improved, sympathetic version of the evangelical premillennialist representation of the Jews. LaHaye and Jenkins have little appreciation for the Jewish faith, which, in their novel, keeps Jews fanatically hostile to Jesus and the Christian gospel. Yet in their novels the Jewish community has given rise to extraordinary figures and serves as a nursery to the future evangelists and leaders of the true faith. The novel thus reflects a new wave of evangelical–Jewish relations, a reflection of the intensive involvement of evangelicals with Jews and Israel from the 1970s to the 2000s.

Notes

1. Tim LaHaye and Jerry B. Jenkins, *Left Behind* (Wheaton, Ill.: Tyndale House, 1995), 6–14.
2. For details on this eschatological hope, see, for example, Hal Lindsey's (with Carole C. Carolson) best-seller *The Late Great Planet Earth* (Grand Rapids, Mich.: Zondervan, 1970).
3. Ernest Sandeen, *The Roots of Fundamentalism: British and American Millenarianism, 1800–1930* (Grand Rapids, Mich.: Baker Book House, 1978).
4. A. G. Mojtabai, *Blessed Assurance: At Home with the Bomb in Amarillo, Texas* (Boston: Houghton Mifflin Company, 1986).
5. Yaakov Ariel, *Evangelizing the Chosen People: Missions to the Jews in America 1880s–2000* (Chapel Hill: University of North Carolina Press, 2000).
6. For example, Barbara Tuchman, *Bible and Sword* (London: Macmillan, 1983).
7. See William E. Blackstone, *Jesus Is Coming*, 3rd. ed. (Los Angeles: Bible House, 1908), 211–213, 236–241.
8. See Yaakov Ariel, "An American Initiative for a Jewish State: William Blackstone and the Petition of 1891," *Studies in Zionism* 10 (1989), 125–137.

9. Blackstone stated this in a letter to Woodrow Wilson, November 4, 1914, and in a telegram to Warren G. Harding, December 10, 1920. Blackstone Personal Papers at the Billy Graham Center, Wheaton, Illinois.

10. See Yaakov Ariel, "William Blackstone and the Petition of 1916: A Neglected Chapter in the History of Christian Zionism in America," *Studies in Contemporary Jewry* 7 (1991), 68–85.

11. William L. Pettingill, J. R. Schafler, and J. D. Adams, eds., *Light on Prophecy: A Coordinated, Constructive Teaching, Being the Proceedings and Addresses at the Philadelphia Prophetic Conference, May 28–30, 1918* (New York: The Christian Herald Bible House, 1918); Arno C. Gaebelein, ed., *Christ and Glory: Addresses Delivered at the New York Prophetic Conference, Carnegie Hall, November 25–28, 1918* (New York: "Our Hope" Publication Office, 1919).

12. See, e.g., George T. B. Davis, *Fulfilled Prophecies That Prove the Bible* (Philadelphia: Million Testaments Campaign, 1931); and Keith L. Brooks, *The Jews and the Passion for Palestine in Light of Prophecy* (Los Angeles: Brooks Publications, 1937).

13. James Gray, "Editorial," *Moody Bible Institute Monthly* 31 (1931), 346.

14. See Dwight Wilson, *Armageddon Now! The Premillenarian Response to Russia and Israel since 1917* (Grand Rapids, Mich.: Baker Book House, 1977).

15. See Louis T. Talbot and William W. Orr, *The New Nation of Israel and the Word of God* (Los Angeles: Bible Institute of Los Angeles, 1948); M. R. DeHaan, *The Jew and Palestine in Prophecy* (Grand Rapids, Mich.: Zondervan, 1954); Arthur Kac, *The Rebirth of the State of Israel: Is It of God or Men?* (Chicago: Moody Press, 1958); and George T. B. Davis, *God's Guiding Hand* (Philadelphia: Million Testaments Campaign, 1962).

16. John Walvoord, *Israel in Prophecy* (Grand Rapids, Mich.: Zondervan, 1962), 19.

17. E.g., L. Nelson Bell, "Unfolding Destiny," *Christianity Today* (1967), 1044–1045.

18. See, e.g., Peter L. Williams and Peter L. Benson, *Religion on Capitol Hill: Myth and Realities* (New York: Oxford University Press, 1986); Allen D. Hertzke, *Representing God in Washington* (Knoxville: University of Tennessee Press, 1988); Mark Silk, *Spiritual Politics* (New York: Touchstone, 1989); and Michael Lienesch, *Redeeming*

America: Piety and Politics in the New Christian Right (Chapel Hill: University of North Carolina Press, 1993).

19. Evangelical tracts of the period give evidence to such notions. The most "classical" of them is Lindsey's *The Late Great Planet Earth*.

20. Peter Grose, *Israel in the Mind of America* (New York: Alfred A. Knopf, 1983), especially 38, 256, 293.

21. Cf. Aba Eban, *Autobiography* (New York: Random House, 1977), 187.

22. See Martin Gardner, "Giving God a Hand," *New York Review of Books*, August 13, 1987, p. 22.

23. Cf. Silk, *Spiritual Politics*; Liensch, *Redeeming America*.

24. James McWhirter, *A World in a Country* (Jerusalem: B.S.B. International, 1983), 160–174; interviews with Marvin and Merla Watson, Jerusalem, October 16, 1992, and Menahem Ben Hayim, Jerusalem, October 14, 1992.

25. Van der Hoeven, "If I Forget Thee O Jerusalem," *Sukkoth Brochure* (Jerusalem: International Christian Embassy, 1984), 4.

26. On the various activities of the embassy, see its brochure, "The Ministry of the International Christian Embassy Jerusalem" (Jerusalem: International Christian Embassy, 1992).

27. Cf. Merrill Simon, *Jerry Falwell and the Jews* (Middle Village, N.Y.: Jonathan David, 1984).

28. Cf. Joan Didion, "Mr. Bush and the Divine," *New York Review of Books*, November 6, 2003, 82.

29. Kai Kjaer-Hansen and Bochil F. Skjott, *Facts and Myths about the Messianic Congregations in Israel* (Jerusalem: United Christian Council in Israel in Cooperation with the Caspari Center, 1999).

30. Cf., e.g., Tim LaHaye and Jerry B. Jenkins, *Nicolae: The Rise of Antichrist* (Wheaton, Ill.: Tyndale House, 1997), 225–250.

31. David E. Harrel, *Oral Roberts: An American Life* (Bloomington: Indiana University Press, 1985), 137.

32. A striking example of the Israeli failure to understand the evangelicals and their motives can be found in Michael Pragai's book *Faith and Fulfillment* (London: Valentine Mitchell, 1985). The author, who served as the head of the department for liaison with the Christian churches and organizations in the Israeli Ministry of Foreign Affairs for many years, did not fully comprehend the nature of the evangelical support of Zionism and of the differences between conservative and mainline/liberal churches.

33. E.g., David M. Eichorn, *Evangelizing the American Jew* (Middle Village, N.Y.: Jonathan David, 1978).
34. E.g., Robert L. Lindsey, *Israel in Christendom* (Tel Aviv: Dugit, 1961).
35. Per Osterlye, *The Church in Israel* (Lund: Gleerup, 1970); Cf. Ariel, *Evangelizing the Chosen People*, 277–278; Daniel Ben Simon, "Doing Something for Judaism," *Haaretz*, December 18, 1997, English edition, 1–2; e.g., a letter circulated through electronic mail by Noam Hendren, Baruch Maoz, and Marvin Dramer, March 1997.
36. "Israel Looks on U.S. Evangelical Christian as Potent Allies," *Washington Post*, March 23, 1981, p. A11.
37. LaHaye and Jenkins, *Left Behind*, 80.
38. See Arno C. Gaebelein, "Jewish Leadership in Russia," *Our Hope* 27 (1921), 734–735; James M. Gray, "The Jewish Protocols," *Moody Bible Institute Monthly* 22 (1921), 589; and William B. Riley, *Wanted—A World Leader!* (Minneapolis: Authors, n.d.), 41–51, 71–72.
39. Cf. Yaakov Ariel, "Jewish Suffering and Christian Salvation: the Evangelical-Fundamentalist Holocaust Memoirs," *Holocaust and Genocide Studies* 6 (1991), 63–78.
40. Marc H. Tanenbaum, Marvin R. Wilson, and A. James Rudin, *Evangelicals and Jews in Conversation* (Grand Rapids, Mich.: Baker Book House, 1978).
41. David Brickner, *Future Hope: A Jewish Christian Look at the End of the World* (San Francisco: Purple Pomegranate Productions, 1999).
42. Cf. Yaakov Ariel, "Counterculture and Missions: Jews for Jesus and the Vietnam Era Missionary Campaigns," *Religion and American Culture* 9, no. 2 (Summer 1999), 233–257.
43. E.g., Tim LaHaye and Jerry B. Jenkins, *Soul Harvest: The World Takes Sides* (Wheaton, Ill.: Tyndale House, 1998), 245.
44. Ibid., 246–250; Tim LaHaye and Jerry B. Jenkins, *Assassins: Assignment Jerusalem, Target: Antichrist* (Wheaton, Ill.: Tyndale House, 1999), 9–13.
45. Raymond L. Cox, "Time for the Temple?" *Eternity* 19 (January 1968), 17–18; Malcolm Couch, "When Will the Jews Rebuild the Temple?" *Moody Monthly* 74 (December 1973), 34–35, 86.
46. Lindsey, *The Late Great Planet Earth*, 32–47.
47. Cf. Gideon Aran, "From Religious Zionism to Zionist Religion: the Roots of Gush Emunim," *Studies in Contemporary Jewry* 2 (1986), 118.

48. *Mishna, Kelim* 1, 8. Cf. "Har Ha Bayit" in *HaEncyclopedia HaTalmudit* (The Talmudic Encyclopedia, Jerusalem, 1970) vol. 10, 575–592.
49. Cf. Numbers 19.
50. Cf. Ehud Sprinzak, *The Ascendance of Israel's Radical Right* (New York: Oxford University Press, 1991), 279–288.
51. See Jerusalem District Court Archive, Criminal File 69/173.
52. Ibid.
53. On Jewish groups aiming at building the Temple, see Sprinzak, *Ascendance of Israel's Radical Right*, 264–269, 279–288.
54. Cf. Jeffrey, *Armageddon*, especially 108–150.
55. E.g., Don Stewart and Chuck Missler, *The Coming Temple: Center Stage for the Final Countdown* (Orange, Calif.: Dart Press, 1991), 157–170.
56. Quoted in Robert I. Friedman, *Zealots for Zion* (New York: Random House, 1992), 144.
57. Ibid., 144–145.
58. On Chuck Smith, see Donald E. Miller, *Reinventing American Protestantism* (Berkeley: University of California Press, 1998).
59. On Dolphin and his premillennialist thinking and connections, see Dolphin's extensive website, www.Ldolphin.org; see also a series of tracts the Californian physicist has published, copies in Yaakov Ariel's collection.
60. Stewart and Missler, *Coming Temple*, 157–170.
61. See Yisrayl Hawkins, *A Peaceful Solution to Building the Next Temple in Yerusalem* (Abilene, Tex.: House of Yahweh, 1989).
62. On the premillennialist fascination with the lost ark, see Doug Wead, David Lewis, and Hal Donaldson, *Where Is the Lost Ark?* (Minneapolis: Bethany House Publishing, n.d.); Don Stewart and Chuck Missler, *In Search of the Lost Ark* (Orange, Calif.: Dart Press, 1991).
63. Lawrence Wright, "Forcing the End," *The New Yorker* 74, no. 20 (July 20, 1998), 42–53; Jewish Telegraph Agency, September 2, 1999, www.jta.org/sep99/02-cows.htm.
64. See, e.g., C. W. Sleming, *These Are the Garments* (Fort Washington, Pa.: Christian Literature Crusade, n.d.); Wead, Lewis, and Donaldson, *Where Is the Lost Ark?*; Stewart and Missler, *In Search of the Lost Ark*; Thomas Ice and Randall Price, *Ready to Rebuild* (Eugene, Oreg.: Harvest House, 1992).
65. E.g., LaHaye and Jenkins, *Left Behind*, 415; LaHaye and Jenkins, *Nicolae*, 369; Tim LaHaye and Jerry B. Jenkins, *Tribulation*

Force: The Continuing Drama of Those Left Behind (Wheaton, Ill.: Tyndale House, 1996), 208.

66. LaHaye and Jenkins, *Tribulation Force*, 277.
67. LaHaye and Jenkins, *Left Behind*, 70.
68. Ice and Price, *Ready to Rebuild*.
69. E.g., Gershom Gorenberg, "Israel Pushes Out 'Elijah' for Promising to Bring the Redemption," *The Jerusalem Report*, September 27, 1999.
70. Cf. Melani McAlister, "An Empire of Their Own," *The Nation*, September 22, 2003.
71. Cf., e.g., Jesus/Christians website: www.cust.idl.net.au/fold/Teach.html; "Left Behind: Bad Fiction; Bad Faith," http://christianity.about.com/cs/adultchristianity /a /leftbehind.htm.
72. Charles Y. Glock and Rodney Stark, *Christian Beliefs and Antisemitism* (New York: Harper Torchbooks, 1966).
73. L. Ianniello, press release by the Anti-Defamation League, New York, January 8, 1986.

6

What Social and Political Messages Appear in the Left Behind Books?

A Literary Discussion of Millenarian Fiction

AMY JOHNSON FRYKHOLM

Stories about the end of time have always been a part of Christianity. There have been stories about disaster and redemption, about Babylon and the New Jerusalem. There have been stories of violence and destruction as well as everlasting peace and overwhelming happiness. In every place and at every time these stories have been told, they not only have envisioned the end of time, but they also have instructed readers and listeners about their own time and place. This is just as true of the Left Behind series as it has been for the multiplicity of other stories Christians have told about the end of time over two millennia.

What does the Left Behind series say about our own time and place? What are the social and political messages conveyed through these stories? When attempting to answer these questions, we must remember that all writing is embedded in social and cultural understandings. Writers are part of a social world.

Even though every story is the creation of an author, it is also a part of history and social context. Writers have no choice but to draw on this history and this context as they write, and often, in the process of doing that, they draw on stereotypes, unexamined assumptions, and political ideologies. In its examination of the Left Behind series, this chapter looks not only at what messages the authors *intend* to send to us about our world, but also some messages the authors may be less aware of sending. I explore what some of the unexplored and implicit assumptions of the books might be.

The social and political messages of Left Behind speak both to the grand scale of global politics and to the small scale of everyday, interpersonal interaction. Both of these scales of perspective are rooted in social understandings about how the world works and how the world should work. These messages often offer a diagnosis of what is wrong with our world as it exists and how it might be improved. At the same time, however, stories like those in the Left Behind series are multi-layered. They rarely say only one thing in a straightforward way. Instead, the messages can be complex and contradictory; the actions and words of the characters can stand in opposition to each other or be derived from tangled views about both the past and the future. In this chapter, I by no means exhaust what the Left Behind series has to say about our world as it currently exists, but I address a set of issues central to the Left Behind message and meaning.

Global Unity and the Threat of the Antichrist

These are times of enormous controversy regarding the relationship of the United States to the rest of the world. Whether the question is an international environmental treaty, our place in the United Nations, or the attack on the World Trade Center, each instance provides an opportunity to reflect on the U.S. place in the world and our interaction with international bodies and other countries. Should we stand alone in armed conflicts or only participate as part of a body of nations? Should we act independently on foreign policy issues or seek the help of allies? Should we sign international treaties that restrict our activities or should we develop our own separate policies? Each of these questions contains its own complexities and each individual circumstance raises its own problems, but each of them also points to the question of the United States' role in the world. This is where Left Behind intervenes to offer an understanding of the United States in the world that is very specific and part of a long tradition supporting U.S. isolationism.

In every instance, a reading of Left Behind hints that treaties, alliances, and participation in the United Nations all pave the way for the coming of the antichrist. The series is suspicious of such interactions, and, even though it only constructs images of future scenarios, it still offers reason to fear them now. In order to see how this is so, we must recognize that stories about the rapture and tribulation are woven out of two elements. First, these stories are derived from the circumstances of the particular time and place from which they are written. Second, they draw from a stock of images and plots that remain the same from story to story. For example, every story about rapture and tribulation provides some depiction of the antichrist. Where the antichrist comes from, how he gains his power, even what he looks like vary from story to story, but all contain this central figure. In each story of rapture and tribulation, the antichrist unites the world to form a One World Government. Since the end of the nineteenth century, people who have believed in dispensational premillennialism (usually without ever calling it that) have believed that the antichrist will come in peace and preach unity and brotherhood, but he will be full of lies and deceit. Once the world is united under one government, with the antichrist as the head, he will use this position to tyrannize the world.

In Left Behind's treatment of this formulaic scenario, the antichrist's regime eclipses an American government beset by moral failure. Authors Tim LaHaye and Jerry Jenkins refer to the president as the "Carpathia-emasculated President Gerald Fitzhugh."[1] The President quickly concedes his authority to the

United Nations and thus to Nicolae Carpathia, the antichrist. The strong political message contained here is both a critique and a warning. The critique points to the weakness and corruption of the federal government. Godless, worldly, without a backbone, the U.S. government is one of the first to crumble to Nicolae Carpathia's demands.

It might seem for a moment, then, that the Left Behind series is anti-American and unpatriotic. But it is neither. Instead, the legitimacy that the federal government concedes when it becomes a part of the antichrist's regime is transferred to the Tribulation Force. While the force is, on one hand, also an international group, it has its roots and its leadership in the United States. This is no accident. Beneath the corrupt government, the series hints at another "America," more true to its ideals than the America represented by political leaders. This is an America that still persists in its ideals. We catch a glimpse of this other America in *Tribulation Force*, when hero Buck Williams confronts Carparthia. "I am motivated by truth and justice," Buck tells the antichrist, who sarcastically responds, "Ah, the American way! Just like Superman."[2] Buck, Rayford Steele, and the other members of the Tribulation Force represent the true America, uncorrupted by politics and unencumbered by international treaties and alliances that make it vulnerable to the antichrist.

In asserting that the "real" America is separate from the government, Left Behind joins an important strain of American culture that claims that the nation is not best represented by official institutions. Part of our tradition of individualism is to claim that real Americans are not found in the government, but instead in people who are social outsiders—the cowboy, the pioneer, the person who starts out poor and isolated and makes himself rich. Our stories about ourselves come back time and time again to stories of the isolated and persecuted hero who intervenes to save society, but then leaves it again. We can find this story widely spread in American culture, in classic westerns, in movies like *Star Wars*, and in books like those in the Left Behind series.

The caution contained in Left Behind's understanding of the U.S. government has to do with the books' treatment of the United Nations as a vehicle of the antichrist. The political message is clearly a warning against association and participation with such international organizations. The books imply that a better, more God-ordained path for the United States is self-determination and a willingness to forgo cooperation in order to act autonomously. The implications of this resistance to international cooperation are obvious. Such a view dictates that the United States stand alone, outside of international partnerships and obligations.

In the Left Behind series, the One World Government takes the form of Carpathia's Global Community. Early in the first novel we learn that the Global Community's promise of bringing the world together and uniting people for peace is a lie. Carpathia actually intends to inflict violence and death, not peace and universal harmony. At the same time, his rhetoric is one that promotes peace and "universal brotherhood." He claims to imagine a world united with common goals and common understanding, a world in which wars are no longer fought and weapons no longer dictate foreign policy. "The world will be a better place in which to live. . . . Our destiny is a utopian society based on peace and brotherhood," he tells Buck.[3] Carpathia promotes helping third-world nations economically and working toward disarmament. He suggests that no one in the world should be hungry or in need of shelter. Surely these are lofty goals; indeed, some might even consider them goals worthy of Christians' attention. Why, then, in the context of the story, are they evil?

In part, we can better understand this by focusing on the "premillennial" aspect of dispensational premillennialism. Premillennialism is an understanding about the end of time that emerged out of arguments about society in the eighteenth and nineteenth centuries. In the United States in the nineteenth century, the prevailing view of the end of time was an optimistic one. This view was that human beings could work together to bring about the kingdom of God on earth. In other words, humans had a God-given opportunity to create the millennium—a time of universal peace and happiness. When they succeeded, Christ would come and reign over the earth. Scholars have called this view "postmillennialism." The "post" refers to the coming of Christ *after* the millennium is instituted on earth.

Not everyone agreed with this view. As the nineteenth century progressed, some became convinced that human beings would never achieve the millennium on earth. In fact, they saw society not improving but rapidly declining. This was especially true as the Industrial Revolution and mass urbanization transformed American life. Many conservative Protestants saw these as signs that traditional life was being destroyed and the world was changing, but not for the better. In this context, a view called "premillennialism" became prevalent. Premillennialism is largely a pessimistic view. It posits that the world will fall into rapid decline morally, spiritually, and economically. At some point, Christ will return to earth to save the world from its misery. In this view, Christ will usher in the millennium without human help. Over the course of the twentieth century, with its violent wars and rapid social changes, many conservative Protestants saw this view confirmed.

As Jeanne Kilde explained in chapter 2, the idea of the rapture and tribulation grew out of this pessimistic view of the fate of the world. The Left Behind series emerges out of the same trajectory. In the view of the series' authors, efforts to make the world a better place are a direct contradiction to the idea that Christ alone can save humanity through his second coming. Attempts to create "utopia" on earth are not particularly useful because of humanity's sinful nature and the imminent coming of Christ. Furthermore, premillennialists feel that these are efforts by humans to try to live without God, to demonstrate that they do not need God. Thus world peace, disarmament, the elimination of world hunger, or other plans to make the globe a better place are seen as part of the devil's work, doomed to failure and full of lies.

From the late nineteenth century onward, conservative Protestants have been very suspicious of the way the modern world breaks down boundaries. One of the things that the social changes of the early twentieth century produced was an increasingly international understanding of the world. Even though the Internet, satellites, and other forms of mass communication are recent developments of the global community, people in the late nineteenth and early twentieth centuries also had reason to believe that their world was rapidly expanding. Chain stores were replacing small, local operations; corporations were growing and locating themselves in more than one country; people were coming to the United States from all over the world, giving citizens a tangible sense of the world outside U.S. borders; new technology allowed people to communicate across vast distances. These changes were very unsettling for those who wanted to cling to traditional life, which was focused around the local, not the international. Values, families, and religion were centered in small communities.

Conservative Protestants were reluctant for the United States to join the League of Nations and later the United Nations. They saw these things as threats to the boundaries of the United States and felt that this internationalism was a threat not only on the local level but also on the national. Many conservative Protestants still see world unity, common goals, and attempts for nations to work together as attempts by human beings not only to build the Tower of Babel but also to bring about the destruction of the United States. John Walvoord, a prophecy teacher to whom Jerry Jenkins and Tim LaHaye dedicated the fifth novel in the series, *Assassins*, wrote in 1964 that the United Nations was playing a role in prophecy by emphasizing the global rather than the national and by teaching people to think globally. In his view, this was not a positive development; he saw the United Nations as a way for the antichrist to take power over the world.[4] For many who agree with Walvoord's worldview, any sign that the world is drawing together for peace or harmony is interpreted as a "sign of the end," not the coming of the millennium but the coming of the antichrist.

At different moments over the history of this belief, fear of the One World Government has meant various things. In the early part of the twentieth century, the One World Government was associated with capitalism and vast economic changes taking place. Later, during the cold war, it was associated with the Soviet Union and communism. In the Left Behind series, the fear of the One World Government manifests itself in a portrayal of the United Nations. Although the exact target of the fear shifts with the particular circumstances of each time and place, the general fear of world unity remains in place.

Fear of the One World Government is not the only manifestation of the fear of world unity in the Left Behind series. The books also depict a One World Religion under the figurehead Pontifex Maximus Peter Mathews. In this case, all of the world's religions join together and emphatically declare that belief is irrelevant and that all religions are in fact the same thing. The pope-like characteristics of Pontiff Peter have led Catholics to declare the Left Behind series anti-Catholic. Clearly this figure and the Enigma Babylon One World Faith embody a fear of ecumenism and a fear of religious bodies, like governments, joining together. If a One World Religion is as much to be feared as a One World Government, following that logic, any unification of religious bodies portends evil. From this perspective, when the Lutherans and the Episcopalians decide to share one communion, we can take that as evidence of Satan's work in the world. When Christian and Buddhist leaders meet together in an attempt to find common ground, we can take that as a sign of the end times. In this worldview, disagreement is prized above agreement and division above unity.

The more we follow this logic, the more tangled it becomes. On one hand, a One World Religion points to the coming of Christ. It is one of many factors that usher in the end of the world. Presumably this is good, since all Christians celebrate the second coming of Christ. On the other hand, unity among religions and nations is evidence of Satan's work in the world, something of which Christians ought to be wary (notwithstanding the obvious contradiction that Christians themselves want to convert everyone to Christianity and produce a One World Religion). This kind of confusion has the potential to cause political paralysis. Christians should not get involved with organizations like the United Nations and perhaps even should avoid political candidates who seem friendly toward them. But, ultimately, Christians of this worldview believe that they have very little control over the future. It is already "written in advance," as the raptured pastor of Irene Steele's church puts it.[5] For this reason, whether there is political support for the United Nations or not, the antichrist is coming and we can do little more than try to convert others in the meantime.

From yet another perspective, the Tribulation Force itself develops a form of "global unity" in the form of the Christian Cooperative. United by faith and committed to defying the antichrist's regime, Christians work together to exchange goods throughout the world. Why is this form of global cooperation better than the antichrist's form? What makes the Christian Cooperative better than the Global Community? Let me suggest one possibility. The Tribulation Force is an organization run by American Protestant Christians. Its beliefs, its forms of organization, its ways of thinking and acting, while claiming to be universally Christian, in fact reflect a very small and very specific part of Christianity. The religious language that the Tribulation Force speaks, its rallies in stadiums, its Christian Cooperative— all of these are very specific American Protestant ways of interpreting and spreading the meaning of Christianity. Thus one important difference between the Tribulation Force and the Global Community, besides the fact that one is aligned with God and the other with Satan, is that one is dominated and run by American Protestants and the other is dominated and run by foreigners whose way of understanding and interpreting religion is, in the view of the authors, wrong. In a world that is rapidly globalizing, the Tribulation Force imagines a way that America maintains its dominance and worldly power. It casts this power in a spiritual light and imbues it with religious significance; it imagines American Protestantism as the center of God's universe.

The message in all of this is a contradictory one. On one hand, the United States has no central role to play. Biblical prophesiers have long agreed about this. Hal Lindsey's *The Late Great Planet Earth* contains chapters on Russia, China, and Israel, but it says little about what role the United States might play.[6] On the other hand, the books participate in an important American mythology. In the rhetoric of the books, Americans are the world's most natural leaders. The world's believers embrace without question American Protestant language, methods, and beliefs. When a character becomes a part of the Tribulation Force—whether he or she is Chinese, Egyptian, or Greek—the Tribulation Force's bunker in the United States becomes his or her second home.

While the Left Behind series clearly draws on American mythology, does any of this have any impact on actual political decisions? That is a difficult question to answer. Belief in the rapture and tribulation has had some explicit impact on U.S. policy throughout its history. One famous example comes from the Reagan administration's secretary of the interior, James Watt. As a believer in the imminent rapture, Watt saw no reason to introduce policy that would protect the environment for future generations.[7] In his view, there simply would not be any future generations. One historian has recently suggested that President George W. Bush has effectively used prophetic language, like the kind in the Left Behind books, to justify his decision to go to war against Iraq and reject multiple international treaties. When he insists on the need for the United States to stand alone, to act against allied governments, and to set its own agenda, he strikes a chord with the millions of dispensationalist believers in the United States who fear that joining with other nations sets a path toward the antichrist. When we hear political rhetoric that supports our worldviews, we tend to offer both explicit and implicit support to these beliefs and thus bolster their power. In this way, perhaps, such beliefs can have an important impact on how decisions in the United States are made.

Despite overt political statements on abortion and gender, the Left Behind series has very little else to say about what humankind should do to make the world a better place. It is the antichrist who talks about such things, not Christians.

The political message we get from this is fairly clear—attempts at world peace, talk about disarmament, treaties, and other cooperation among nations is suspect. Christians should try to convert other people to Christianity and save individual souls, but beyond that, they have little responsibility for the state of the world. Christ will come to solve those problems; meanwhile, humankind will only make them worse. In Left Behind's view, our world is threatened by global unity. As we become more and more connected to one another, we pave the way for the coming of the antichrist. The only hope we have is that Christ will rapture the church and take true Christians away. Otherwise, the world itself is doomed. This view is very much in contrast to other Christians' views that emphasize the importance of activity and work in the world. Many Christians believe it is a Christian's responsibility to shape the future of this world, rather than waiting for its end.

Reflecting on the One World Government and its meanings should lead us to question what place we see ourselves having in the "global community." Do we agree with the authors of the Left Behind series that globalism is a diabolical way of thinking that paves the way for the antichrist? Or do we believe that nations and people should strive to work together for peace on earth? In what ways does globalization threaten our communities and traditions? Or what do we have to learn from other cultures and other traditions? Are there different kinds of globalization that need to be evaluated differently? For almost a century, the story of One World Government has told of fears and uncertainties in the face of rapid social change. How we respond to these fears is an important part of reflecting on the relationship between religion and culture, tradition and change.

Gender

On the issue of the One World Government, the Left Behind series looks very similar to the many novels about the rapture that came before it. The authors stay very much within the tradition of the rapture narrative to tell the story of the antichrist's

rise to power, even though the precise fears that drive such a
story vary in different eras. On the issue of gender and feminism, however, the Left Behind series is very different from what
came before it. Its social and political messages about women
are highly complex and often very subtle. In order to understand how the social position of women is treated, we need to
look both at what characters *say* and what they *do*. On the surface, in the rhetoric of the characters, the authors appear to
view feminism as an enemy to Christianity in its attempt to
usurp and equalize the traditional power relationships between
men and women. Feminism is blamed for destroying the family,
for encouraging abortion, and for disrupting the God-ordained
order of the world. When we look at what characters do, however, the picture becomes considerably more complicated. The
relationships between men and women hint at far more equality
and complexity than the rhetoric would seem to allow.

Traditional rapture fiction begins with the rapture of a devout
Christian woman. She is usually raptured from her home while
her worldly husband is left behind. He returns from work to
find supper burning on the stove and his wife gone. Very rarely,
in rapture fiction, is a man raptured first and his wife left
behind. One exception is Don Thompson's movie *Thief in the
Night*, in which a young woman is left behind while her husband is raptured. But this scenario is very rare in rapture stories.
More traditionally, these stories rely on the piety of women in
order to point out their husband's worldly failings. In part, this
is because, historically, the rapture narrative was part of a
movement to bring more men to church. Fundamentalist
preachers wanted men to know that they could not rely on their
wives' spirituality to get them to heaven. They had to be saved
themselves. In this way, the rapture narrative often served as a
warning to men. "You need to get right with God," the story
warned, "or you are going to be left all alone on this earth to
face untold suffering." But the story also served as a warning to
women. The devout Christian woman who is raptured is always
an exceptional wife and mother. She is not only a good
Christian but also an extremely good housekeeper. Part of the

reason she is rewarded with rapture is because she has fulfilled her domestic duties as well as her spiritual duties. Thus the narrative warned women who did not fulfill these roles that they may not be raptured. In a novel written in the 1950s, *Raptured* by Ernest Angley, one girl who is left behind blames non-Christian mothers. On the morning after the rapture, Hester confronts a woman. "Tears were rolling down Hester's cheeks. She was thinking that if her mother had taken her to church and taught her in the right way, she might not have been left behind either; but she had no encouragement. 'Mothers like you have a lot to think about this morning,' she cried."[8] The responsibility for mothers is very strong in this tradition, and they are easily blamed for the failings of those around them.

In the traditional rapture narrative, women have another role as well. The devout woman leaves behind not only a worldly man, but also a young female protégée (like Hester)—sometimes her daughter, sometimes simply a neighbor over whom she has exerted some influence. These are women who did not heed her warnings before the rapture but who convert immediately afterward. They become the protagonists of this early rapture fiction and then are captured and tortured by the antichrist. While the woman's husband is condemned to hell, this young woman becomes the martyred saint of rapture fiction.

Like other rapture fiction, *Left Behind*, the first book in the series, begins with a worldly man and his raptured wife. The opening lines of *Left Behind* make this distinction clear. "Rayford Steele's mind was on a woman he had never touched. With his fully loaded 747 on autopilot above the Atlantic en route to a 6 A.M. landing at Heathrow, Rayford pushed from his mind thoughts of his family."[9] Notice how Rayford is clearly associated here with worldly things, especially adultery and his "fully loaded 747." Family and, eventually we learn, religion are the very things he is pushing from his mind. Meanwhile, at home, his wife's mind is on precisely these two things. She is raptured; he is left behind.

This, however, is where Left Behind's similarity with other rapture fiction ends. Rayford follows a distinctly different trajectory from his predecessors. Rather than taking the mark of the beast and being condemned to eternal damnation, Rayford converts to his wife's faith. The story of how he integrates his manhood with his Christian faith is an important part of the Left Behind narrative. He not only becomes more religious; he also becomes more domestic. Early on, becoming a Christian means learning to identify with his wife. He starts to perform domestic duties—cooking and cleaning—and starts to understand how, for his wife, faith was something she expressed through her home. He learns to express his emotions and to be a good father. But then, as if troubled by how feminine he is becoming, he goes off in a fury to kill Nicolae Carpathia. His rage comes in part, he says, from no longer feeling important. "The danger in his present role wasn't the same. . . . For now, Rayford was just meeting contacts, setting up routes, in essence working for his own daughter. . . . [It] wasn't the same. He didn't feel as necessary to the cause."[10] With his daughter Chloe directing the resistance operations, Rayford feels lessened by his role as his daughter's employee, somehow less of a man than he once was. His response is rage, and an angry masculinity completely overwhelms his faith. Rayford's Christian "witness," as well as his role as a leader in the Tribulation Force, is threatened by this new passion.

As Rayford becomes a Christian leader, he learns both to assert his authority and to be humble about it. He must learn to be more emotional and listen more carefully to those around him. In Rayford, we see all the contradictions in gender identity that are present in the contemporary "Promise Keepers" movement. As "servant-leaders," men in the Promise Keepers are supposed to assert their authority as men, but they also are supposed to learn to be more expressive and emotional. They are supposed to learn to be better husbands and fathers through more attentive listening to their wives. While the Promise Keepers movement has been criticized as strongly anti-feminist, the responsibility that men bear for improving their relationships and humbling themselves suggests that this is a patriarchy of word more than deed. Like Rayford, Promise Keepers seek a compromise between masculinity and the softening demands of Christianity.

The situation for Rayford's daughter Chloe is equally complex. In the traditional story of rapture and tribulation, Chloe would be the protagonist. She would stand firm against the antichrist, but eventually would be tortured and killed by him. She would be spiritually strong but weak in other ways. In the Left Behind series, Chloe instead becomes the CEO of an underground Christian organization. Even as she performs this essential duty and has her father as an employee, she talks about female submission to male authority and is a kind of stay-at-home mom in the Tribulation Force's bunker.

In the fourth book in the series, *Soul Harvest*, Chloe is pregnant, but nonetheless she wants to go to Israel with her husband Buck. She is angry with him for deciding that she should not go, saying: "Don't parent me, Buck. Seriously, I don't have a problem submitting to you because I know how much you love me. I'm willing to obey you even when you're wrong. But don't be unreasonable. And don't be wrong if you don't have to be. . . . [D]on't do it out of some old-fashioned, macho sense of protecting the little woman. I'll take this pity and help for just so long, and then I want back in the game full-time. I thought that was one of the things you liked about me. . . . Am I still a member of the Tribulation Force, or have I been demoted to mascot now?"[11]

These passages are complex and even contradictory. First of all, Chloe uses the rhetoric of female submission to male authority that is typical of many contemporary evangelical leaders. For example, she says that she will "obey" Buck even when he is wrong. Yet Chloe also strongly articulates her views. She refuses to become an object and even demands full participation in the work of the Tribulation Force. She both submits and asserts herself, negotiating for a position that will allow her to be Christian mother and Christian warrior. Later the situation becomes even more complicated as Chloe becomes CEO of the Christian Cooperative. Still later in the series, Chloe leaves for an adventure in Greece while Buck stays at home with their son.

From these examples, we can see that Chloe is neither the domestic saint nor the martyred heroine of previous rapture fiction. While she certainly would not say she is a feminist, she is a strong, articulate, savvy businesswoman, and even though she says that she submits to Buck's authority, we rarely see examples of it.

The Left Behind series also contains examples of gender stereotypes less complicated than the depictions of Rayford and Chloe. Hattie Durham exists in the novels as a warning of the dangers of women who refuse to submit to Christian male authority. Hattie is a rebel. She does not listen to Rayford; she does not obey the Tribulation Force when members tell her where to go and where not to go. At every turn, until her Christian conversion, she denies Rayford's authority and flaunts her independence. The result is danger for the Tribulation Force and her own misery. Some people might argue that Hattie's suffering comes from her refusal to accept faith, but as a woman, she faces a different set of problems than other unbelieving characters like Chaim Rosenzweig. Most of these problems center around her status as a woman outside the faith. As the embodiment of the Whore of Babylon, a figure from the book of Revelation, she has a disastrous affair with Carpathia, becomes pregnant, and gives birth to a deformed and dead baby (in contrast to Chloe's healthy and happy little boy), is attacked and tortured by locusts, and is poisoned and imprisoned. Everyone in the Tribulation Force knows that if she would give her life to Christ and submit to Rayford as the force's leader everything would be fine. But over and over again, she refuses. Because Hattie stands outside the Tribulation Force and refuses to submit, she is, as the books tell us, "unlovable."

We know from the very opening lines that Rayford is attracted to Hattie, that she is alluring and beautiful. But this image of Hattie is confused by another image of her as stupid. The books move back and forth between telling us that Hattie is a fascinating, if dangerous, woman and telling us that she lacks intelligence. She is repeatedly referred to as "vapid," "naïve," and "without a clue." In one scene, Hattie tells Rayford that the rapture has put abortion clinics out of business—all unborn babies have been taken from their mothers' wombs. She imagines that abortion workers—her sister is one—are disappointed at their loss of business and compares abortion to "owning a gas station and nobody needing gas or oil or tires anymore."

In this passage, the authors intend to portray people who work in abortion clinics as cynical, even evil people who are motivated by money. Anti-abortion politics run as a theme through all the books. Abortion, which is portrayed by feminists as an issue of women's control over their own bodies, is portrayed in the Left Behind series as the evil choice of selfish and deluded women. But the even more subtle message of the passage is that Hattie is ridiculous. Throughout their conversation, Rayford thinks "he had never found Hattie guilty of brilliance," that "he shouldn't waste his energy arguing with someone who clearly didn't have a clue," and that "irony was lost on her." He subtly mocks her through his responses to her assertions about abortion clinics and their employees until it seems that this is an entirely different Hattie from the one who had been so provocative for Rayford at the beginning of the novel.[12] Why does Rayford make fun of Hattie? Is he trying to punish her for being so attractive to him even while she is evil?

This portrayal of Hattie Durham as a bad woman is as disparaging as the portrayal of homosexual characters in the series. Characters like Verna in *Tribulation Force* and *Nicolae* and Guy Blod in *The Indwelling* point out what false or bad sexuality looks like. The authors contrast homosexuality with images of real masculinity and femininity in characters like Buck and Chloe. When Verna tries to usurp Buck's power, we learn that she is actually a lesbian. She mimics masculine power, but because it does not "rightfully" belong to her, the story mocks her and puts her in her place. Guy Blod, the man Carpathia has commissioned to make a sculpture, is similarly ridiculous in his effeminate mannerisms. Like Verna, he is mocked, and the books make it clear that Guy is not a "real" man.

Because fiction both reflects the worldviews of the culture from which it comes and influences that culture, we might argue that the Left Behind series gives us an interesting and contradictory picture of the role of gender in evangelicalism. This picture is considerably more complex than it once was. Women are both submissive and assertive. Men are both dominant and humble. Questions about the place of the family in contemporary life and about the roles of women and men in marriages and society are explored in the Left Behind story. As with the One World Government, the depiction of gender in the novels can help us to examine how such relationships function in our own time and place. Where do we experience the disjunction between rhetoric and action? What demands do we make on the people around us to fulfill roles and live up to expectations based on their gender? Where do our ideas about gender come from, and how do they change from one family to the next and one generation to the next?

Race

As with gender, when we consider the messages that the Left Behind series sends about race, we must look both at what characters say and what they do. On the surface, the Tribulation Force is a multicultural band of Christians sharing their faith through a difficult time. On a deeper level, the books give true authority to white men, men like Rayford, and use men of color to submit to this "rightful" authority for reasons the books cannot explain. Rayford's position of authority is unusual because he is not the pastor—a converted Jew named Tsion Ben-Judah has taken that role. Traditionally, religious authority has been located with the pastor, but Rayford is not particularly knowledgeable spiritually. Instead, his authority is located somewhere else. But where? Rayford himself wonders. In *The Indwelling*, during a moment of self-doubt, Rayford questions his role as leader of the Tribulation Force. "Smarter people were in the Force, Rayford knew, including his own daughter and son-in-law. And where on earth was a more brilliant mind than that of Tsion Ben-Judah? And yet they all naturally looked to Rayford for leadership."[13] The word "naturally" stands out as one that needs to be examined. Why is Rayford's leadership natural? No reason is ever given for why Rayford should have assumed leadership, yet repeatedly, new members of the Tribulation Force, especially non-whites, acknowledge his leadership and submit to it.

The first example of this comes with the introduction of Dr. Floyd Charles, an African American doctor who saves the lives of several members of the Tribulation Force and also of Hattie. He becomes a member of the force and moves into the safe house after his position at the hospital is threatened. Dr. Charles is not around long. In treating Hattie, he receives the poison from her body and dies. But before that, he takes time to affirm Rayford's authority. Dr. Charles comes to Rayford with a troubling problem. Despite Hattie's depravity, the doctor finds himself attracted to her, even in love with her. He begins his conversation with Rayford by apologizing for snapping at him during the delivery of Hattie's stillborn child. "You're the chief," he tells Rayford. "I need you to know that I know that and respect it." Rayford denies this in the next sentence. "There's no time for hierarchy anymore," he says. But the story line constantly disputes this. Rayford is at the head of the hierarchy. Dr. Charles acknowledges this, and Rayford's denial only serves to point out what both of them know to be true.[14]

In a later book, this same sequence is repeated. This time Rayford is troubled about his "little, dark friend," Albie, a Kuwaiti and a Muslim convert to Christianity. The situation is more complicated because Rayford is concerned that, despite the mark on Albie's forehead, he is not really a Christian. As they are flying to rescue Hattie, Albie tells Rayford that he is not being a very good leader. "If I may say so, I expected you to be more decisive. I am just playacting, yet I appear more of a leader than you are. . . . Decide. Tell me, tell the people in the Strong Building, and do it."[15] From Albie's speech, we learn that even as he pretends, for the sake of the enemy forces watching them, that he is Rayford's superior, this is just an act. The real authority belongs to Rayford. He wants Rayford to tell him what to do. He urges Rayford to take over that authority—especially authority over him. Like Dr. Charles, Albie submits to Rayford and asks Rayford to be in command.

This acknowledgment of Rayford's leadership is not something that white men in the books do. Ken Ritz, the maverick, John Wayne type pilot, does not tell Rayford, "You're the chief." Buck does not ask Rayford to tell him what to do. That role is left to "dark" men like Dr. Charles and Albie. In this way, the books assert the rightness of white men's power over black men, of white men in positions of leadership and men of color as followers. This power dynamic is important for reasons that the books leave unexplained and unexplored. It subtly confirms the power relations of our own social world, where white men hold positions of power they do not want to concede.

The authors of the Left Behind series would likely disagree with this analysis of race in the books. What different explanations might they provide? Are we unfair to read against the authors' own intentions? The depiction of race in the series also might encourage us to question how race functions in our own churches, schools, and communities. Who are the "natural" leaders, and why is their leadership natural? Are some people encouraged to submit to the authority of others for reasons we cannot articulate or explain?

Consumer Culture

For much of their history, stories about the rapture and tribulation have been stories about trying to escape the modern world and its attack on traditional structures of order and power. They have imagined Christians either leaving the world through the rapture or being martyred during the tribulation. The world that these stories described was one that needed to be destroyed completely in order for the millennium to come. As we have already seen, the Left Behind series makes some significant changes to the way this story is told. Unlike previous rapture fiction, which roundly condemns consumer culture as part of the corrupt modern world, the Left Behind books fully endorse and engage in it.

The relationship between Christianity and consumer culture has long been a complicated one. On one hand, when consumer culture claims that this world is the only one that matters, that buying things and looking good will make a person happy, Christianity has claimed that there are things of greater significance. Christianity has suggested that buying things will never fully satisfy a person, that the material world is only partial and incomplete. People need spiritual food as well as material food. For some Christians, this has meant situating themselves in opposition to consumer culture, resisting demands to buy more and asserting instead the rightness of a simple life that makes room for spiritual things.

On the other hand, most American Christians participate in consumer culture along with other Americans. They spend Saturdays at the mall, read magazines, watch television, and go to the movies. Christians often buy explicitly Christian products— T-shirts, books, bumper stickers, CDs, and so on—but all of these things are very much products of consumer culture. Churches, youth groups, and religious organizations rarely raise complaints against the dominance of consumer mentality; instead they often use this mentality to "sell" their own organizations to a consuming public. We "shop" for churches; we "buy" into religious programs.

In Christian fiction depicting the rapture, however, this has not always been the case. Rapture fiction has been a place where Christians, especially conservative Christians, expressed fears and anxieties about a world that seemed bent of gratifying material rather than spiritual needs. Rapture fiction—a genre born about the same time as the rise of consumerism in the United States—saw consumer culture as dangerous to the human soul. One of the ways rapture fiction expressed protest was by "rapturing" poor people and leaving wealthy people behind to suffer. Wealthy and worldly people, people hungry for money and things, were depicted as being the first to give their souls to the antichrist, the first to line up to take the mark of the beast. The mark of the beast, in particular, was a sign of anxiety about consumer culture. It was something one had to receive to participate in the economy, to acquire and use goods. The mark was a way for conservative Christians to express concerns about the conformity of modern life and the dominance of computers. Prophecy writers have imagined the mark as a barcode or a microchip implanted in the human body, taking away human freedom and making humans slaves to the market.

Along with criticism of wealth and fear of being enslaved to consumer culture, this fiction also expressed anxiety about technology. In rapture fiction before *Left Behind*, technology was something that the antichrist used. For example, in a book of rapture fiction published in 1971, Salem Kirban depicts technology as a device the antichrist uses to spy on Christians, to capture and kill them. People who become Christians after the rapture are at the mercy of the antichrist's technology. They do not fight back. They suffer as martyrs and die.[16]

All of this should help us to understand how different the Left Behind series is in its messages about consumer culture from previous rapture fiction. In the Left Behind novels, worldly status and wealth are not bad, but good. Consumer goods are not the deceitful work of the antichrist, but tools for God's plan. And technology is not in the hands of the antichrist so much as it is something that Christians use in their fight against the Global Community. We see this in *Nicolae* when Buck and Chloe go to buy a new car. Buck uses his Global Community credit card to buy the biggest, fanciest SUV he can find.

> "Do you feel like you just spent the devil's money?" Chloe asked Buck as he carefully pulled the new earth-toned Range Rover out of the dealership and into traffic.
>
> "I *know* I did," Buck said. "And the Antichrist never invested a better dollar for the cause of God."
>
> "You consider spending almost a hundred thousand dollars on a toy like this an investment in our cause?"
>
> "Chloe," Buck said carefully, "look at this rig. It has everything. It will go anywhere. It's indestructible. It comes with a phone. It comes with a citizen's band radio. It comes with a fire extinguisher, a survival kit, flares, you name it. It has four-wheel drive, all-wheel drive, independent suspension, a CD-player that

plays those new two-inch jobs, electrical outlets in the dashboard that allow you to connect whatever you want directly to the battery."[17]

Notice how, for Buck, the SUV is an expression of himself. "It has everything. It will go anywhere. It's indestructible," just like Buck himself. Buck loves the SUV, not just for what it can do for the "cause of God"; he loves it for itself. The books do not criticize Buck for this passion for consumer goods—they praise him. Buck loves to buy things; he dresses well and always looks good, like a rugged magazine model. He has both worldly prestige and Christian faith and does not need to compromise either.

Furthermore, Christians use technology against the antichrist, rather than the other way around. In a direct reversal from previous rapture fiction, Christians use technology to spy on the antichrist. They are the smartest and most computer savvy. Certainly Carpathia has technology and uses it diabolically, but the Christians use it better and use it smarter. Inside the antichrist's empire, the best technological minds are actually Christians, hiding their identity to help the cause. At one point, Buck explains to the Tribulation Force's technician what they need. "I need five of the absolute best, top-of-the-line computers, as small and compact as they can be, but with as much power and memory and speed and communications abilities as you can wire into them. . . . I want a computer with virtually no limitations. I want to be able to take it anywhere, keep it reasonably concealed, store everything I want on it, and most of all, be able to connect with anyone anywhere without the transmission being traced."[18] Buck describes computers in a way similar to his description of the SUV. Like the SUV, the computers must be able to go anywhere and have "virtually no limitations." Buck wants all the latest in technology and lets Donny, the technician, know that he is willing to pay anything for them. "Let me assure you that money is no object," he says. Donny responds, "You're speaking my language, Mr. Williams." It is clear that technology and the spending of money are now friends to Christianity, no longer to be feared.

The religious language in the books takes on certain shades of consumer culture as well, producing subtle shifts in the ways that the characters talk about their spiritual lives. Before Buck and Chloe are married, Buck carries out a flirtation with a secretary, Alice. As he offers Alice a ride home in his new car, Buck's love for cars becomes mingled with his newfound religious salvation: "Alice waited while he unlocked the door. 'Nice car.' 'Brand new,' he answered. And that was just how he felt."[19] Since this short statement comes at the end of a section, we do not know exactly why Buck feels "brand new." Does he feel "brand new" because he has just become a Christian? Is "brand new" a synonym for "born again"? Or does he feel "brand new" because he has a new car? Or because he is flirting with Alice and her flattery makes him feel good? Or is it all of these things at once? Buck's religious identity becomes intertwined with both the things that he buys and his masculinity. The computers, the SUV, this new car are all expressions of the manly Christian Buck. If Christian men often have doubted the relationship between masculinity and faith, Buck seems to solve this problem by buying things that confirm his masculine identity.

Another way that the religious language of the books becomes enmeshed with consumer culture is the way that the characters describe conversion as "transaction." As Rayford looks down from a helicopter at the destruction caused by an earthquake, he thinks about Hattie and hopes for her conversion. "Was it possible she might have received Christ before this? Could there have been somebody in Boston or on the plane who would have helped her make the transaction?"[20] Conversion to Christianity is described as a business transaction or a commodity exchange. Ken Ritz puts it, "So once I join up I get the secret mark on my forehead?"[21] Conversion is something like a business deal or a bargain—the "secret mark" is received in exchange for "joining up." This is a dramatic change from the mostly organic metaphors—like being "born again" or being "washed in the blood of Christ"—used to describe conversion by previous generations of Christians. Here conversion is a "transaction" conducted between the believer and God, a business deal that comes with benefits and everlasting assets.

The Left Behind series does not see Christianity as something that needs to be opposed to consumer culture. It sees consumerism and products as potential benefits and tools for the Christian life. Rather than using rapture fiction to protest consumer culture, these novels praise goods and technology. This depiction of consumer culture might cause us to question the relationship between the spiritual world and the material world. Are the Christians of Left Behind called to be "in the world, but not of the world," or is that distinction no longer important? As readers, how should we respond to this presentation of consumer culture? What is the relationship between materialism and spirituality? Do consumer goods threaten the Christian life or aid it?

Using Left Behind to Read the World

"This millenniums old account reads as fresh to me as tomorrow's newspaper," Pastor Barnes says in the second book in the Left Behind series, *Tribulation Force*. He is talking about the Bible and the end times scenario derived from ancient biblical texts. For him, and for the authors of the series, the Bible is "history written in advance." Everything that is going to happen in the end times is recorded in the Bible; we only need to know how to read it properly. Although this way of reading the Bible raises many issues, including issues of biblical interpretation and prophecy, I want to focus on the effect that it has on the way we interpret everyday life. For many people who read the series, the stories that are told there are both truth and fiction. They are truth in the sense that they are based on biblical scenarios that many people take to be prophetical accounts of what will happen. At the same time, these are fictional accounts of characters living in a time that has not yet come. Because the Left Behind series is for many people both truth and fiction, it has a powerful effect on the way they understand the world. As truth, it tells them what is actually coming, possibly in their very own lifetimes. As fiction, it provides vivid pictures for readers to invest in. They become absorbed in the lives and events of characters who may even become as real as their neighbors. This vivid fictional world is powerful in shaping the world to which readers return after they put down the book.

So how does the series shape that world? One thing that it provides is a lens through which the world can be interpreted. When readers turn on the television and see the account of a catastrophic event in China, Iraq, or New York, they already have some available categories for interpretation. Some of those categories may come from family, from church, from social context, or from what they knew or understood from previous events like this one. Left Behind also offers tools for interpretation. If the series provides clues to tomorrow's newspaper, then it may help to understand today's newspaper as well. Readers may see an economic summit as the coming of the One World Government or the rise of a powerful leader as a hint of the antichrist. They may find themselves wondering if this or that earthquake is a sign of the end times or if events in the Middle East are directly linked to the scenarios outlined by the books. All of these are ways that the Left Behind series helps to provide a lens through which readers might begin to see and understand the world. In this sense, the series is much more than fiction. It provides insight into the present moment and helps readers interpret the bewildering pace of world events. The books might even give readers a sense of self-justification and self-righteousness. As they watch world events unfold, as they watch television or read the newspaper, they know a secret the rest of the world does not know. They have a method for interpreting these events and putting them into a scheme of logic. They are no longer random, but part of a foreordained plan for the world set in place by God himself.

How reliable readers think Left Behind is in providing a lens for interpreting both the present and the future depends, of course, on their understanding of the Bible. If the Left Behind books are accurate depictions of what the Bible teaches, then readers may praise the series for bringing these realities to life.

The series offers vivid mental images that they can use to remind themselves of the plan God has for the world. If readers do not subscribe to this view in the least, they may simply discard the books as "nice stories" and be only briefly reminded of them when they see something in the news that hints of the scenarios they offer. But even if readers disagree with the scenario the books provide for the end times, the series still offers a picture that becomes, in a complicated way, a part of the way that they see the world. This is one reason why examining the messages that Left Behind has for our time and place can be so important. We can learn to see not only through our own lenses, but we also can learn to see the lens itself.

The Left Behind books are a form of entertainment. Although the authors hope they will edify readers and perhaps even lead some to make a commitment to Christianity, their main purpose is to entertain. They want to tell a fast-paced, action-packed story with adventure and drama that will capture and hold readers' attention. Given that the books are meant as entertainment, are we being unfair by analyzing them the way we have? Are we over-analyzing and over-reading?

Whether we watch television, go to the movies, pick up *Sports Illustrated*, read the latest John Grisham novel or the latest in the Left Behind series, we are receiving messages about our world. These forms of entertainment are telling us what is important and what is not important, what to think and how to think it. That is not to say that we are helpless when it comes to popular culture. We can accept or reject the messages. We can examine them critically or forget about them entirely. But all of these things shape the world that we live in and also shape our understanding of that world. For that reason, critical reflection on what "entertains" us, taking time to understand what messages are being sent and whether those messages fit with our own values and beliefs, is a worthwhile occupation. It helps to understand ourselves and our world better.

The Left Behind series is enormously popular. People are reading the books, giving them to friends, buying a dozen copies as gifts, and talking about them everywhere. Why? What does the series say that speaks so clearly to its audience? What is it about our world that resonates with the "future" that Jerry Jenkins and Timothy LaHaye have imagined? Although these reflections on the social and political messages of Left Behind have not been able to answer that question entirely, we gain some insight into the current state of our own religious and social condition. Perhaps in the midst of the vast social changes of the last few decades—changes brought on by the women's movement, civil rights, rapidly changing technology, the end of the cold war, and other social and political forces—Left Behind restores a sense of order. In the series, everyone and everything has its proper place, even if that means re-establishing old hierarchies rather than imagining new equality. We know who is saved and who is damned. We know the outcome of history and what all these seemingly random events mean. Good is clearly separated from evil. Questions all have answers. In this way, despite the chaos the tribulation appears to bring, the world of Left Behind is a simpler one than the one we live in and confront every day. At the same time, the books tell us, we have no reason to deny ourselves anything. As Christians we can consume without guilt the best cars, the best computers, and the best clothes. Christianity is compatible with worldly beauty, worldly status, and worldly goods. Perhaps this combination of moral simplicity with material comfort is part of the pleasure that reading the books brings and accounts for their singular and extraordinary popularity.

Notes

1. Tim LaHaye and Jerry B. Jenkins, *Nicolae: The Rise of Antichrist* (Wheaton, Ill.: Tyndale House, 1997), viii.
2. Tim LaHaye and Jerry B. Jenkins, *Tribulation Force: The Continuing Drama of Those Left Behind* (Wheaton, Ill.: Tyndale House, 1996), 131.
3. LaHaye and Jenkins, *Nicolae*, 128.
4. John Walvoord, *The Church in Prophecy* (Grand Rapids, Mich.: Zondervan, 1964), 179–180. Cited in Paul Boyer, *When Time Shall Be No More* (Cambridge, Mass.: Harvard University Press, 1992), 264.

5. Tim LaHaye and Jerry B. Jenkins, *Left Behind: A Novel of Earth's Last Days* (Wheaton, Ill.: Tyndale House, 1995), 214.

6. Hal Lindsey with Carole C. Carlson, *The Late Great Planet Earth* (Grand Rapids, Mich.: Zondervan, 1970).

7. Grace Halsell, *Prophecy and Politics: Militant Evangelists on the Road to Nuclear War* (Westport, Conn.: Lawrence Hill & Company, 1986), 8. Paul Boyer, *When Time Shall Be No More*, 141.

8. Ernest Angley, *Raptured: A Novel of the Second Coming of the Lord* (Akron, Ohio: Winston Press, 1950), 105.

9. LaHaye and Jenkins, *Left Behind*, 1.

10. Tim LaHaye and Jerry B. Jenkins, *Assassins: Assignment: Jerusalem, Target: Antichrist* (Wheaton, Ill.: Tyndale House, 1999), 4.

11. Tim LaHaye and Jerry B. Jenkins, *Soul Harvest: The World Takes Sides* (Wheaton, Ill.: Tyndale House, 1998), 307.

12. LaHaye and Jenkins, *Left Behind*, 266–268.

13. Tim LaHaye and Jerry B. Jenkins, *The Indwelling: The Beast Takes Possession* (Wheaton, Ill.: Tyndale House, 2000), 70.

14. Tim LaHaye and Jerry B. Jenkins, *Apollyon: The Destroyer Is Unleashed* (Wheaton, Ill.: Tyndale House, 1999), 110–113.

15. Tim LaHaye and Jerry B. Jenkins, *The Mark: The Beast Rules the World* (Wheaton, Ill.: Tyndale House, 2000), 24–28.

16. Salem Kirban, *666* (Wheaton, Ill.: Tyndale House, 1970).

17. LaHaye and Jenkins, *Nicolae*, 25.

18. Ibid., 45–46.

19. LaHaye and Jenkins, *Tribulation Force*, 19.

20. LaHaye and Jenkins, *Nicolae*, 407.

21. LaHaye and Jenkins, *Soul Harvest*, 275.

Study Guide

Discussion Questions for Small-Group Consideration or Personal Reflection

Chapter 1   How Popular Are the Left Behind Books ... and Why? (Forbes)

1. Does some knowledge about the backgrounds of authors Tim LaHaye and Jerry Jenkins influence the way you read the novels? Why or why not? If it does influence you, in what way?
2. Why do you think the Left Behind novels have been so popular?
3. On the basis of your acquaintance with people who have read the Left Behind series, do you think they read the books simply as entertainment? Are they attracted to the religious beliefs in the books? Does reading the books influence the viewpoints and the lives of readers? If so, in what ways? If not, why not?
4. One criticism of the Left Behind books, and of the belief system on which they are based, is that it creates an "us-versus-them" mentality. The complaint is that it divides the world too easily into good and bad, black and white, with no shades of gray. Do you think this is true? If so, is it a helpful way to look at the world or not?

Chapter 2   How Did Left Behind's Particular Vision of the End Times Develop? (Kilde)

1. Kilde observes that, throughout history, times of strife have prompted Christians to focus on ideas of the end times, while attention to the end times has been less popular when things are going well for Christians. Why would this be the case? Is it true now?

2. Over the centuries of Christian history, many persons have predicted that "the end is near." Does that make you skeptical when people make similar claims today? Should it, or is today's situation different?
3. Many persons believe that the United States plays a special role in God's plan for humanity. Do you agree with this belief? Have you seen this belief expressed in American culture beyond the Left Behind books?
4. Some critics worry that belief in Jesus' imminent return tends to undercut social responsibility. If a person is convinced that life on earth will deteriorate until Christ intervenes, why would he or she worry about protecting the environment, combating poverty, or working for peace? Is this a fair criticism?

Chapter 3   What Does the Bible Say About the End Times? (Reasoner)

1. One major division among Christians is whether certain portions of the Bible should be read literally or symbolically. How would you summarize these two approaches, in your own words? With which approach are you most sympathetic?
2. Another basic disagreement exists about how to understand the biblical book of Revelation. Do the visions of John refer to the persecution of early Christians in the Roman empire? Do they provide a coded prediction of the future, two thousand years later? What other viewpoints are possible? How should a person decide?
3. Do you think the Bible foretells a rapture, or not?
4. Given that Christians disagree about the details of an end-times scenario, does it make a difference which details one accepts? Does one's choice of a particular viewpoint about the end times necessarily tie the person to certain principles of biblical interpretation? Is your own view of the end times important in how you read the Bible or how you live your life?

Chapter 4   When Do Christians Think the End Times Will Happen? (Grenz)

1. This chapter discusses three major Christian belief systems about the end times: postmillennialism, premillennialism, and amillennialism.

Premillennialism is then divided into two subgroups: dispensational premillennialism and historic premillennialism. How would you explain the basic differences between them, in your own words? Which view is closest to your perspective? Why?

2. Do you expect a literal earthly era in which God reigns for a thousand years at the end of history? Or do you see most of this discussion of the end times as symbolic or allegorical? What leads you to take one position or another?

3. Grenz comments that there has been a "long-standing absence in many churches of any talk about a future end of the age." Do you think that is true? Should there be more focus on this topic, or less?

4. Which come first, religious beliefs or political and social events? Grenz suggests that premillennial theology developed first and then events, such as the Russian Revolution, confirmed the beliefs and broadened their appeal. In other chapters Kilde and Frykholm suggest that theology developed in response to events. With which view do you agree? Can they be combined in some way?

Chapter 5 How Are Jews and Israel Portrayed in the Left Behind Series? (Ariel)

1. What characters and scenes in the various Left Behind books portray Jews or the nation of Israel? Do these portrayals fit with the analysis offered by Yaakov Ariel, or do you interpret them differently?

2. This chapter discusses a "paradox" in evangelical Christian understandings of Judaism that is reflected in the Left Behind books. Jews and Israel are seen as crucial in the last days, because of the reestablishment of Israel and the rebuilding of the Jerusalem Temple, but Jews must convert to Christianity in order to be saved. Thus, would you call the novels pro-Jewish, anti-Jewish, or some other alternative? Why?

3. There is a debate among Christians about whether Christians should try to evangelize Jews. What is your view?

4. Ariel argues that Christian millennial beliefs have influenced U. S. foreign policy regarding Israel. Do you agree that such an influence has existed in recent American politics? In your view, is such an influence appropriate and beneficial, or not?

Chapter 6   What Social and Political Messages Appear in the Left Behind Books? (Frykholm)

1. Do you view international organizations (like the United Nations or the European Union) positively or negatively? Why?
2. "Globalization" and "global community" have become controversial terms, from a great variety of political and social perspectives. How do you understand the terms? Do they represent a threat or a promise?
3. Do your religious beliefs influence your evaluation of international organizations and globalization (the topics of questions 1 and 2)? How do your views compare with the perspective in the Left Behind novels?
4. Have you reflected on the roles of gender and race in the Left Behind novels before reading Amy Frykholm's chapter? Do you agree with what she sees as the message of the books on these two topics?
5. Does consumer culture threaten the Christian life or aid it?

Glossary

amillennialism A particular understanding of the millennium, or the thousand-year reign of Christ on earth, which asserts that it should be viewed symbolically rather than literally. Augustine was an early advocate of this view, which has been widely held by Christians ever since. Although some amillennialists understand the millennium to be currently in effect, others see it as a metaphor for spiritual perfection attainable through Christ.

antichrist A false Christ or enemy of Christ. In premillennial dispensationalist thought, the individual or institution that will deceive the people of the world in order to achieve global domination. Once this individual or institution has gained the trust of the people, he/it will reveal himself/itself as the embodiment of evil and the enemy of Christ. Some millenarians throughout Christian history have variously identified the Roman Catholic Church, the papacy, Adolf Hitler, the Soviet Union, the United Nations, and communism, as well as other individuals, groups, and ideas, as the antichrist.

apocalypse, apocalyptic literature From the Greek word *apokalypsis*, meaning "unveiling," "disclosure," or "revelation." The biblical book titled The Revelation to John is also called the Apocalypse. Scholars use the term "apocalyptic literature" to refer to a genre of writings that reveal divine mysteries, particularly those associated with the punishment of enemies and the reward of those faithful to God. Apocalyptic literature and thought tends to rely on dreams or visions, is highly symbolic, and frequently refers to an end of human history. The books of Daniel and Revelation are biblical examples, though there are many nonbiblical apocalyptic texts as well (e.g., First Enoch).

Armageddon A mountain (Harmageddon), mentioned in Revelation 16:16, that is often associated with the ancient city of Megiddo in Palestine, where decisive battles had been fought. Some millenarians believe that Armageddon will be the location of the final battle between Christ and the forces of evil (Satan), which will occur during the end times. The name of the site frequently is generalized to refer to this final battle itself.

C.E. "Common Era." Many people use these initials instead of A.D. (Anno Domini—Year of Our Lord) to refer to the years since the birth of Jesus Christ. C.E. is a more neutral designation, recognizing that this dividing point in the calendar has become a common standard in the western world for Christian and non-Christian alike. B.C.E. indicates time "Before the Common Era."

chiliasm From the Greek *chilioi*, meaning "thousand," this is another word for millennialism and refers to the belief in a thousand-year reign of Jesus Christ at the end of time.

chosen people A term used in the Hebrew scriptures to describe the Israelites, who were taken under Yahweh's particular care. Some Christian theologians have argued that with Christ's atonement for human sin, Christians supplanted Jews as God's chosen people. Others, however, retain the view that Jews remain God's chosen people.

dispensationalism A term referring to the notion that God has organized sacred and human history, from beginning to end, in a series of eras, or "dispensations." A common modern dispensationalist scheme alludes to seven dispensations: (1) the Age of Innocence, which began with Adam; (2) the Age of Conscience, which began with the expulsion from Eden; (3) the Age of Government, which began with the flood; (4) the Age of Promise, which began with Abraham; (5) the Age of Law, which began with Moses; (6) the Age of Grace, which began with Jesus' death and resurrection; and (7) the Millennium. God is viewed as dealing with humanity differently in each era. The term frequently is used to refer to premillennial dispensationalism.

end times The culmination of God's plan for human history, which includes the return of Jesus Christ to earth to judge the living and the dead. In premillennial dispensationalist thought, the period encompassing the series of events believed to occur when Christ returns.

eschatology From the Greek *eschatos*, meaning "last," and *logos*, meaning "word," eschatology is thinking or reasoning about the end— the study of last things. It includes various beliefs regarding individuals' futures (resurrection or punishment, heaven or hell, etc.) or the end of history (the second coming of Jesus Christ, climactic cosmic events at the end of time, a final judgment, a new age, etc.).

evangelicalism   Rooted in the Greek *euangelion*, meaning "good news" or "good message" and referring to the gospel of salvation through Jesus Christ. "Evangelical" can be a confusing term because, when referring to groups of Christians, different persons use the term with different definitions in mind. In Europe, for instance, "evangelical" usually means simply "Protestant." For much of U.S. history, "evangelical" referred to Christians who emphasized the importance of a personal conversion experience, faith in Jesus Christ, commitment to the full authority of scripture as a guide for faith and life, and the necessity of being a witness for the gospel message, and scholars continue to use the term in this way. Until the early twentieth century, a majority of Protestants in the United States called themselves evangelical. With the development of liberal Protestantism, many mainline Protestant denominations deemphasized the term along with the strong focus on scriptural authority and witnessing. Today the term frequently is used generally to include a variety of conservative Christians, from fundamentalists to Pentecostals to Southern Baptists.

exegesis   From the Greek *eksagō*, meaning "to lead out" or "bring out," exegesis refers to the critical examination and analysis of texts, particularly scriptural or biblical texts.

fundamentalism   A Protestant perspective that formed in the early twentieth century in opposition to modernism. Fundamentalists seek to uphold what they see as the essential beliefs of the Christian faith ("fundamentals"). Key principles include the inerrancy of the Bible, its literal interpretation, and historicity of supernatural events such as the virgin birth and the second coming of Christ. Fundamentalism is a notoriously slippery term, and scholars debate which groups fall under its mantle. Many see fundamentalism as evangelicalism in a more militant form.

futurism   A branch of premillennial dispensationalism that asserts that events described in prophetic scriptures and associated with the end times have not yet occurred but remain in the future to be sparked by Jesus' return. John Nelson Darby advanced this position in the 1830s. See "**historicism**."

glorious appearing   A term used by premillennial dispensationalists to denote the **parousia** (see entry), or second coming, of Jesus Christ.

historicism   A branch of premillennial dispensationalism that asserts that ongoing historical events have been predicted in the Bible and that, by identifying key events, one can estimate when the second coming of

Jesus or the end times will occur. Historicism was favored by millenarians for centuries and was used to encourage Christians to be "on the lookout" for signs that scriptural prophecies were being fulfilled and the end times were about to commence. In the 1830s John Nelson Darby's proposal of **futurism** (see entry) challenged this view. To this day, premillennial dispensationalists debate the historicist and futurist positions.

judgment, final judgment, Day of Judgment   In messianic thought, the resurrected Christ is expected to return to earth to judge the living and the dead, thus pronouncing the eternal punishment or reward for each individual.

mark of the beast   In literal interpretations of Revelation, this phrase refers to a symbol that will be inscribed on every individual during the tribulation as a sign of loyalty to false prophets or the antichrist. The term often is associated with the "number of the beast," 666, mentioned in Revelation 13:18.

messiah   From the Hebrew *māšăh*, meaning "the anointed." The messiah, in Jewish thought, will deliver the Jewish people.

messianic thought   Ideas and stories informed by notions of the messiah.

millennium, millennialism, millennialist   From the Latin *mille*, meaning "thousand," millennium refers to a thousand-year reign of Christ, usually seen as a period of peace and harmony on earth. Millennialists are persons who hold particular views about the millennium. Three common views within Christianity are premillennialism, postmillennialism, and amillennialism. (See separate entry for each term.)

millenarianism, millenarian   Other words for millennialism and millennialist.

modernism   A theological movement that began in the late nineteenth century among both Protestants and Catholics who interpreted Christianity in light of then-recent scientific and philosophical thought. Responding to scientific evidence of evolution, including the age of fossils, and new investigations into the historical compilation of biblical texts, modernists asserted that Christians could harmonize their beliefs and the Bible with these new findings.

orthodox, orthodoxy   In its most general sense, orthodox means holding proper or correct beliefs. This is in opposition to heresy, which is improper belief. Certain Jewish and Christian groups use the capitalized term, Orthodox, to name their particular religious group and to indicate their conviction that they hold the truth.

parousia   Greek term meaning "arrival" or "presence." This term is used to refer to the second coming of Jesus Christ.

postmillennialism   A particular view of the millennium, or a thousand-year period of peace and harmony on earth, which asserts that Christ's second coming to earth will occur at the conclusion of the millennium. Thus, Christ's second coming is "postmillennial," or after the millennium. Advocates of this view believe that positive developments on earth, including Christian conversions and/or social improvement, can help prepare the way for Christ's second coming. Postmillennialism in various forms was a very common view in early American history, particularly in the nineteenth century.

posttribulationism   A branch of premillennial dispensationalism that asserts that the rapture will occur after the tribulation (see entry).

premillennialism   A particular view about the millennium, or the thousand-year reign of Christ, which asserts that Christ's second coming to earth will occur prior to the millennium. Thus, Christ's second coming is "premillennial," or before the millennium. Persons holding this view generally believe that situations on earth will deteriorate until Christ returns to do battle with the forces of evil. Only then will the millennium begin.

premillennial dispensationalism   A view of the end times that unites premillennial thought with a distinctive time line of eras, called dispensations, and events. Developed by John Nelson Darby and others and widely disseminated in the twentieth century in the *Schofield Reference Bible*, this view asserts that the end times will consist of the following order of events: the Rapture, the Tribulation, Jesus' second coming and the battle of Armageddon, the millennium, the battle of Gog and Magog, the final judgment, and the new heaven and new earth. This is the viewpoint held by the authors of the Left Behind books. This view is also known as dispensational premillennialism.

pretribulationism   A branch of premillennial dispensationalism that asserts that the rapture will occur before the tribulation.

proof text, proof-text method   A method of biblical interpretation that cites scriptural passages as proof of theological or doctrinal ideas. The proof-text method is used by premillennial dispensationalists to demonstrate scriptural derivation of the dispensational scheme. It also has been used by historicist premillennialists to associate specific historical events with biblical passages as a means of suggesting that the end times are upon us or imminent. Many biblical scholars use the phrase "proof text" in a derogatory sense, arguing that taking scriptural verses out of context and ignoring the original meanings of texts are inappropriate methods for exegesis.

prophecy   The inspired utterance of an individual (a prophet), which is seen as the revelation of a divine entity. Some believe that such utterances disclose or predict the future.

proselytize   To induce someone to convert to a particular religion or faith.

quietism   A term referring to a mystical seventeenth-century practice of meditation on God that required the extinction of the will and disengagement from worldly events. It is used more generally to indicate religiously based disengagement with the world.

rapture, secret rapture   In premillennial dispensationalist thought, the initial event of the end times, in which all true Christians will be swept up to heaven to remain with Christ during the seven years of tribulation on earth. Although the idea of being swept up has been discussed throughout Christian history, John Nelson Darby used the term "secret rapture" to denote the event and made it a centerpiece of his thought.

second coming, second advent   Other terms for the parousia (see entry), referring to the expectation that Jesus, the resurrected Christ, will return to earth to redeem humanity.

tribulation, great tribulation   In premillennial dispensationalist thought, a period of seven years on earth in which the antichrist will rise to power and wreak havoc on humanity. True Christians will be spared the horror of these events, having experienced the rapture prior to the beginning of the tribulation.

Zionism   A worldwide movement to restore the nation of Israel to Palestine, which is considered the Jewish people's historic homeland.

Suggestions for Further Reading from a Variety of Perspectives

An Annotated Bibliography

Ariel, Yaakov. *On Behalf of Israel: American Fundamentalist Attitudes Toward Jews, Judaism, and Zionism, 1865–1945.* Brooklyn, N.Y.: Carlson Publications, 1991.

In this book, Ariel, the author of chapter 5 in our collection, tells the story of the rise of the dispensationalist wing of fundamentalist Christianity, the viewpoint that undergirds the Left Behind books. Ariel explains how the restoration of Israel was a key component of their end-times beliefs, which led to fundamentalist Christian political support for the nation of Israel.

Balmer, Randall. *Mine Eyes Have Seen the Glory: A Journey into the Evangelical Subculture in America.* New York: Oxford University Press, 1989, 1993.

Balmer's book is something of a travelogue of stories introducing the reader to varieties of American evangelicalism. Chapter 3 "On Location," focuses on Donald Thompson, the director of the film *A Thief in the Night*, and discusses the tremendous influence his movie about the rapture had on evangelicals in the 1970s and 1980s.

Boyer, Paul. *When Time Shall Be No More: Prophecy Belief in Modern American Culture.* Cambridge, Mass.: Harvard University Press, 1992.

A study of the multifaceted role that end-times prophecy has played throughout the history of the United States. Boyer traces apocalyptic thought from the early colonists through the present day, showing how belief in prophecy has impacted a variety of national events and situations. His discussion of the impact on the cold war and more recent politics is especially interesting.

DeMar, Gary. *End Times Fiction: A Biblical Consideration of the* Left Behind *Theology*. Nashville, Tenn.: Thomas Nelson Publishers, 2001.

DeMar, an evangelical author who otherwise agrees with LaHaye on many Christian beliefs and social issues, disagrees with the end-times beliefs reflected in the Left Behind books. DeMar seeks to provide a detailed biblical refutation of Tim LaHaye's approach, including critiques of his views of the rapture, the tribulation, the glorious appearing, the antichrist, and more. In many cases DeMar believes that the biblical passages describe events that happened to Christians in the era when Revelation was written, when Christians were persecuted in the Roman empire.

Frykholm, Amy Johnson. *Rapture Culture: "Left Behind" in Evangelical America*. New York: Oxford University Press, 2004.

Frykholm, author of chapter 6 in this collection, studies the genre of rapture fiction in American culture, including the Left Behind series and many other novels. Her work draws on extensive interviews with readers of the novels, and she analyzes their appeal.

Gorenberg, Gershom. *The End of Days: Fundamentalism and the Struggle for the Temple Mount*. New York: Oxford University Press, 2000.

Gorenberg is a journalist, an associate editor and columnist for *The Jerusalem Post*, and a resident of Israel. He discusses the roles played by Jewish, Christian, and Muslim fundamentalisms in the turmoil of the Middle East, with considerable attention to Christian millennial thought. The second chapter includes specific comments about the Left Behind books.

Grenz, Stanley J. *The Millennial Maze: Sorting Out Evangelical Options*. Downers Grove, Ill.: InterVarsity Press, 1992.

Topics discussed by Grenz in chapter 4 in this collection are considered in greater detail in *The Millennial Maze*, which compares four different positions held by Christian evangelicals: postmillennialism, dispensational premillennialism, historic premillennialism, and amillennialism.

As an evangelical theologian himself, Grenz also offers his analysis of the strengths and weaknesses of each of the four positions.

Hill, Craig C. *In God's Time: The Bible and the Future.* Grand Rapids, Mich.: William B. Eerdmans Publishing Company, 2002.

Hill, a professor of New Testament at Wesley Theological Seminary, represents a mainstream scholarly perspective that takes biblical references to the future seriously, as an expression of hope. However, Hill rejects the "ultra-literal" interpretation on which the Left Behind books are based and even includes a ten-page appendix specifically responding to the series. Although written by a biblical scholar, the book avoids jargon and is intended for general readers.

Jewett, Robert. *Jesus Against the Rapture: Seven Unexpected Prophecies.* Philadelphia: Westminster Press, 1979.

Jewett, a New Testament professor now retired from Garrett-Evangelical Theological Seminary, wrote this book in the era when Hal Lindsay's (with Carole C. Carlson) *The Late Great Planet Earth* was popular. Jewett argues that the historical Jesus would have disagreed with sensationalist voices who expect an imminent rapture and who offer predictions of doom.

Koester, Craig R. *Revelation and the End of All Things.* Grand Rapids, Mich.: William B. Eerdmans Publishing Company, 2001.

The opening chapter of this book provides an interesting, brief history of how Revelation has been interpreted over the centuries. The rest of the volume works through the various sections of Revelation, making current "mainline" scholarship about Revelation available to general readers. Koester, a New Testament professor at Luther Seminary, sees his work as an alternative to the Left Behind views.

LaHaye, Tim. *Rapture Under Attack.* Sisters, Ore.: Multnomah Publishers, 1998.

Originally published in 1992 under the title *No Fear of the Storm*, this revised version was published following the appearance of the first three books in the Left Behind series. LaHaye's intention is to defend the pretribulation rapture theory against what he sees as "savage attack" by persons who do not read the Bible literally and by those who advocate midtribulation or posttribulation views.

LaHaye, Tim, and Jerry B. Jenkins. *Are We Living in the End Times?* Wheaton, Ill.: Tyndale, 1999.

Although the Left Behind books are fiction, LaHaye and Jenkins believe that the underlying outline of events is biblically based and will occur in history. In this volume they "lay out twenty reasons for believing that the Rapture and Tribulation could occur during our generation."

LaHaye, Tim, Jerry B. Jenkins, with Norman B. Rohrer. *These Will Not Be Left Behind: Incredible Stories of Lives Transformed after Reading the Left Behind Novels.* Wheaton, Ill.: Tyndale House Publishers, 2003.

Rohrer, the actual writer of this volume, compiles and summarizes thirty-one stories of people who reported changed lives as a result of reading these novels, plus excerpts from additional e-mail messages. The book illustrates the intention of the Left Behind authors to prompt Christian conversions and changed beliefs.

LaHaye, Tim, and David Noebel. *Mind Siege: The Battle for Truth in the New Millennium.* Nashville, Tenn.: Word Publishing, 2000.

For those who want to learn more about LaHaye's perspectives on religion and social issues, this volume, cowritten with Noebel, is a recent exposition of his views. The book calls Christians to oppose what LaHaye sees as secular humanism and its "five basic tenets," which he defines as atheism, evolution, amorality, human autonomy, and globalism. The discussion includes comments about public schools, abortion, gay and lesbian rights, feminism, and other subjects.

Lindsey, Hal, with Carole C. Carlson. *The Late Great Planet Earth.* Grand Rapids, Mich.: Zondervan Publishing House, 1970.

This was the best-selling "nonfiction" book of the 1970s in the United States. It argued for a view of the end times very similar to the beliefs underlying the Left Behind series. Lindsey was very specific in identifying various prophecies in Revelation with specific current events, thus implying that the rapture would occur in the 1980s.

Metzger, Bruce M. *Breaking the Code: Understanding the Book of Revelation.* Nashville, Tenn.: Abingdon Press, 1993.

Metzger is the chairperson of the translation committee for the New Revised Standard Version (NRSV) of the Bible and a former

New Testament professor at Princeton Theological Seminary. This is a very brief study book intended for use in local churches. Metzger says that people should be "wary of turning Revelation into a kind of almanac or time chart of the last days."

Nelson, Dwight K. *What "Left Behind" Left Behind.* Fallbrook, Calif: Hart Books, 2001.

This is a critique by a Seventh-Day Adventist pastor. Nelson represents a denomination that has focused on literal expectations of a second coming, but Seventh-Day Adventist views differ in many details from the Left Behind perspective.

Olson, Carl E. *Will Catholics Be Left Behind?: A Critique of the Rapture and Today's Prophecy Preachers.* San Francisco: Ignatius Press, 2003.

Olson describes himself as a former fundamentalist and dispensationalist who entered the Catholic church in 1997. Now the editor of *Envoy* magazine, a "journal of Catholic apologetics and evangelization," Olson wrote this book to provide an "exhaustive Catholic critique" of the viewpoint expressed in the Left Behind novels.

Ryrie, Charles Caldwell. *Dispensationalism.* Revised and expanded edition. Chicago: Moody Publishers, 1999.

Ryrie, a professor emeritus at Dallas Theological Seminary, is well known in part because his name appears on several study Bibles. He also is acknowledged as a leading advocate of classic dispensationalism, and this book frequently is cited as a primer that seeks to counteract misconceptions about dispensationalism and to provide a positive presentation of the subject.

Sandeen, Ernest R. *The Roots of Fundamentalism: British and American Millenarianism, 1800–1930.* Chicago: University of Chicago Press, 1970.

This historical examination of the development of fundamentalism contains the most comprehensive account to date of the early nineteenth-century conferences and discussions surrounding premillennial dispensationalism. It also provides a full picture of the late nineteenth-century discussion of premillennial dispensationalism in the United States.

Strozier, Charles B. *Apocalypse: On the Psychology of Fundamentalism in America*. Boston: Beacon Press, 1994.

Written by a historian who is also a practicing psycholanalytic psychotherapist, this book explores the role of apocalyptic ideas in contemporary everyday life through a series of interview-based case studies of individual believers. Strozier presents the stories of individuals who believe in end-times prophesy in a way that allows reader to gain insight into how these beliefs address moral and social concerns shared by most Americans.

Weber, Eugen. *Apocalypses: Prophesies, Cults, and Millennial Beliefs through the Ages*. Cambridge, Mass.: Harvard University Press, 1999.

Historian Weber chronologically surveys a long list of beliefs about the end of the world, including panic surrounding the sack of Rome in 410 C.E., medieval predictions, and modern movements. The book leaves readers with a strong sense of how widespread and various such beliefs have been over the past two thousand years.

Wojcik, Daniel. *The End of the World as We Know It: Faith, Fatalism, and Apocalypse in America*. New York: New York University Press, 1997.

Written by an expert in folklore, this volume examines how end-times beliefs and themes have been conveyed through various forms of popular culture, from books to films to comic books to rock music. The book includes a chapter on Hal Lindsey and dispensationalist beliefs, as well as discussions of apocalypticism among Catholics and the rise of apocalyptic themes in the nuclear age.

List of Contributors

Yaakov Ariel holds a Ph.D. from the Divinity School of the University of Chicago. He has written extensively on the relationship between Jews and evangelicals, and his most recent book is *Evangelizing the Chosen People: Missions to the Jews in America, 1880–2000* (2000). He is currently an associate professor in the Department of Religious Studies at the University of North Carolina, where he teaches courses on religion in America, Judaism, and evangelicalism.

Bruce David Forbes holds a Ph.D. in the history of Christianity from Princeton Theological Seminary. He is the author of several articles on popular culture and on Indian-white relations in the United States, and he recently coedited *Religion and Popular Culture in America* (2000). He is an ordained United Methodist minister, and he currently holds the Arthur L. Bunch Chair in Religious Studies at Morningside College in Sioux City, Iowa, where he teaches courses on American religion.

Amy Johnson Frykholm holds a Ph.D. from the Program in Literature at Duke University. Her scholarly research, and her book *Rapture Culture: Left Behind in Evangelical America* (2004), focus on American religious culture. She currently is teaching courses on American literature and culture in Kiev, Ukraine, with the Fulbright program.

Stanley J. Grenz holds a D.Th. in systematic theology from Ludwig-Maximilians University in Munich, Germany. He has authored and co-authored several books on contemporary theological and religious issues, the most recent being *The Social God and the Relational Self: A Trinitarian Theology of the Imago Dei* (2001). He is an ordained Baptist minister, and he is currently serving as the Pioneer McDonald Professor of Theology at Carey Theological College in Vancouver, British Columbia, where he teaches courses in both theology and ethics.

Jeanne Halgren Kilde holds a Ph.D. in American Studies from the University of Minnesota. She has published several articles on religious space and architecture and is the author of *When Church Became Theatre: The Transformation of Evangelical Architecture and Worship in Nineteenth-Century America* (2002). She currently teaches courses on religion in America as a visiting assistant professor in the Department of Religious Studies at Macalester College in St. Paul, Minnesota, and she also codirects Macalester's Lilly Project in Work, Ethics, and Vocation.

Mark Reasoner holds a Ph.D. in New Testament and early Christian literature from the University of Chicago. He has published several articles on New Testament topics, including Paul and the book of Romans. His recent book is *The Strong and the Weak: Romans 14.1–15.13 in Context* (1999). He is an associate professor of biblical studies at Bethel College in St. Paul, Minnesota, where he teaches courses in the fields of biblical studies and humanities.

Index